Testbuilder for TOEFL iBT™

Pamela Vittorio

Macmillan Education
Between Towns Road, Oxford OX4 3PP
A division of Macmillan Publishers Limited
Companies and representatives throughout the world

Testbuilder for TOEFL iBT™
ISBN 978-0-2304-0970-5

Text © Pamela Vittorio 2011

Design and illustration © Macmillan Publishers Limited 2011
First published 2011

All rights reserved; no part of this publication may be reproduced, stored in a retrieval system, transmitted in any form, or by any means, electronic, mechanical, photocopying, recording, or otherwise, without the prior written permission of the publishers.

Design by xen
Illustrated by Oxford Designers & Illustrators
Picture research by Rebecca Sodergen
Audio produced by John Marshall Media

Author's acknowledgements
I'd like to thank Al Tanzer for his dedicated help and advice and special thanks to "the crew" for their support. With deepest appreciation to my family and parents for their patience and for always being a phone call away. I also would like to express sincere thanks to the editors and staff at Macmillan Education.

The publishers would like to thank Tammy LeRoi Gilbert and Louise Tester.

The author and publishers would like to thank the following for permission to reproduce their photographs:

Alamy/Sally and Richard Greenhill p33, Alamy/Image Source p24, p27, Alamy/Dennis MacDonald p22, Alamy/MBI p61 (t).
Corbis/Dirk Anschütz p57, Corbis/Odilon Dimier/PhotoAlto p64, Corbis/Greg Hinsdale p29, Corbis/Image Source p32, Corbis/Juice Images p62 (t), Corbis/Moodboard p34 (b), Corbis/Ocean p54, Corbis/Purestock/SuperStock p21, Corbis/Redchopsticks p25.
Getty/PhotoAlto Agency p62 (b).
Macmillan Publishers Ltd p34 (t).
Photolibrary/Kablonk! P58, Photolibrary/Clarissa Leahy p51, Photolibrary/moodboard p52, Photolibrary/sodapix p61 (b), Photolibrary/M Thomsen p36.
Rex Features/moodboard p55.

With thanks to BBC News for kind consent to re-draw the colossal squid comparison diagram on p13.

These materials may contain links for third party websites. We have no control over, and are not responsible for, the contents of such third party websites. Please use care when accessing them.

Printed and bound in Thailand
2015   2014   2013   2012   2011
10   9   8   7   6   5   4   3   2   1

CONTENTS

Introduction	5
Test 1	6
Reading	6
Listening	21
Speaking	31
Writing	35
Test 2	37
Reading	37
Listening	51
Speaking	60
Writing	63
Further practice and guidance	65
Reading	65
Listening	113
Speaking	139
Writing	150
Key and explanation	153
Listening scripts	178
CD track listing	188
Scoring sheet	190
Test 1 answer sheet	191
Test 2 answer sheet	192

INTRODUCTION

The *Testbuilder for TOEFL iBT*™ book introduction

The *Testbuilder for TOEFL iBT*™ is designed to help students practice items and refine their skills for the TOEFL iBT™. This book has been created for all students preparing for the TOEFL iBT™ who have taken the test prior to using this book and have a score of 70 and above.

The *Testbuilder for TOEFL iBT*™ contains:
- Two full-length practice TOEFL iBT™ exams.
- A Further practice and guidance section in each of the skill areas: Reading, Listening, Speaking, and Writing.
- Answer Key with explanations for the two tests.
- Answer Key for the Further practice and guidance section.
- Listening and Speaking scripts.
- Two CDs.

The two tests reflect the level and types of questions found in the TOEFL iBT™ exam.

In the Further practice and guidance section, you will find information on the four TOEFL iBT™ skills areas:
- Reading practice
- Listening practice
- Speaking practice
- Writing practice.

The Further practice and guidance pages include plenty of skills-building items as well as additional practice questions based on the two tests. By reviewing the questions, reading texts, listening and speaking scripts, and writing responses, you will learn commonly used academic vocabulary, expressions, and key words.

Steps to building your skills for the TOEFL iBT™

1. Take Test 1. Use the answer sheet on page 191 to mark your answers. Use a no. 2 pencil to mark your answer choices.
2. Check your answers with the Key and explanations for Test 1 at the back of this book.
3. Use the Scoring sheet on page 190 to approximate your TOEFL iBT™ score.
4. Focus on the areas in which you need improvement. Read and do the practice items in the Further practice and guidance section of this book. You can choose to do any or all of the items for Test 1 and check your answers in the Key.
5. Take Test 2. Use the answer sheet on page 192 to mark your answers.
6. Check your answers with the Key and explanations for Test 2 at the back of this book.
7. Review any parts of the Further practice and guidance section that you need. Then do the practice items for Test 2.

For further information about the TOEFL iBT™, registration, and scoring rubrics for all sections of the test, please visit the official ETS website at www.toefl.org.

TEST 1

READING 80 minutes

This section measures your ability to comprehend academic reading passages in English. There are four passages in this section.

Each passage is followed by **12 to 14 questions** with directions for each question. Some of the questions in this section will be worth more than 1 point.

You will have **20 minutes** to read each passage and answer the questions. You have **80 minutes** to complete the entire section.

Set a timer for **80 minutes**. Read each passage and answer the questions within the time allowed. Follow the directions for each type of question. Fill in your answers on the answer grid on page 191.

Questions 1–14 are based on the following passage.

Passage 1 The controversy of a hoax: the Lost Colony of Roanoke

1   Settled by English colonists in the late sixteenth century, Roanoke Island lies off the coast of what is now the state of North Carolina. It is best known as the home of "the Lost Colony." In 1587, the explorer Sir Walter Raleigh dispatched a ship bound for the New World, carrying a group of approximately 117 people—including their new governor, John White. The captain was supposed to take them farther north, to Chesapeake Bay near Massachusetts, but instead dropped the passengers at Roanoke Island—the site of the first, unsuccessful English colony. Governor White realized that supplies were low and sailed back to England to acquire more food, promising to return in three months. However, the war between England and Spain prevented White from voyaging back to the island for three years. When White finally returned to Roanoke in 1590, he found that the settlers had disappeared. The entire site had been abandoned without a trace of the colonists having been there. The only clue that White found was the word "CROATOAN" carved into a fence post, and the letters CRO etched into a tree trunk. There was nothing else to indicate where the colonists had gone or the manner in which they had left.

2   This centuries-old case of the Lost Colony has long puzzled scholars who have tried to reconstruct the events that led to the colonists' vanishing act. Both historians and archaeologists have been unable to piece together exactly what happened to the colonists. The most popular theory holds that they simply abandoned the area. It has long been believed that they went to Croatoan Island—known today as Hatteras. Scholars speculated that the colonists may have gone to live with the Croatoans—a tribe of Native Americans with whom they had had very friendly relations.

3   However, any scholarly inquiries regarding this 350-year-old mystery nearly came to a halt in 1940 when the *Saturday Evening Post* newspaper published a story claiming that it was "solved." The story upheld the angle that a few of the colonists had survived—among them, Governor John White's daughter Eleanor Dare, her husband Ananias, and their infant daughter Virginia. Eleanor had allegedly inscribed her story on a series of 48 stones so that her father would know what had happened to them. The article included photographs of some of the stones that the reporter said had been found in swamps and various other places in North and South Carolina, as well as Georgia, all within a 400-mile radius of each other. The stones were given to Dr. Haywood Pearce, a professor of American History at the University of Atlanta, who examined them and took his story to the media. The text on the stones was simple, but written in what appeared to be sixteenth-century Roman letters. Pearce thought that the stones were authentic and the *Post* printed the story.

4   In 1941, an investigative reporter named Boyden Sparkes published a follow-up story declaring the Dare stones to be a **hoax**. He systematically proved, with supporting evidence from experts, that the words written on the rocks in an Elizabethan-era Roman script had been fabricated, and the dates on the rocks could not be scientifically proven. After Sparkes's exposé on the hoax, Professor Pearce's academic integrity was compromised in the fraud, and he subsequently dropped out of sight.

5 Fifty years later, Robert W. White's book *A Witness for Eleanor Dare* revisited the story of the Dare stones. White raised the question of the stones' authenticity by stating that Sparkes had created the controversy in order to get publicity about the mystery of the Lost Colony, but moreover, to seek monetary gain for himself. White's examination of the evidence reintroduced the possibility that the stones were not fake. However, historians and archaeologists alike have still not reached an agreement about this potential physical evidence of the Lost Colony. Despite the controversy, one of the infamous Dare stones is now on exhibit at the Lost Colony Center for Science and Research in Williamston, North Carolina.

6 Questions about the colonists' fate still exist: Did they assimilate with the Croatoan Indians? Did they attempt to sail back to England and were lost at sea? Did they all succumb to disease or harsh weather? These questions and the authenticity of the Dare stones continue to be one of the most enduring unsolved mysteries of early American history.

Glossary

hoax: a deceptive act; something that leads people to believe an act or event is real

1 According to paragraph 1, the "Lost Colony" is

   A the island of Roanoke.

   B a group of English settlers.

   C the state of North Carolina.

   D an area of Chesapeake Bay.

2 According to paragraph 1, the author implies that the colonists

   A were governed by Sir Walter Raleigh.

   B forced John White to return to England.

   C had planned to land on Roanoke Island.

   D had originally intended to settle in Chesapeake Bay.

3 The word etched in paragraph 1 is closest in meaning to

   A cut into.

   B drawn.

   C printed.

   D erased.

4 The phrase vanishing act in paragraph 2 is closest in meaning to

   A disappearance.

   B performance.

   C behavior.

   D struggle.

5 In paragraph 2, why does the author mention the theory about the colonists' disappearance?

   A to connect the word "CROATOAN" with the possible whereabouts of the colonists

   B to contrast the different opinions of the historians and archaeologists

   C to offer more speculation about where they might have gone

   D to support the work done by scholars to solve the mystery

6 The word it in paragraph 3 refers to
   A 1940.
   B a story.
   C the mystery.
   D the newspaper.

7 The word allegedly in paragraph 3 is closest in meaning to
   A irrefutably.
   B illegally.
   C unbelievably.
   D supposedly.

8 In paragraph 4, what does the author say about the script on the stones?
   A It was from the Elizabethan era.
   B It was not easy for experts to read.
   C No one could prove it was from the sixteenth century.
   D Scientists could not sequence the stones by their dates.

9 According to paragraph 4, what does the author imply about Professor Pearce after Boyden Sparkes published his hoax story?
   A He tried to reach an agreement with Sparkes.
   B He left his position at the university.
   C He was fired from his job.
   D He lost his sight.

10 Which of the following best represents the important information in the highlighted sentence from paragraph 5? Answer choices that are *incorrect* change the meaning or leave out necessary information.
   A In 1991, Robert White published a book about the mystery of the Lost Colony that re-examined a 1940s hoax.
   B Robert White's 1991 book investigates the story of the Dare stones, claiming that Sparkes's hoax story was a ruse created for publicity and financial gain.
   C The story of the Dare stones needed to be told again, so Robert White questioned the authenticity of the stones in his controversial 1991 book.
   D Fifty years after Sparkes's hoax controversy, Robert White discussed the need to find out if the mystery of the Lost Colony was still unsolved or not.

11 Why does the author mention White's examination of the evidence in paragraph 5?
   A to make people aware of the unsolved mystery
   B to show that the Lost Colony was not completely forgotten
   C so that readers will reconsider the authenticity of the Dare stones
   D to exemplify how Sparkes's desire for money might have harmed history

12 The word infamous in paragraph 5 is closest in meaning to

   A unknown.

   B notorious.

   C memorable.

   D disreputable.

13 In paragraph 6, the author raises several questions on theories about the colonists' fate EXCEPT

   A they could have settled with a Native American tribes on the island.

   B they may all have died from a fatal illness.

   C they attempted to return to England.

   D they moved south to warmer climates.

14 **Directions**: Complete the table below to organize information about the controversy surrounding the Lost Colony of Roanoke. Match the statements below to the topic to which they belong. Look at the chart on your answer sheet and select **three** answers for row **1** and **three** answers for row **2**. **This question is worth 3 points.**

[On the actual test, you will drag your answer choices to the spaces where they belong.]

The historical events	Select three
Theories and controversy	Select three

Answer choices

   A While their governor is in England collecting food and supplies, 117 people mysteriously disappear from Roanoke Island.

   B Eleanor Dare, husband Ananias, and their infant daughter are the only survivors of the Roanoke colony.

   C The mystery was deemed "solved" when a newspaper published a story about stones that had messages from Eleanor Dare to her father carved into them.

   D Scholars had no clues to determine the colonists' fate except for Governor White's account that he had found the word "CROATOAN" carved into a post, and the letters CRO etched into a tree trunk.

   E The 1941 investigative report by Boyden Sparkes disputed the findings of a well-known professor and destroyed the man's reputation by claiming the Dare stones to be a hoax.

   F The colonists suffer during the harsh winter and are unable to survive on the island.

   G Robert White's 1991 book refutes Sparkes's claims and reintroduces the idea that the whereabouts of the Lost Colony might be found in further examination of the Dare stones.

   H The colonists abandoned the Roanoke settlement and moved south to Croatoan Island, where they lived with the Native American tribe there.

   I The first colony on Roanoke Island is a complete failure, thus inspiring the second group of colonists to build a home in Chesapeake Bay in 1587.

Questions 15–27 are based on the following passage.

Passage 2 Sustainable architecture and green building

1   The concept of being environmentally conscious, or "green," has become more prevalent in twenty-first-century U.S. culture. It has begun to affect the manufacturing of everything from non-toxic household cleaning products to motor vehicles powered by alternative sources of energy. However, one way of being "green" that is perhaps not as apparent to the viewer but of equal importance in being environmentally conscious, is the construction of buildings that are considered "sustainable." Sustainable buildings are those that do not impose on the environment or rely on the over-utilization of energy or natural resources. There are four main principles of sustainability, which include consideration of the health and stability of all living things and their environmental diversity, as well as the economic opportunities of humanity.

2   Sustainable architecture consists of environmentally conscious design techniques. In the past, the demolition of an old building meant that all or most of the debris of the building would end up in a landfill or a waste disposal site. Today, architects can plan and design a building that uses recycled materials, such as wood, concrete, stone, or metal. These materials are salvaged from the demolition of an older building and can be appropriately incorporated into a new construction. Architects and construction supervisors may also choose to recycle more organic parts of demolished buildings, such as wooden doors, windows and other glass, ceramics, paper, and textiles.

3   A problem that has often arisen has been with how a site crew—whether it is demolition or construction crew—determines and sorts what is "waste" and what is recyclable. Architects and environmental scientists have to decide whether or not a material is appropriate for use in new construction and how it will impact the environment. They must evaluate the materials from the demolition and determine what those materials contain, and if they meet the standards set by the U.S. government's Environmental Protection Agency (the EPA). If the debris from the demolition contains hazardous materials that are harmful to the environment or to the consumer, such as **asbestos**, then the material is not salvageable. Use of asbestos for insulation and as a form of fire retardation in buildings and fabrics was common in the nineteenth century. Asbestos was once used in shingles on the sides of old buildings, as well as in the insulation in the interior walls of homes or other construction. In new "green" construction, insulation that was once asbestos-based can be replaced with recycled denim or constructed with *cellulose*—a fibrous material found in paper products. The same assessment applies to wood or wallboard painted with toxic **lead**-based paints. In addition, gas-flow regulators and meters on both water and gas heating systems constructed prior to 1961 must be carefully evaluated to determine that they do not contain dangerous substances such as **mercury**. Mercury can be harmful to humans and the environment if it is spilled during the removal of these devices.

4   These factors contribute to the use of sustainable materials and construction practices in commercial buildings as well as residential homes. When the intended construction is a new home, the owners themselves may now participate in deciding what recycled materials go into building their homes. Homeowners may also decide on aspects such as the indoor air quality, sources of energy and water efficiency, and the consistency of the soil on which to build the home. About two percent of all homes built in the U.S. in 2005 were deemed "green." Some reports predict that this number will increase in the next five to ten years, so that the number of "green" buildings may surpass ten percent of the number of newly constructed homes.

5   In terms of energy and natural resources, sustainable architecture may incorporate many alternative energy sources—energy that is not harmful to the environment and does not rely on mineral-based fuels like coal or oil. Some utility companies around the world are offering wind and solar power as alternatives to electricity. In the U.S. today, these options are available to homeowners and commercial building management. Along with the capability to use recyclable materials in residential or commercial constructions, as well as options for generating power from renewable energy sources, society can contribute to the concept of a greener way of life.

Glossary

asbestos: a mineral with fibrous qualities that has highly dangerous effects on humans

lead: a poisonous metal used in paint to extend its durability and improve appearance

mercury: an element used in instruments of measurement and toxic in liquid form

15 The word prevalent in paragraph 1 is closest in meaning to

  A rare.

  B unusual.

  C widespread.

  D valuable.

16 In paragraph 1, the author implies that

  A all buildings impose on the environment.

  B the concept of being green has not influenced manufacturers.

  C uses of alternative energy are apparent to the consumer.

  D some companies manufacture vehicles that are not powered by gasoline.

17 According to paragraph 1, which of the following is true?

  A Today's cleaning products and appliances harm the environment.

  B All construction follows the concept of sustainable architecture.

  C Sustainable buildings do not overuse electricity, oil, or gas.

  D Construction of "green" buildings is an old idea.

18 In paragraph 2, the word salvaged is closest in meaning to

  A lost.

  B saved.

  C buried.

  D destroyed.

19 According to paragraph 2, environmentally conscious design incorporates which of the following?

  A materials from a landfill

  B new wood, stone, or concrete

  C debris from a demolished building

  D safe, organic, recycled materials

20 In paragraph 3, why does the author mention both demolition and construction crews?

  A to demonstrate that choosing recyclable materials is challenging for both crews

  B to give an example of how choosing materials is not easily determined on a site

  C to illustrate the types of crews that sort waste and recyclables

  D to contrast the work of the two types of crews on a site

21 The word they in paragraph 3 refers to

  A the EPA.

  B the site crew.

  C architects and environmental scientists.

  D the materials from the demolition.

22 In paragraph 3, the author mentions all of the following hazardous materials found in debris from a demolition site EXCEPT

   A lead.

   B mercury.

   C cellulose.

   D asbestos.

23 In paragraph 4, why does the author mention the influence of homeowners on the use of construction materials and energy sources?

   A to illustrate ways that people are becoming more aware of sustainable architecture

   B to criticize the past construction of residential homes in the United States

   C to show that homeowners now have green options for their homes

   D to give an example of sustainable architecture in everyday life

24 In stating that About two percent of all homes built in the U.S. in 2005 were deemed "green" the author means that

   A a small percentage met the level of efficiency standards set by the government.

   B homeowners used exclusively recyclable materials in new-home construction.

   C most American homes were overusing energy and natural resources.

   D architects have recently built very few green buildings.

25 The following sentence can be added to paragraph 5. Look at the four letters that indicate where the following sentence could fit in paragraph 5. Mark the letter **A**, **B**, **C**, or **D** on your answer sheet.

   So, instead of using traditional gas heat or electricity powered by a generator, American homeowners or building management may now choose greener energy sources.

   [**A**] In terms of energy and natural resources, sustainable architecture may incorporate many alternative energy sources—energy that is not harmful to the environment and does not rely on mineral-based fuels like coal or oil. Some utility companies around the world are offering wind and solar power as alternatives to electricity. [**B**] In the U.S. today, these options are available to homeowners and commercial building management. [**C**] Along with the capability to use recyclable materials in residential or commercial constructions, as well as options for generating power from renewable energy sources, society can contribute to the concept of a greener way of life. [**D**]

26 In paragraph 5, the author uses the phrase renewable energy sources to mean

   A resources that are easy to use.

   B energy from mineral-based resources.

   C energy sources that are naturally refilled.

   D energy sources that are purchased by homeowners.

27 **Directions**: Complete the table below to organize information about the building materials mentioned in the passage. Sort the types of materials found in a demolition site according to their qualities. Look at the corresponding number on your answer sheet and select **three** answers for row **1** and **three** answers for row **2**. **This question is worth 3 points**.

Salvageable building materials	Select three
Non-recyclable building materials	Select three

Materials

    A wooden doors covered with lead-based paint

    B ceramic tiles from a kitchen or bathroom floor

    C newspapers and textiles found on the site

    D a 1950s gas heater

    E plastic cups and take-out containers

    F stone and concrete from interior walls

    G water pipes from the sewer system

    H shingles of asbestos-based construction

    I insulation consisting of cellulose

Questions 28–41 are based on the following passage.

Passage 3 Discovery of a colossal squid

1 Colossal squid (*mesonychoteuthis hamiltoni*) were once only imagined as the sea-monsters of myths, like those portrayed in author Jules Verne's eighteenth-century novel *Twenty Thousand Leagues Under the Sea*, or illustrated in other works of science fiction. Today, the existence of colossal squid has been validated. Even larger than the giant squid, the aptly named colossal squid is also a much heavier creature. However, despite its daunting size, recent research has speculated that it may not be such an aggressive predator as was previously thought. Instead of hunting its prey, the colossal squid may be a "sit and float" predator that waits for fish to swim by, unaware of its presence, before ambushing its prey.

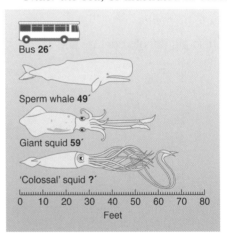

2 An elusive creature, it is rare that marine biologists or fishermen have ever seen a living colossal squid. In fact, scientists did not verify the true existence of the colossal squid until about 1925, when parts of its tentacles and spiked beak were found in the stomach of a sperm whale, one of its main predators. Over the past century, scientists have identified fewer than ten specimens of colossal squid, and most have only been identified from examining the remains found in the stomachs of sperm whales, or, its other main enemy, the sleeper shark.

3 All squid are scientifically classified in the *cephalopoda* class of animals. The term is derived from Greek roots meaning *head* and *foot*. Cephalopods are invertebrates, lacking a backbone or spinal column. Squid, like octopus and cuttlefish, belong to the same subclass of cephalopods called *Coleoidea*. Squid have a distinct head, a mantle and eight arms, two fins, and two pairs of tentacles. The colossal squid differs from the giant squid in that it has hooks on the tentacles. Another difference is in the distribution of giant squid in the oceans surrounding New Zealand whereas the colossal squid seems to prefer colder, deeper waters. Colossal squid are more likely to inhabit the Ross Sea in the region near Antarctica. Another notable difference is that the colossal squid can weigh over a thousand pounds and may be up to 40 feet long. These squid can move through the water to a submerged depth of about 6,560 feet.

4 In 2003, fishermen in the Ross Sea caught a colossal squid of almost 20 feet in length with enormous eyes and razor-sharp hooks on its tentacles. From examining the physiology of this specimen, scientists realized that because of *dimorphism*—a difference in size between the genders, the female of the species are atypically much larger than the males. Thus, the discovery of an enormous male colossal squid indicates the possible existence of even larger female squid.

5 Scientists proved this theory in 2007 when fishermen in the Ross Sea captured a colossal squid that was feeding on toothfish. This female squid weighed over a ton and was nearly 33 feet long. The fishermen also filmed the squid on video. This enabled scientists to examine it, to some extent,

as a live specimen. They were unable to contain the live squid, but preserved it in ice and took it to New Zealand for further study. In spring of 2008, scientists thawed the squid and began a thorough examination, which allowed them to obtain much more information on the lethal hooks of its tentacles.

6 Determining the age of the colossal squid has been difficult, which means that if age is a factor in size, there could be even larger colossal squid in the deep sea. Both scientists and observers of the colossal squid have investigated how these squid came to be "colossal" and how this benefits the animal's survival. This is a phenomenon known as *deep-sea gigantism*. Deep-sea gigantism is a tendency where invertebrates, such as squid and octopus, or crustaceans such as lobsters, grow much larger than invertebrates that swim in shallow waters. It has also been determined that gigantism improves longevity of the species because it slows down the squid's **metabolism**.

7 Another factor that may cause gigantism is the frigid temperature of the deep sea. Biologists believe there is a correlation between the body temperature and size of the colossal squid. Their larger size enables the colossal squid to conserve body heat in a frigid environment, thus giving them another edge over their competition.

Glossary

metabolism: chemical reactions in the body's cells that convert food into energy

28 In paragraph 1, why does the author mention Jules Verne's novel?

   A to exemplify modern literature containing illustrations of colossal squid

   B to contrast the portrayal of colossal squid in literature with other works of science fiction

   C to give an example of how colossal squid were once thought to be myths

   D to show the difference between the portrayal of sea monsters in eighteenth century and contemporary fiction

29 According to paragraph 1, what is true about colossal squid?

   A They did not exist in the eighteenth century.

   B They were once only imagined in science fiction books.

   C They are named because of their vicious dispositions.

   D Scientists validated their existence nearly a century ago.

30 In paragraph 1, what does the author imply by stating that the colossal squid is now believed to be a "sit and float" predator?

   A The squid was once thought to exist only in very deep water.

   B Scientists now describe colossal squid as an aggressive predator.

   C Ideas about how colossal squid hunt their prey are controversial.

   D Scientists know exactly how colossal squid catch prey.

31 The word elusive in paragraph 2 is closest in meaning to

   A strange.

   B obvious.

   C evasive.

   D indescribable.

32 Which of the following sentences best expresses the essential information in paragraph 2?

  A The remains of a colossal squid were identified in the stomach of a shark.

  B Scientists identified the spiked beak and parts of the tentacles of a colossal squid in the stomach of a sperm whale.

  C Fewer than 10 specimens of colossal squid were found in the stomachs of its main predators.

  D The existence of the colossal squid was determined in 1925 by examining parts of 10 different specimens.

33 In paragraph 3, the author mentions that giant squid have all of the following in common with the colossal squid EXCEPT

  A fins.

  B hooks.

  C mantles.

  D tentacles.

34 According to paragraph 3, what is true about octopus and cuttlefish?

  A They do not have backbones.

  B They do not have fins or mantles.

  C They have hooks on their tentacles.

  D They swim in very cold, deep water.

35 The word submerged in paragraph 3 is closest in meaning to

  A sunken.

  B floating.

  C plunged.

  D immersed.

36 In paragraph 4, what does the author imply about the size of colossal squid?

  A that the male of the species is always larger

  B that the size of the female colossal squid is not typical in most other species

  C that it is impossible to predict how large a female colossal squid might be

  D that the enormous size of the male colossal squid has no bearing on the size of a female

37 In paragraph 5, the phrase Scientists proved this theory in 2007 means

  A the prediction that the female colossal squid would be much larger was true.

  B ideas about the size of colossal squid were dependent on water temperature.

  C the enormous male squid found in 2003 was evidence of their belief.

  D the examination of the specimen from 2003 was inconclusive.

38 In paragraph 5, the word lethal is closest in meaning to

  A strong.

  B extreme.

  C revitalizing.

  D deadly.

39 The following sentence can be added to paragraph 6. Look at the four letters that indicate where the following sentence could fit in paragraph 6. Mark the letter **A**, **B**, **C**, or **D** on your answer sheet.

Experts claim that their large size favors survival because the squid are intimidating to their predators.

Determining the age of the colossal squid has been difficult, which means that if age is a factor in size, there could be even larger colossal squid in the deep sea. [**A**] Both scientists and observers of the colossal squid have investigated how these squid came to be "colossal" and how this benefits the animal's survival. [**B**] This is a phenomenon now known as *deep-sea gigantism*. [**C**] Deep-sea gigantism is a tendency where invertebrates, such as squid and octopus, or crustaceans such as lobsters, grow much larger than invertebrates that swim in shallow waters. [**D**] It has also been determined that gigantism improves longevity of the species because it slows down the squid's **metabolism**.

40 In paragraphs 6 and 7, what does the author imply about the correlation of the colossal squid's size with the temperature of the water?

    A The icy water temperature makes them more aggressive.

    B The water temperature has no effect on the squid's behavior.

    C The colossal squid's size and icy temperatures may affect its lifespan.

    D It is unlikely that smaller squid are living in the colder waters of the ocean.

41 Directions: A sentence that introduces a short summary of the passage is provided below. Complete the summary by choosing **three** answer choices that represent the most important ideas of the passage. There are sentences that may not be included in the summary because they are minor points or do not express the ideas presented in the passage. Read each sentence and mark your answer choices on the sheet. **This question is worth 2 points**.

This passage describes the rarely seen colossal squid and some of its features.

Answer choices

    A The main predators of the colossal squid are the sperm whale and the sleeper shark.

    B The female colossal squid—larger than the male of the species—can intimidate its predators due to its uncommonly large size.

    C Until the early twentieth century, the existence of the colossal squid was a myth.

    D The discovery of the colossal squid sheds light on the phenomenon of gigantism in deep-sea creatures.

    E Like most deep-sea creatures, colossal squid are uncommonly large.

    F In recent years, a closer examination of captured specimens of colossal squid have revealed more details about its size, weight, and the lethal hooks on its tentacles.

Questions 42–54 are based on the following passage.

Passage 4 Cultural aspects of genealogy

1 To social scientists, the field of genealogy is not typically considered a legitimate area of scholarly research. However, its relevance to cultural and historical anthropologists in understanding the connections among people in society is indisputable. The genealogical method, or, way of using symbols and diagrams to create a record of kinship connections, is an important technique of *ethnography*. Ethnography, therefore, is two things: a method that both cultural and historical anthropologists use to conduct research about a group of people, and, the written record of that research. Genealogy uses ethnographic tools because it includes both **kinship** connections and written records of the families. This is better known as a "family tree," which is a diagram of a person's ancestry.

2 Cultural anthropologists can collect data on family backgrounds to further exploration of kinship connections within a society. Genealogical research reveals significant facts that can be analyzed in order to see how descent, marriage, and kinship ties play a role in the development of a given society over time. These principles are the social building blocks of many nonindustrial-based societies: societies that are "kin based." For example, genealogical records were perhaps most important to the aristocracy of Europe. Throughout history and even today, in upper-class families, one's **pedigree** determined whether a couple could wed. For example, there was no barrier to Charles, Prince of Wales and Lady Diana Spencer marrying because of her impeccable lineage. Similarly, in the U.S., one's lineage often played a role in uniting families of a particular socio-economic level—such as the marriage between President John F. Kennedy and Jacqueline Bouvier.

3 The American public's fascination with genealogy may have started in 1976 with the publication and television mini-series of author Alex Hailey's acclaimed book, *Roots*, the story of his eighteenth-century African ancestors from the time of their enslavement to the emancipation proclamation in the U.S. The popularity of genealogy as a "cultural phenomenon" has grown to a point where people worldwide are subscribing to various ancestry websites, becoming members of genealogical societies, and even having their DNA tested, all in order to trace their family trees. In addition to a recent rise in the number of Internet-based genealogical research companies, genealogy has also generated commercial appeal by way of television broadcasting. Today, programs on television about "finding your roots" are ubiquitous. The premise of one show, for example, is investigating the family trees of American celebrities. These features, combined with a celebrity factor, have boosted the interest in genealogy in the U.S. and Canada by nearly half a million people.

4 This cultural phenomenon may seem like a fad, but at the same time, its historical and more scholarly implications are not lost to cultural anthropologists and researchers in other disciplines. For archivists—the library science specialists who deal with documenting, preserving, and organizing old records—the field of genealogy and the needs of genealogical researchers are very important. There is no special credential or degree-bearing requirement for becoming a "professional" genealogist. Many people have become genealogists simply because of an interest in their own family history.

5 The genealogist must learn how to reconstruct family trees based on the information provided by an individual as well as have a deep knowledge and understanding of the sources, in order to reconstruct another person's family tree. Other skills include understanding how to work with a variety of records: registers from religious institutions, population **census reports**, deeds to land, immigration and emigration records, as well as other primary sources. Anyone conducting genealogical research must know how to read these documents and interpret the data. Often, the researcher must also be able to decipher script or handwriting on records from different eras and from various regions of the world.

6 Genealogists often find that researching a family tree is a multi-faceted task. The family tree often becomes much more than a list of names and dates on a diagram. It reaches a deeper level—one that explores the personality, character, lifestyle, and humanity of the individuals it represents. This is perhaps the desired result of genealogical research: to create a more holistic and realistic picture of families and kinship ties, and in turn, societies, as they change and grow over time.

Glossary

kinship: family connection

pedigree: documented proof of lineage or ancestry

census reports: systematic surveys conducted by a government to record data about the country

42 According to paragraph 1, what is true about the field of genealogy?

　A Its research is questionable.

　B It is not a real field of study.

　C Cultural and historical anthropologists dispute its relevance.

　D It helps anthropologists reconstruct the links among people in society.

43 In paragraph 1, the author's description of ethnography mentions all of the following EXCEPT

　A it includes recorded documents.

　B it is a research method.

　C it is a diagram.

　D it is a technique.

44 Which of the following best represents the important information in the highlighted sentence from paragraph 2? Answer choices that are *incorrect* change the meaning or leave out necessary information.

　A Genealogists can discover significant research by studying a given society.

　B By studying kinship ties, genealogists are able to examine the development of society.

　C The role of marriage and kinship ties in a society's development may be revealed by the analysis of genealogical research.

　D By researching certain social ties over time, genealogists can significantly analyze how a society develops.

45 Why does the author mention the aristocracy in paragraph 2?

　A to show that American genealogy was unimportant

　B to point out a social group that was not kin-based

　C to show similarities between the upper class and aristocracy

　D to illustrate how one's background could influence one's marriage ties

46 The word lineage in paragraph 2 is closest in meaning to

　A property.

　B heritage.

　C connection.

　D inheritance.

47 According to paragraph 3, the author mentions all of the following as factors that have made genealogy a cultural phenomenon EXCEPT

　A television shows on the subject of genealogy.

　B the number of Internet-based research sites.

　C the involvement of celebrities.

　D the importance of DNA testing.

48 The word ubiquitous in paragraph 3 is closest in meaning to

　A ever-present.

　B universal.

　C censored.

　D restricted.

49 The following sentence can be added to paragraph 3. Look at the four letters that indicate where the following sentence could fit in paragraph 3. Mark the letter **A**, **B**, **C**, or **D** on your answer sheet.

Stations in the U.K., Canada, and U.S. have broadcasted shows based on themes of discovering one's ancestry.

The American public's fascination with genealogy may have started in 1976 with the publication and television mini-series of author Alex Hailey's acclaimed book, *Roots*, the story of his eighteenth-century African ancestors from the time of their enslavement to the emancipation proclamation in the U.S. [**A**] The popularity of genealogy as a "cultural phenomenon" has grown to a point where people worldwide are subscribing to various ancestry websites, becoming members of genealogical societies, and even having their DNA tested, all in order to trace their family trees. In addition to a recent rise in the number of Internet-based genealogical research companies, genealogy has also generated commercial appeal by way of television broadcasting. [**B**] Today, programs on television about "finding your roots" are ubiquitous. [**C**] The premise of one show, for example, is investigating the family trees of American celebrities. [**D**] These features, combined with a celebrity factor, have boosted the interest in genealogy in the U.S. and Canada by nearly half a million people.

50 The word fad in paragraph 4 is closest in meaning to

  A fashion.

  B manner.

  C trend.

  D whim.

51 According to paragraphs 4 and 5, all of the following are true about professional genealogists EXCEPT

  A they must be able to find and use data from source materials.

  B they read and interpret various handwritten documents.

  C they may research another individual's family tree.

  D they must have credentials in order to do research.

52 In paragraph 6, the word It refers to

  A a list of names.

  B the family tree.

  C genealogy.

  D a diagram.

53 The word holistic in paragraph 6 is closest in meaning to

  A partial.

  B complex.

  C complete.

  D segmented.

54 Directions: A sentence that introduces a short summary of the passage is provided below. Complete the summary by choosing **three** answer choices that represent the most important ideas of the passage. There are sentences that may not be included in the summary because they are minor points or do not express the ideas presented in the passage. Read each sentence and mark your answer choices on the sheet. **This question is worth 2 points.**

Genealogy has become more relevant in anthropological studies as a technique of ethnography.

Answer choices

A The principles of genealogical study, such as kinship ties and marriage, may play a role in the development of nonindustrial-based societies.

B Largely due to the public's fascination with Alex Hailey's novel, the media introduced sources for genealogy enthusiasts, from Internet resources to television programs.

C Archivists examine data and preserve records for professional genealogists in order to conduct research.

D Professional genealogists utilize databases and a variety of records in order to conduct research on another person's ancestry.

E Genealogists interpret records and documents that are not easy to decipher.

F The results of genealogical research may reveal a deeper understanding of family trees and the kinship connections that influence societies.

This is the end of the Reading section.

LISTENING approximately 50 minutes

This section of the TOEFL iBT™ measures your ability to understand conversations and academic lectures in English. There are two conversations followed by five questions each, and four lectures followed by six questions each, for a total of 34 questions in this section. You will have approximately **50 minutes** to answer all of the listening questions.

Mark your answers on the answer sheet on page 191. As you listen, you may take notes on the conversations and lectures. The symbol 🔊 means that you will hear but not see part of the question.

Play CD 1, tracks 1 to 47 and do not stop the recording while you complete this section of the test.

Questions 1–5 are based on the following conversation.

Conversation 1 Office hours

🔊 1.1–1.7 Listen to a conversation between a student and a teaching assistant.

1 What are the speakers mainly discussing?

   A the problems in the statistics syllabus

   B how to put together a study plan

   C the main chapters of the statistics book

   D if the students are going to take a test or a quiz

2 What is the main reason the student is meeting with the teaching assistant?

   A because she is lost

   B because she missed the last class

   C because she doesn't know how to study

   D because the professor does not have office hours today

3   What does the teaching assistant say about the chapters of the book?

    (Choose two answers)

    A Chapter one is mostly introductory material.
    B Chapter two is longer than chapter one.
    C Chapter two only discusses distributions.
    D Chapter two is on descriptive statistics.

4   Listen again to part of the conversation. Then answer the question

    What does the student mean when she says this?

    A That she is amused but realizes the test will not be short.
    B That his joke is funny because the test will be short.
    C That probabilities are sometimes amusing.
    D That she thinks statistics is a joke.

5   What does the teaching assistant suggest?

    A The student should attend class more regularly.
    B The student should attend a group study session.
    C The student should review over one hundred pages of the textbook.
    D The student should prepare for the study session by reading the entire textbook.

Questions 6–10 are based on the following conversation.

Conversation 2 Consulation

1.8–1.14 Listen to a conversation between a student and a staff member at the registrar's office.

6 Why does the student visit the registrar's office?

  A to confirm his class schedule

  B to evaluate his coursework

  C to discuss his transfer credits

  D to get permission to take a class

7 What is the staff member's attitude toward the student?

  A surprised

  B annoyed

  C impressed

  D disappointed

8 Listen again to part of the conversation. Then answer the question.

  What does the staff member mean when she says this?

  A She has never visited Cairo.

  B She thinks she lost some of the student's paperwork.

  C She is apologizing for missing another appointment.

  D She realizes she may have overlooked some information.

9 Why does the student want to take the paleontology class?

  A to fulfill his degree requirements

  B to complete his course schedule

  C to transfer to another school

  D to get a good evaluation

10 What did the student say he did prior to visiting the registrar's office?

  (Choose two answers)

  A He met with his advisor.

  B He picked up his transcripts.

  C He passed his prerequisite courses.

  D He filled out all the necessary forms.

Questions 11–16 are based on the following lecture.

Lecture 1 History of printing

🎧 1.15–1.21 Listen to part of a lecture in a history of design class.

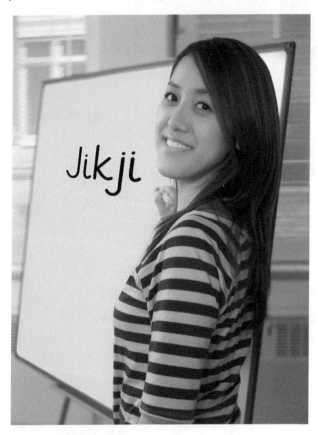

11 What does the professor mainly discuss?

   A the origins of metal movable type

   B disagreements over the invention of movable type

   C how metal movable type printing changed over time

   D experiments in the recreation of ancient movable type

12 What does the professor imply about using wood to create written Chinese language characters?

   A It did not represent characters accurately.

   B It took a lot of time to carve a block of text.

   C It was not efficient because it wore out quickly.

   D It could not be separated into individual characters.

13 What does the professor say about the significance of Jikji?

   A Its discovery led to advances in printing techniques.

   B It is not an example of the beeswax method of molding type.

   C Its authenticity is the subject of an ongoing controversy.

   D It proves that metal movable type was invented in China.

14 According to the professor, how do we know that Jikji was created using the beeswax method?

   A The document mentions the technique on its last page.

   B The original clay molds used to print it have been preserved.

   C Researchers could only create the original style using the method.

   D It was the only technique in use at the time Jikji was printed.

15 According to the professor, what are two differences between the German and Korean printing methods?

   (Choose two answers)

   A the nature of the metal

   B the shape of the characters

   C the materials used to create the paper

   D the time it took to create the parchment

16 Listen again to part of the lecture. Then answer the question.

   Why does the professor say this?

   A to signal that she is changing the subject

   B to correct a mistake that she has made

   C to return to a previous point

   D to convey that she is avoiding irrelevant information

Questions 17–22 are based on the following lecture.

Lecture 2 Computer forensics

1.22–1.28 Listen to part of a lecture in a computer science class.

17 What does the professor mainly discuss?

  A an overview of the field of computer forensics
  B the reasons for the rise of computer forensics
  C changes in the field of computer forensics
  D research into the effectiveness of computer forensics

18 Listen again to part of the lecture. Then answer the question.

  Why does the professor say this?

  A to remind the students that they have already seen the statistics
  B to imply that the average yield of computer theft has remained the same
  C to imply that the growth of computer crime is obvious
  D to make a comment about the validity of the statistics

19 Why does the professor talk about the abstract nature of data?

  A to stress how the role of computers is expanding
  B to describe a common procedure for converting files
  C to explain why computer crime is so widespread
  D to illustrate the difficulty of adhering to established law

20 What does the professor imply about the pressure to produce fast results?

  A It has had a devastating effect on computer forensics.
  B It is a vital to successfully completing an investigation.
  C It provides a necessary counterweight to legal procedures.
  D It presents a persistent problem for computer forensic specialists.

21 Why does the professor mention the tape that the police use?

  A to stress that investigators must be in touch with authorities
  B to emphasize the importance of isolating the investigation
  C to assert that investigators must keep the scene contained
  D to caution against the improper recovery of evidence

22 According to the professor, what is true about volatile data?

On your answer grid, mark the correct box for each numbered statement. The answer is worth 2 points.

	True	False
1 It is a threat to the security of the investigation.		
2 It cannot be easily documented without damaging it.		
3 It is lost when the computer is turned off.		
4 It results from an attempt to destroy data.		

Questions 23–28 are based on the following lecture.

Lecture 3 Flowering plants

🔊 1.29–1.37 Listen to part of a lecture in a botany class.

23 What does the professor mainly discuss?

   A the dispute over whether the transition to angiosperms was gradual or abrupt

   B recent evidence for the coexistence of angiosperms and gymnosperms

   C the implications of the discovery of an ancient species of flowering plants

   D new ideas about the reasons for the rapid rise of flowering plants

24 What does the professor say about the theory that dinosaurs caused the expansion?

   A The theory has been disproved by subsequent evidence.

   B It is the most plausible account of the trigger event.

   C It is based on a popular misconception about dinosaurs.

   D There is no evidence to prove or disprove the theory.

25 Why did angiosperms have difficulty sharing space with gymnosperms?

   A Fallen gymnosperm leaves kept the soil low in nutrients.

   B Gymnosperms took all the nutrients from the soil.

   C Tall gymnosperm trees blocked necessary sunlight.

   D Thick gymnosperm roots blocked tender angiosperm roots.

26 Listen again to part of the lecture. Then answer the question.

   Why does the professor say this?

   A to remind students that she has already given the answer
   B to imply that the answer is too obvious to mention
   C to solicit a response from the students
   D to suggest that the answer is unknown

27 According to the lecture, what is positive feedback?

   A a growth cycle in rich soil stimulated by shedding and decomposition of leaves
   B the decomposition of a plant that has been taken over by another plant
   C the ability of all plant life to absorb nutrients from the surrounding soil
   D the occurrence of a minor catastrophe that influences plant growth

28 Two of the answer choices below are used in the passage to describe angiosperms and three are used to describe gymnosperms. Complete the table by matching appropriate answer choices to the type of plant they describe.

   Organize the answer choices into the categories where they belong. One answer will not be used. **This question is worth 2 points**.

Angiosperms	*Choose two*
Gymnosperms	*Choose three*

Answer choices

   A have thicker leaves
   B grow more slowly
   C lose leaves faster
   D need more nutrition
   E grow near the poles
   F are extinct

Questions 29–34 are based on the following lecture.

Lecture 4 Early American literature

🔘 1.38–1.47 Listen to part of a discussion in an American literature class.

Washington Irving

James Fenimore Cooper

29 What is the discussion mainly about?

  A a dispute between two American authors

  B the origins of distinctly American literature

  C the difference between American and British English

  D the influence of American writers on European literature

30 Listen again to part of the discussion. Then answer the question.

  Why does the professor say this?

  A to return to his previous topic

  B to postpone the topic until later

  C to signal that a digression is to follow

  D to prevent the student from interrupting

31 What does the male student say identifies an author as an American author?

  A They must be born in America.

  B They must be an American citizen.

  C They must write in an American style.

  D They must be recognized by Europeans.

32 Why does the professor mention the writers of the U.S. Constitution?

  A to offer another example of American writers

  B to stress the British origin of American English

  C to give the student an example of an earlier type of script

  D to imply that there is no real distinction between British and American English

33 What does the male student imply about Captain John Smith's writing?

  A His writing style does not reflect American English.

  B He cannot be the first American author.

  C He is considered to be a British writer.

  D He developed a new style of English.

34 According to the professor, what did Cooper and Irving have in common?

  (Choose two answers)

  A They were admired in Europe.

  B They were primarily novelists.

  C They were born in the same year.

  D They provided a foundation for other authors.

This is the end of the Listening section.

You should take a ten-minute break before beginning the Speaking section of the test.

SPEAKING approximately 20 minutes

In this section of the test, you will have the opportunity to demonstrate your ability to speak clearly and coherently on a variety of subjects. There are **six** tasks in this section with special directions for each task. You should answer each question as thoroughly as possible.

Tasks 1 and 2 are independent speaking tasks. After you hear and read each question you will have **15 seconds** to prepare your response and **45 seconds** to speak and record your response.

Tasks 3 and 4 are integrated speaking tasks. For these two tasks, you will read a short text and then hear part of a discussion or short lecture that is connected to the text. You will have **45 seconds** to read the text. After you play the listening track, you will see a question about what you have just read and heard. You will have **30 seconds** to plan a response and **60 seconds** in which to answer the question.

You will hear a tone on the CD indicating when your preparation time is up and you should begin your response. You may begin speaking when you hear the tone.

Tasks 5 and 6 are integrated speaking tasks. For these tasks, you will hear a short conversation or lecture. Then you will read a question related to what you have just heard. You will have **20 seconds** to plan your response and **60 seconds** in which to answer the question.

You will hear a tone on the CD indicating when your preparation time is up and you should begin your response. You may begin speaking when you hear the tone.

You should record all your responses on your computer or use a recording device. Then you can play back your responses and check them against the sample responses at the back of this book.

Speaking task 1

 Do you agree or disagree with the following statement?

Experience in life is just as important as knowledge from books.

Use specific reasons and examples to support your answer.

Preparation time: 15 seconds   Response time: 45 seconds

Speaking task 2

 Which do you prefer? Would you rather communicate with your friends on the phone, via e-mail, or face-to-face every day?

Give reasons and examples to support your choice.

Preparation time: 15 seconds   Response time: 45 seconds

Speaking task 3

Reading time: You have 45 seconds to read the passage. Set your timer and begin reading. You may take notes.

Read the following notice from a university institute regarding their summer internships.

> The Office of Academic and Research Programs of the World Cultural Institute is pleased to announce the Summer Internship Program. Through the program, students will be able to apply for full-time summer internships within one of the many divisions of the World Cultural Institute. Internships are available for both undergraduate and graduate students and all positions are paid. Please note that only current students of All-State University are eligible. Students graduating in May are not eligible. Applicants must be in good academic standing and should submit a résumé that details their relevant work and educational experiences, along with a cover letter stating their interests, qualifications, and the internship they are applying for. If responding by e-mail, all applicants must state the name of the internship in the subject line of the e-mail.

🔊 1.50–1.52 Now listen to two students discussing this notice. You may take notes as you listen.

Read and listen to the question. When you hear the tone, begin recording your answer.

> The woman expresses an opinion about possibly applying for the summer internship program. State her opinion and her reasons for being concerned about applying.

Preparation time: 30 seconds   Response time: 60 seconds

Speaking task 4

Reading time: You have 45 seconds to read the passage. Set your timer and begin reading. You may take notes.

Read the following passage on ozone depletion.

> According to the U.S. government's Environmental Protection Agency (EPA), the main substances that destroy the ozone are chlorofluorocarbons (CFCs) and hydro-chlorofluorocarbons, (HCFCs), which are chemicals found in products like fire extinguishers and pesticides. These ozone-depleting substances are released into the upper ozone layer and destroy it very slowly over time. The EPA has prohibited nonessential use of all products containing CFCs and HCFCs. In order to prevent further depletion of the ozone, the EPA and other agencies around the world have taken precautions. With wider restrictions on products that contain ozone-depleting chemicals, the governments believe that the ozone layer should return to a more normal state by 2050.

 Listen to part of a lecture in a geological sciences class. The professor is discussing ways to repair the ozone layer. You may take notes as you listen.

Read and listen to the question. When you hear the tone, begin recording your answer.

> The professor's lecture is about beliefs about the ozone layer. Using information from the passage and the lecture, discuss what the professor says about the ozone layer and why it is a controversial subject.

Preparation time: 30 seconds   Response time: 60 seconds

Speaking task 5

 Listen to a conversation between a student and a librarian. You may take notes as you listen.

The student and the librarian discuss two possible solutions to the student's problem. Describe his problem and explain which of the two solutions you prefer, and why.

Preparation time: 20 seconds   Response time: 60 seconds

Speaking task 6

 Listen to a professor in an anatomy and physiology class. You may take notes as you listen.

Using points and examples from the talk, explain the two types of muscles presented by the professor.

Preparation time: 20 seconds   Response time: 60 seconds

This is the end of the Speaking section.

WRITING 50 minutes

This section measures your ability to write in an academic setting. There are two writing tasks.

Task 1 requires you to read a passage and listen to a lecture. Then you will answer a question based on what you have read and what you have heard. You will have **3 minutes** to read the passage and take notes on the passage. You will then listen to a lecture, which is also about **3 minutes** long. You may take notes. You have **20 minutes** to plan and write your response.

For **task 2**, you will answer a question based on your own knowledge and experience. You will read the question and then have **30 minutes** to plan and write your response.

Writing task 1

After you listen to the lecture, write a response to a question that asks you about the relationship between the reading and the lecture. Try to answer the question as completely as you can, based on what you have read and heard. Do not try to answer the question based on your own personal knowledge.

You will have **20 minutes** to plan and write your response.

Your essay will be judged on the basis of the quality of your writing and how well your response represents the points made in the lecture and their relationship to the passage.

You have **3 minutes** to read the passage. Set your timer for **3 minutes** and begin.

The theory of American philosopher Charles Sanders Peirce (1839–1914) holds that *semiotics*, the study of signs and meaning, was of extreme importance to fields that deal extensively with representation, such as anthropology, cognitive science, epistemology, linguistics, and all the fine arts. According to Peirce, human beings have a desire to place meaning on objects by creating or thinking in signs.

Signs are signifiers for objects. A sign can be an utterance, a spoken or written word, an image, a sound, a smell or flavor, or an action. Peirce stated that nothing is a sign unless it represents an object to someone who interprets and translates the meaning, which he called the *interpretant*. The interpretant is the "sense made out of the sign," or the understanding that we have of that sign. Peirce believed that if either the object or the person interpreting the sign were to be eliminated, the sign itself no longer has meaning. The complexity of Peirce's theory of signs evolved over time. He first divided signs into three groups based on the structure of the signs. A sign could be classified as an *icon*, an *index*, or a *symbol*. If the sign reflects the quality or characteristics of the object, it is an icon. If the interpretant connected to the object is physical or existential—confirming one's existence—then the sign is called an index. Lastly, if the interpretant employs a rule, law, convention, or habit to signify the sign, it is a symbol.

A sign could be, for example, smoke. The smoke represents its object: fire. Similarly, if an anthill exists, then it could be interpreted as a sign for its object, ants. The object is the physical or conceptual thing that the sign represents.

 When you have finished reading, listen to part of a lecture in a philosophy class. You may take notes as you listen.

After the lecture has ended, set your timer for **20 minutes** and begin writing your response to the question below.

> Summarize the points about signs in the lecture, being sure to explain specifically how they support explanations in the reading passage.

Writing task 2

For this writing task, you will write an essay in response to a question that asks you to explain and support your opinion on an issue. You have **30 minutes** to plan and write your response.

Read the question.

> Many celebrities, such as actors, athletes, and rock musicians, often speak about subjects or causes they feel strongly about. Because of their fame, many people listen. Do you think that celebrities make a difference in the world because they voice their opinions? Use specific reasons and examples to support your answer.

Set your timer for **30 minutes** and begin writing your essay.

This is the end of Test 1.

Check your answers with the Key and explanations at the back of the book. Then, use the Further practice and guidance section to review your skills.

TEST 2

READING 80 minutes

This section measures your ability to comprehend academic reading passages in English. There are four passages in this section.

Each passage is followed by **12 to 14 questions** with directions for each question. Some of the questions in this section will be worth more than 1 point.

You will have **20 minutes** to read each passage and answer the questions. You have **80 minutes** to complete the entire section.

Set a timer for **80 minutes**. Read each passage and answer the questions. Follow the directions for each type of question. Fill in your answers on the answer sheet on page 192.

Questions 1–13 are based on the following passage.

Passage 1 Leonardo da Vinci's musical instruments

1   Though most famous for the artistic finesse of his paintings, like the *Mona Lisa* or *The Last Supper*, Leonardo da Vinci (1452–1519) was also a master draftsman, architect, scientist, engineer, inventor, and musician. The genius da Vinci has always been described as the archetype of the "Renaissance man," though he was not a typical man of the fifteenth and sixteenth centuries.

2   Of his many skills, his abilities as a musician have often been disputed. However, among his top talents, he notably listed "engineer" as well as "inventor of instruments" in a letter of introduction he wrote to the Duke of Milan, Italy. Da Vinci described himself as "as capable as any man," in these areas. According to Vasari, da Vinci's biographer, he constructed a silver *lyre*—an ancient stringed instrument—in the shape of a horse's head, which he gave to the duke as a gift. Some historians claimed that da Vinci played it with great skill, comparable to any musician at his patron's court.

3   In his lifetime, Leonardo da Vinci produced nearly 4,000 drawings—many of which were found in his notebooks. One notebook, the *Codex Atlanticus*, contained designs for several musical instruments, including a drum and a *viola-organista*. Because these instruments were never built and played during Leonardo's lifetime, scholars have disagreed on *exactly* what these instruments were and what to call them, or how they would sound. Jean Paul Richter, who translated Leonardo's notebooks in 1883, described the *viola-organista* as a combination of a **zither** and a primitive keyboard. Others have called it a "harpsichord-viola" because it has the strings of a viola and a three-**octave** keyboard, similar in appearance to a modern-day piano. To operate the harpsichord-viola, air would be forced through a **bellows** attached to the keyboard and powered by the player's leg when he marched or walked. Designs for this instrument show that it could be easily carried by use of shoulder straps and a belt placed around the waist of the player.

4   One of two lesser-known notebooks (the *Madrid I*), housed at the Madrid National Library, contained sketches of two other instruments: a bell with a **damper system**, and, a pipe-like wind instrument. This wind instrument was designed to operate by pumping air through a bag attached to the pipes. Da Vinci called this a *pipa*. Scholars have also disagreed on this instrument's true appellation. Some believe it resembled a bagpipe due to the pumping of air and the mouthpiece, while others designated it to be a "triple trumpet" because it looked more like a horn than a bagpipe.

5   Da Vinci's designs for percussion instruments were also quite unusual. Unlike the string and wind instruments, the concepts for these designs were more detailed. Intended for use in parades and pageants, da Vinci's motorized drums were set on a cart that had a crank mechanism containing several rows of curved mallets on either side. The musician could "program" the mechanism by using movable pegs that were inserted into rows of holes on rollers. The player then adjusted the mechanism to a desired rhythm. When the player pulled the cart behind him, the beat could sound continuously as long as the player kept the speed of the cart constant.

6   Scholars have claimed that it is difficult to reconstruct these musical instruments because so few musical instruments from the Renaissance era have survived. In addition, some of the pages of the notebooks were missing, leaving potential instrument makers at a loss. It was not until 2008 that some Italian instrument makers created the first functional model of da Vinci's "harpsichord viola." For the first time in history, people were able to hear how the instrument would sound. Listeners claimed that it sounded somewhat like a violin, but that the wooden mechanism by which it worked was grating and noisy.

Glossary

zither: a type of stringed instrument, played horizontally

octave: an interval of eight musical tones, as in a scale

bellows: a device that delivers a controlled quantity of pressurized air into a controlled location

damper system: a device that muffles the resonance of a bell

1. The word archetype in paragraph 1 is closest in meaning to
   A rival.
   B model.
   C antagonist.
   D counter-example.

2. In paragraph 1, the author states that Leonardo da Vinci was not typical of his time in order to
   A illustrate how da Vinci was similar to his contemporaries.
   B point out that da Vinci was not exceptional during his time.
   C demonstrate that calling da Vinci a "Renaissance man" does not have a literal meaning.
   D show that there were many "Renaissance men" in the fifteenth and sixteenth centuries.

3. In paragraph 2, based on Leonardo da Vinci's letter to the Duke of Milan, which of the following did da Vinci NOT mention as one of his professional skills?
   A patron
   B painter
   C engineer
   D instrument maker

4. According to paragraph 2, the author suggests that da Vinci's skills as a musician were
   A not as good as his other skills.
   B never confirmed in a public forum.
   C less than the standard of other musicians.
   D equivalent to the skills of most musicians.

5. According to paragraph 3, why did scholars disagree on what to call da Vinci's musical instruments?
   A because they were too complicated to build
   B because they were complex combinations of several unusual instruments
   C because there were no clear instructions on how to construct them
   D because da Vinci had not given these instruments appropriate names

6. What can be inferred from paragraph 3 about the *viola-organista*?
   A Because the piano had not yet been invented, it was difficult to know how to describe it.
   B It could not easily be played in a stationary position.
   C It was different from the harpsichord-viola.
   D Air was not necessary to make it work.

7 The following sentence can be added to paragraph 3. Look at the four letters that indicate where the following sentence could fit in paragraph 3. Mark the letter **A**, **B**, **C**, or **D** on your answer grid.

In the fifteenth century, the piano had not yet been invented.

In his lifetime, Leonardo da Vinci produced nearly 4,000 drawings—many of which were found in his notebooks. One notebook, the *Codex Atlanticus*, contained designs for several musical instruments, including a drum and a *viola-organista*. **[A]** Because these instruments were never built and played during Leonardo's lifetime, scholars have disagreed on *exactly* what these instruments were and what to call them, or how they would sound. **[B]** Jean Paul Richter, who translated Leonardo's notebooks in 1883, described the *viola-organista* as a combination of a zither and a primitive keyboard. Others have called it a "harpsichord-viola" because it has the strings of a viola and a three-octave keyboard, similar in appearance to a modern-day piano. **[C]** To operate the harpsichord-viola, air would be forced through a bellows attached to the keyboard and powered by the player's leg when he marched or walked. **[D]** Designs for this instrument show that it could be easily carried by use of shoulder straps and a belt placed around the waist of the player.

8 According to paragraph 4, what can be inferred about Leonardo da Vinci's *Madrid I* notebook?

    A Scholars had not widely recognized or examined the notebook's contents.

    B The notebook contained sketches for an instrument operated by the wind.

    C The notebook consisted of fewer pages than his other notebooks.

    D The *Madrid I* journal also included architectural designs.

9 The word appellation in paragraph 4 is closest in meaning to

    A construction.

    B ability.

    C calling.

    D name.

10 In paragraph 5, the phrase curved mallets means

    A the beat of the drum.

    B a type of drumstick.

    C rounded pegs.

    D shaped carts.

11 According to paragraph 5, the player of the motorized drum could do all of the following to change the beat of the drum EXCEPT

    A use different mallets.

    B bring the cart to a complete stop.

    C move the pegs in the mechanism.

    D speed up or slow down while pulling the cart.

12 The word it in paragraph 6 refers to

    A the wooden mechanism.

    B the instrument.

    C a violin.

    D history.

13 Directions: A sentence which introduces a short summary of the passage is provided below. Complete the summary by selecting **three** answer choices that represent the most important ideas in the passage. Some sentences do not belong in the summary because they express minor ideas or ideas that are not presented in the passage. **This question is worth 2 points.**

Leonardo da Vinci, the original Renaissance man, was gifted in areas ranging from science and engineering to painting and music.

Answer choices

- **A** Da Vinci's biographer noted his creation of musical instruments, as well as his superior musical abilities.
- **B** Through some of da Vinci's notebooks, scholars learned that he designed musical instruments such as woodwind, a keyboard-like instrument, and motorized drums, which were never constructed during his lifetime.
- **C** Da Vinci's designs for musical instruments were so complicated that no one could ever build them and thus, they were neither definable nor heard.
- **D** Scholars believed that it was impossible to reconstruct da Vinci's instruments because they had not been created during his life.
- **E** Though scholars never believed that da Vinci's instruments could be reconstructed, one of his instruments was recently built and played in public for the first time.
- **F** When one of his instruments was reconstructed, people did not enjoy hearing it because it was very noisy.

Questions 14–26 are based on the following passage.

Passage 2 The search for Earth-like planets

1   Astronomers have discovered more than 400 *exoplanets*, or, planets outside our solar system. Some of these planets have Earth-like qualities. However, many of these exoplanets are as large as Jupiter, and it is unlikely that they are habitable. A planet in the "habitable zone" means the planet is located at a distance from its sun suitable enough to allow for the existence of water on its surface. This is called the "**Goldilocks** position," meaning the planet is neither too hot, nor too cold.

2   In order to find planets that are light years from our own solar system, astronomers use two types of telescope, each with sensitive instruments that employ special techniques, to aid in the acquisition of data: ground-based and orbiting telescopes. In 2007, a team of Swiss scientists discovered the first Earth-like planet outside of our solar system, *Gliese 581*, estimated to be approximately 50 percent bigger than Earth. Located about 20.5 light years from our world, Gliese 581 orbits a **red dwarf** star. To identify this new planet, the astronomy team used a *spectroscopic* instrument known as HARPS, which is linked to a 3.6-meter telescope at the European Southern Observatory in La Silla, Chile. Spectroscopic instruments use a Doppler, or "wobble" technique, to identify radial velocity—how fast a star moves toward or away from the point of observation. By analyzing the wavelength of light emitted from a star, the instrument is therefore able to calibrate the mass of a planet in the star's orbit. With the wobble technique, astronomers are only able to perceive a planet that is less than 160 light years from Earth. Employing this technique can be slow, because astronomers must wait for the planet to make one complete orbit of its sun in order to confirm their data.

3   Though earth-bound telescopic systems like HARPS at La Silla play a prominent role in space exploration, orbiting telescopes, like the Hubble Space Telescope and the Kepler Orbiting Telescope, can provide astrophysicists with different data. Circling 380 miles above the Earth, the Hubble Space Telescope (HST) is about the size of a yellow school bus. Soon after its launch in 1990, astronomers were shocked to find that images sent back by the Hubble were slightly blurry due to a defective mirror. To remedy this problem, NASA created a special lens for the Hubble, similar to the way eyeglasses correct human eyesight. In a special mission, a team of astronauts serviced the Hubble by mounting this corrective lens. They also added several other specialized instruments, including an infrared camera and a spectrograph, which is used to analyze light. Among the Hubble's discoveries are new planets, newly born stars, various **nebulae**, and even collisions of **asteroids** on the planet Jupiter. In

joint observation with several ground-based telescopes, the Hubble found several exoplanets that exist in a habitable zone from their stars. It is also credited with the discovery of a molecule of methane gas in the atmosphere of a Jupiter-sized exoplanet, supporting the theory of life forms in space.

4   In 2009, NASA launched the Kepler Orbiting Telescope. Its primary task is to focus on or, "stare at" the stars. Instead of orbiting the Earth like the Hubble, it "trails" the Earth, meaning it travels behind the Earth's orbit around the Sun. The Kepler's mission is to observe about 150,000 stars and determine if these stars contain planetary systems, most particularly, habitable planets. Unlike the La Silla and Hubble telescopes, the Kepler Orbiting Telescope uses a *photometric* instrument to measure light emanating from a star. When a planet passes in front of a star (similar to an observation of Mercury or Venus crossing in front of the Sun), the Kepler telescope analyzes a change in the intensity of light emitted by that star. This process allows astronomers to evaluate and examine the data further to determine if one or more planets may orbit the star.

5   The Kepler Orbiting Telescope accomplished its primary objective in 2010: to find Earth-like planets. It discovered seven planets—some almost as large as Jupiter—beyond our solar system. While many astrophysicists and astro-biologists have argued the unlikelihood of life forms on other planets, the data from the Kepler Orbiting Telescope suggests the contrary.

Glossary

Goldilocks: the female character in a fairy tale who tested the food, chairs, and beds of three bears, in order to find the one that was "just right"

red dwarf: a star with low surface temperature, mass, and size

nebulae: clouds of dust that exist in outer space

asteroids: small or minor planets resembling stars

14   According to paragraph 1, what is true about exoplanets?

   A Most of them are considerably smaller than the planet Jupiter.

   B Those that are as large as Jupiter probably cannot sustain life.

   C They are found within our solar system.

   D They are larger than the Earth.

15   In paragraph 1, why does the author use the phrase "the Goldilocks position"?

   A to support the concept of Earth-like exoplanets

   B to demonstrate the unlikelihood of a planet being Earth-like

   C to illustrate the differences between a habitable and uninhabitable planet

   D to explain the conditions needed for a planet to be considered habitable

16   In paragraph 2, all of the following are true about *Gliese 581* EXCEPT

   A it is half the size larger than Earth.

   B it is probably in a habitable zone.

   C it is in our solar system.

   D it has its own sun.

17 In paragraph 2, which of the following best expresses the essential information in the highlighted sentence? *Incorrect* answer choices change the meaning or leave out essential information.

   A Wobble techniques are used to demonstrate the use of a spectroscope.

   B Using the wobble technique, spectroscopic instruments can determine a star's speed.

   C A star can move very fast away from the Earth, therefore it is necessary to use a wobble technique.

   D In radial velocity, a star can move so quickly that it wobbles, which can be seen by using a telescope.

18 The word blurry in paragraph 3 is closest in meaning to

   A clear.

   B cloudy.

   C stormy.

   D indistinct.

19 According to paragraph 3, what problem did the Hubble Space Telescope have?

   A Its mirror was flawed.

   B NASA damaged its mirror.

   C A lens on its camera was broken.

   D It did not have an infrared camera.

20 The word It in paragraph 3 refers to

   A observation.

   B the Hubble Space Telescope.

   C a molecule.

   D a habitable zone.

21 Why does the author mention the molecule of methane in paragraph 3?

   A to support his statement about habitable planets

   B to give evidence of one of the Hubble Space Telescope's uses

   C to give the Hubble credit for the discovery of a new gas

   D to illustrate the possibility for the existence of other life forms in the universe

22 According to paragraph 4, what can be inferred about the Kepler's main purpose?

   A to search for new planets

   B to focus on threatening asteroids

   C to trail closely behind the Earth's orbit

   D to determine if star systems contain potentially habitable planets

23 Look at the four letters that indicate where the following sentence could fit in paragraph 4. Where would it best fit the paragraph? Mark the letter **A**, **B**, **C**, or **D** on your answer sheet.

In this way, the Earth's shadow does not obstruct the images made by the telescope's cameras.

In 2009, NASA launched the Kepler Orbiting Telescope. **[A]** Its primary task is to focus on or, "stare at" the stars. **[B]** Instead of orbiting the Earth like the Hubble, it "trails" the Earth, meaning it travels behind the Earth's orbit around the Sun. **[C]** The Kepler's mission is to observe about 150,000 stars and determine if these stars contain planetary systems, most particularly, habitable planets. Unlike the La Silla and Hubble telescopes, the Kepler Orbiting Telescope uses a *photometric* instrument to measure light emanating from a star. When a planet passes in front of a star (similar to an observation of Mercury or Venus crossing in front of the Sun), the Kepler telescope analyzes a change in the intensity of light emitted by that star. **[D]** This process allows astronomers to evaluate and examine the data further to determine if one or more planets may orbit the star.

24 The word emanating in paragraph 4 is closest in meaning to

   A changing.

   B radiating.

   C oozing.

   D moving.

25 The author of the passage suggests that

   A the Kepler Orbiting Telescope did not meet its goals.

   B the Kepler's data proves that life beyond our solar system is unlikely.

   C most scientists doubt the usefulness of the Kepler Orbiting Telescope.

   D the discovery of Earth-like planets does not mean they are habitable.

26 Directions: Complete the table by picking **seven** answer choices. Identify the type of telescope and match it to the process or instrument by which it works. **This question is worth 4 points**.

	Type of telescope	
	Ground-based	**Space-based**
	Choose one	*Choose one*
Instrument or process	*Choose three*	*Choose two*

Answer choices

   A infrared camera

   B Kepler

   C La Silla

   D HARPS

   E Doppler

   F photometry

   G spectrometry

   H corrective lens

   I Hubble

Questions 27–39 are based on the following passage.

Passage 3 The development of Keynesian Economics

1 Generally regarded to be the "founder of macroeconomics," twentieth-century British economist John Maynard Keynes's ideas had a resounding effect on global economies. Macroeconomics is the analysis of the behavior of a capitalist nation's economic system as a whole, in regard to such factors as employment, inflation, the balance of trade, and how particular patterns and trends in these factors will influence each other. "Keynesian" economics became known as a school of thought based primarily on his theories about economic policies, money, business cycles, and economic **recession**.

2 John Maynard Keynes, (1883–1946) was born in Cambridge, England. His parents were a well-educated, middle-class couple, which undoubtedly influenced his intellectual development. His mother was a social reformer and his father was an economist and lecturer at the University of Cambridge. Keynes's interest and adeptness in a vast range of subjects were most noticeable during his studies at Eton College. Keynes gained early acceptance at King's College, Cambridge where he earned his bachelor's degree. At both institutions, Keynes had been offered academic scholarships. He excelled in mathematics and took his first BA in that field. He worked briefly as a clerk in the India Office, having passed the service exams by 1906. In his post-baccalaureate pursuits, his inclination was to study philosophy, but with encouragement and persuasion from one of his mentors, he finally decided on economics.

3 Keynes's knowledge and excellence in the field of economics served him well in his appointment as editor of the *Economic Journal*, in 1911. He chose to remain in Cambridge at King's College as a lecturer, where he taught several economics courses such as Theory of Money, the Stock Exchange, and the Money Market; Principles of Economics, and Currency and Banking, as well as two courses specializing in the economics of India: The Currency and Finances of India, and, The Monetary Affairs of India. It was from the combination of his teaching these two latter courses and his position at the India Office that he was inspired to develop the idea for his first book, *Indian Currency and Finance*, published in 1913.

4 From 1914 to 1918, Keynes became an important advisor to the U.K. Treasury, to help with the financing of the war. When World War I ended in 1918, Keynes was appointed to a delegation at the Peace Conference in Versailles, France. His opposition to the terms of the Treaty of Versailles, as it pertained to war reparations imposed on Germany, led him to write the controversial book, *Economic Consequences of the Peace* (1919).

5 In the next decade, Keynes published several treatises and tracts on subjects such as probability and monetary reform. He completed and published his most important text, *The General Theory of Employment, Interest and Money*, during a time when most of the nations of the world were suffering in the grips of the Great Depression. In this work, published in 1936, Keynes established his theories on the world's economy, which became known as the *Keynesian model*, and sought to explain fluctuations in **aggregate** business. The book was widely criticized for being poorly organized and for presenting ideas that were so complicated that they were often incomprehensible to its readers.

6 Despite its flaws, the effects of this book were long lasting. In it, Keynes clearly laid out a foundation for how a government should "run **deficits**" to manage or end a recession. The government creates a budget deficit by borrowing capital and purchasing goods from a world market. The government must then bolster demand and increase taxation and consumption in an effort to stabilize its workforce. During an economic downturn, private individuals do not invest or spend. This creates a cycle where businesses also reduce investments resulting in fewer jobs and less investment. Keynes's idea was that the government should take the place of businesses by investing in public works while simultaneously creating jobs for the unemployed.

7 Initially, Keynes's ideas were met with opposition from most economists. However, in the post-WWI era, U.S. President Franklin Delano Roosevelt wanted to improve the country's economy by investing in public works and financially supporting the nation's farms. In using Keynes's ideas, Roosevelt eventually lowered the unemployment rate and ended the recession.

Glossary

recession: a period of economic downturn with a decline in employment, production, and sales

aggregate: whole

deficits: excess of debits over credits; loss of business operations

27 According to paragraph 1, how did Keynes's ideas influence the field of macroeconomics?

   A He constructed theories that had an impact on all schools of thought.

   B His ideas held solutions to some of the world's major economic problems.

   C His theories drew from many areas and looked at the economic system as a whole.

   D His theories inspired global economies to consider how the patterns of economic balance influenced each other.

28 The word trends in paragraph 1 is closest in meaning to

   A fads.

   B styles.

   C drifts.

   D tendencies.

29 Look at the four letters that indicate where the following sentence could fit in paragraph 2. Where would it best fit the paragraph? Mark the letter **A**, **B**, **C**, or **D** on your answer sheet.

   He resigned after two years in this position, re-entering the world of academia in Cambridge.

John Maynard Keynes, (1883–1946) was born in Cambridge, England. His parents were a well-educated, middle-class couple, which undoubtedly influenced his intellectual development. His mother was a social reformer and his father was an economist and lecturer at the University of Cambridge. **[A]** Keynes's interest and adeptness in a vast range of subjects were most noticeable during his studies at Eton College. **[B]** Keynes gained early acceptance at King's College, Cambridge where he earned his bachelor's degree. At both institutions, Keynes had been offered academic scholarships. He excelled in mathematics and took his first BA in that field. He worked briefly as a clerk in the India Office, having passed the service exams by 1906. **[C]** In his post-baccalaureate pursuits, his inclination was to study philosophy, but with encouragement and persuasion from one of his mentors, he finally decided on economics. **[D]**

30 The word adeptness in paragraph 2 is closest in meaning to

   A talent.

   B flexibility.

   C incompetence.

   D determination.

31 What does the author imply by mentioning Keynes's mentor in paragraph 2?

   A that after university, Keynes was initially indecisive about his career path

   B that Keynes could not become successful in academia

   C that he was not really interested in studying economics

   D that Keynes would have preferred philosophy

32 In paragraph 3, the author mentions all of Keynes's experiences EXCEPT

　　A his involvement in the stock exchange.

　　B his job as a lecturer at King's College.

　　C his position as a clerk in the India office.

　　D his work as an editor at the *Economic Journal*.

33 The word pertained in paragraph 4 is closest in meaning to

　　A ignored.

　　B affected.

　　C sustained.

　　D was relevant to.

34 In paragraph 4, what can be inferred about Keynes's book *Economic Consequences of the Peace*?

　　A Some people disagreed with his viewpoint about policies imposed on Germany.

　　B It was highly unpopular because of its subject matter.

　　C It was not published until many years after the war.

　　D Its subject matter was the Treaty of Versailles.

35 The word its in paragraph 6 refers to

　　A taxation.

　　B the demand.

　　C consumption.

　　D the government.

36 In paragraph 6, the author mentions all of the following factors that might end a recession EXCEPT

　　A buying products from other countries.

　　B boosting the demand for products.

　　C exporting goods overseas.

　　D raising taxes.

37 In paragraph 6, why does the author mention that "a government should run deficits"?

　　A to exemplify the necessity of Keynes's theories

　　B to illustrate how a recession could be resolved

　　C to demonstrate Keynes's support for the concept

　　D to show that running deficits was a good idea

38 According to paragraph 7, what is true about the effect of Keynes's work on the American government's economic policies after the Great Depression?

　　A Although they were unpopular at the time, the U.S. President put Keynes's ideas on economics to use.

　　B Keynes's school of thought forced Americans to think about business as a whole.

　　C Keynesian Economics became a permanent part of the government's economic policy.

　　D Keynes's effect was significant only because it ended the recession.

39 Directions: An introductory sentence for a brief summary of the passage is provided below. Complete the summary by selecting **three** answer choices that express the most important ideas in the passage. Some sentences do not belong because they express ideas that are not presented in the passage or are minor ideas. **This question is worth 2 points**.

Keynes's diverse background and strong interest in economics gave him a special foundation from which he developed theories that still impact society today.

Answer choices

A Keynes's focus on currency and finance contributed to his decision to write books that made a substantial contribution to the concept of the business model.

B Keynes's ideas spanned deficit and debt and explored how a government might be able to improve its economy during a time of recession.

C Though he preferred the world of academia, Keynes's experience as a clerk with the India Office clearly had an impact on his list of publications.

D Despite the fact that some of his publications were complicated or flawed, these works were a foundation for economists and governments who sought to understand how to manage a country's budget in a time of economic downturn.

E President Roosevelt was interested in using the theories in Keynes's books to devise a better plan to end the Great Depression.

Questions 40–52 are based on the following passage.

Passage 4 Meromictic lakes

1 In **temperate** climates, most lakes undergo a normal process where surface waters cyclically mix with waters from the lower layers. This process occurs in spring and fall, when water temperatures are uniformly the same from the surface of the lake to its bottom. A lake can be categorized according to the degree to which the upper and lower strata of its waters turn over and mix. This turnover of surface and bottom layers of water is closely related to seasonal temperatures as well as depth, elevation, and geographical **latitude**. In waters that are deep in proportion to their diameter, the water at the bottom of the lake does not mix with the surface waters, creating two distinct strata. Other factors that affect mixing include the chemical and mineral composition of the lake, as well as wind.

2 In the 1950s, Hutchinson and Loffler classified lakes into six categories. However, experts now agree that there are eight types of lakes. In addition to deep-water lakes, this new classification system also includes shallow-water lakes. Thus, lakes are categorized by depth, temperature, and the pattern by which their waters mix. The two main types are *holomictic* and *meromictic*. These types are further sub-categorized based on the water's temperature and the pattern of mixing that occurs in the lake during the year. For example, some lakes are *animictic*, meaning that they remain ice-covered for the entire year. The distinction of *mixis* (mixing) ranges from lakes with temperatures that rise above 4 degrees Celsius/39 degrees Fahrenheit, and mix once annually, to lakes in tropical climates where the waters may mix several times during the year.

3 In a holomictic lake, the water goes through a cycling whereby the surface waters mix completely at least once per year from top to bottom. This mixing process occurs in spring when normal temperatures rise above 4°C/39°F.

4 In a meromictic lake, stratification of the water exists permanently, whereby surface and bottom waters never mix completely. The upper to surface water, known as the *mixolimnion*, is most affected by wind. Water in the top layers may mix when the temperatures rise above 4°C and the water warms. Mild to moderate winds may cause the waters to mix. A transitional layer, called the *chemocline*, separates the top layer from the sedimentary bottom layer, known as the *monimolimnion*. Because the sedimentary layers do not physically mix with the other layers, the deepest layers of water remain unoxygenated. Because of this, few plants or animals are able to survive in the deeper strata.

5 In most cases, meromictic lakes are extremely deep, with static, undisturbed layers throughout the bottom. This creates an actual historical stratification system, in which scientists are able to take samplings of layers of water from particular points in time.

6 Examples of this type of lake are Round Lake and Green Lake, in New York's Green Lakes State Park. Round Lake's depth is estimated at roughly 55 meters or 180 feet, while its length and width are each almost 700 feet, hence the name, "Round Lake." Similarly, its neighbor, Green Lake, has a depth of 195 feet. Scientists have discovered that certain types of purple bacteria and other single-celled organisms have survived from ancient times in the undisturbed bottom strata of these lakes. Calcium carbonate, a bluish salt solution found in limestone, is prevalent in the lake waters. However, about a third of the way down is a layer of reddish bacteria, which cause that layer of water to appear pink in color. Because its waters are so dense and deep, a meromictic lake generally has a mirror-like surface.

7 Meromictic lakes are rare but can be found all over the world. A large number are in North America in the states of New York, Michigan, and Washington, as well as provinces of Canada such as Ontario and Quebec in the east, and British Columbia in the west. Elsewhere in the world, meromictic lakes are located in Lake Tanganyika in Burundi, Lac Du Bourget, France (its deepest lake), and Lake Fidler, in Tasmania, Australia. Analysis of meromictic lakes is important to the field of *limnology*—the study of inland waters—since the deep strata provide significant information about the formation of the lakes and their geographical record.

Glossary

temperate: moderate climate; not having extreme temperatures

latitude: the parallel lines measured north and south of the Earth's equator

40 According to paragraph 1, cyclical mixing of lake water occurs when

   A the weather and the water are warm.

   B water temperatures vary from top to bottom.

   C water temperatures at different levels are about the same.

   D the water at the bottom does not mix with the surface water.

41 The word strata in paragraph 1 is closest in meaning to

   A parts.

   B layers.

   C states.

   D conditions.

42 According to paragraph 1, which of the following is NOT true about lake water?

   A Wind may affect the mixing of the surface waters.

   B Geographical location can have an effect on cyclical mixing.

   C When a lake's waters are deeper than its diameter, the water has two layers.

   D Chemicals and minerals in the lake are usually only found at the bottom.

43 In paragraph 2, what does the author say about shallow lakes?

   A Scientists did not include them in previous classifications of lakes.

   B Most shallow lakes are ice covered.

   C They are neither holomictic nor meromictic.

   D Shallow lakes have different mixing patterns.

44 In paragraph 2, the water in which of the following lake types exist in temperatures that are always below 4°C /39°F?

   A holomictic

   B meromictic

   C shallow

   D animictic

45 The word transitional in paragraph 4 is closest in meaning to

   A extreme.

   B middle.

   C changing.

   D shadowy.

46 The word unoxygenated in paragraph 4 is closest in meaning to

   A suffocating.

   B without air.

   C lacking oxygen.

   D having too much oxygen.

47 What does the author imply about *meromictic* lakes in paragraph 5?

   A The water strata have historical significance.

   B It takes a long time for the sediment to settle.

   C It is difficult for scientists to find the bottom of a lake.

   D The layers of water indicate different historical periods.

48 In paragraph 6, what is true about organisms found in Green Lake?

   A Some of the organisms have been there for centuries.

   B Organisms do not survive the water mixing.

   C Most of the bacteria are red in color.

   D They contaminate the water.

49 The following sentence can be added to paragraph 6. Look at the four letters that indicate where the following sentence could fit in paragraph 6. Mark the letter **A**, **B**, **C**, or **D** on your answer grid.

   Due to the combination of the lake's depth, these bacteria, and the high concentrations of calcium carbonate, the lake has an aquamarine color.

   Examples of this type of lake are Round Lake and Green Lake, in New York's Green Lakes State Park. Round Lake's depth is estimated at roughly 55 meters or 180 feet, while its length and width are each almost 700 feet, hence the name, "Round Lake." Similarly, its neighbor, Green Lake, has a depth of 195 feet. [**A**] Scientists have discovered that certain types of purple bacteria and other single-celled organisms have survived from ancient times in the undisturbed bottom strata of these lakes. Calcium carbonate, a bluish salt solution found in limestone, is prevalent in the lake waters. [**B**] However, about a third of the way down is a layer of reddish bacteria, which cause that layer of water to appear pink in color. [**C**] Because its waters are so dense and deep, a meromictic lake generally has a mirror-like surface. [**D**]

50 In paragraph 7, what does the author imply about meromictic lakes?

   A Although they may exist on most continents, they are atypical.

   B They occur where the climates are warmest.

   C Climate has little impact on their formation.

   D Canada has the most meromictic lakes.

51 Why does the author mention *limnology* in paragraph 7?

   A to give an example of how meromictic lakes supply data on lake formation

   B to indicate the type of science to which analysis of lake strata is beneficial

   C to illustrate the influence of the scientific research on other fields

   D to support the reasons for studying lake mixing

52 Directions: Complete the table by matching **seven** answer choices. Match the type of lake with its conditions and mixing process. **This question is worth 4 points**.

Lake type	Conditions	Mixing
Select one	Select one	Select one
Select one	Select two	Select one

Answer choices

   A holomictic

   B meromictic

   C animictic

   D mixes at least once per year

   E only surface waters mix

   F never mixes

   G lake water temperature must be above 39°F

   H deep layers are cold and contain little oxygen

   I surface water temperatures may rise above 39°F

This is the end of the Reading section.

TEST 2   LISTENING   **51**

LISTENING approximately 50 minutes

This section of the TOEFL iBT™ measures your ability to understand conversations and academic lectures in English. There are two conversations followed by five questions each, and four lectures followed by six questions each, for a total of 34 questions in this section. You will have approximately **50 minutes** to answer all of the listening questions.

Mark your answers on the answer sheet on page 192. As you listen, you may take notes on the conversations and lectures. This symbol means that you will hear but not see part of the question.

Play CD2 tracks 1 to 40 and do not stop the recording while you complete this section of the test.

Questions 1–5 are based on the following conversation.

Conversation 1 Office hours

2.1–2.8 Listen to a conversation between a student and a professor.

1   What is the student's problem?

   A He didn't do well on his final exam.

   B He didn't do all his coursework.

   C He missed too many classes.

   D He moved away from the school.

2   What does the student want the professor to do?

   A He wants her to give him a new test.

   B He wants an immediate change of grade.

   C He wants her to let him take the class again.

   D He wants her to give him an incomplete in the class.

3 Listen again to part of the conversation. Then answer the question.

What does the professor mean when she says this?

   A You have to deal with this.

   B This is the solution.

   C I can't deal with this.

   D Let's come to an agreement.

4 What is the professor's solution to the student's problem?

(Choose two answers)

   A He has to write a critical essay.

   B He has to fill out a lot of paperwork.

   C He has to re-read all of Shakespeare's plays.

   D He has to have read all the Shakespeare plays.

5 What is the student's attitude about the solution?

   A relieved

   B disappointed

   C shocked

   D ungrateful

Questions 6–10 are based on the following conversation.

Conversation 2 Consultation

 Listen to a conversation between a student and the coordinator at the tutoring center.

6 Why does the student go to the tutoring center?

  A because she doesn't have a clue how to use a computer

  B because she wants help putting her presentation together

  C because she's never used the presentation viewer program before

  D because she's nervous about speaking in front of people

7 Listen again to part of the conversation. Then answer the question.

  What does the man mean when he says this?

  A He wants to know if her presentation will have graphics and animation.

  B He wants to know if she needs a whistle.

  C He wants to know if she needs a timer.

  D He wants to know if she needs sound.

8 What does the man say about using the presentation viewer program?

  A It is an easy program to use.

  B It is a very complicated program.

  C It is not part of the tutoring subjects at the center.

  D It doesn't have as many interesting features as the word processing program.

9 What is the student concerned about?

  (Choose two answers)

  A researching her topic

  B practicing with the presentation viewer program

  C speaking in front of other people

  D how to operate the power source on her computer

10 What does the man advise the student to bring to the tutoring session?

  A her research paper

  B her outline

  C the program

  D her laptop

Questions 11–16 are based on the following lecture.

Lecture 1 Product placement

🔘 2.15–2.19   Listen to a professor giving part of a lecture in an advertising class.

product placement
abnormal return

11 What does the professor mainly discuss?

   A a study of the impact of product placement on film earnings

   B the audience reaction to product placement in films

   C the differences in product placement between 2002 and the present

   D research into the effectiveness of product placement in films

12 What benefit of event study does the professor mention?

   A It allows for assessment of long-term effects of an event.

   B It is particularly designed for product placement.

   C It is a method that has been used for over ten years.

   D It allows researchers to predict trends in the market.

13 What does the professor imply about films that get good reviews from critics?

   A Investor interest in the company rises.

   B Audiences resent product placement.

   C Viewers expect to see more products.

   D Audiences don't notice product placement.

14 According to the professor, what happens when audiences love a film?

　A The audience is in another world.

　B Audiences do not pay attention to products.

　C Audiences are watching the film too closely to notice products.

　D The critically acclaimed films are protected by their audiences.

15 What effect did each of the following factors have on returns? Place a check next to the effect of each factor on returns. **This question is worth 2 points**.

	Strictly positive effect	Strictly negative effect	Both positive and negative
Viewer enjoyment			
Prior notice of placement			
Placement in general			
Highly absorbing plot			

16 Listen again to part of the lecture. Then answer the question.

　Why does the professor say this?

　A to introduce the notion of abnormal returns

　B to make a comment about the researchers' methods

　C to imply that product placement is usually not effective

　D to suggest that stock prices are mostly unpredictable

Questions 17–22 are based on the following lecture.

Lecture 2 Berenice Abbott and Changing New York

2.20–2.25 Listen to part of a lecture in a photography class.

Berenice Abbott
The Work Projects Administration—WPA

17 What is the focus of the lecture?

　　A Doug Levere's re-photography of Abbott's work

　　B Berenice Abbott's Changing New York project

　　C two examples of photography supported by the FAP

　　D the effect of the Depression on Berenice Abbott's work

18 According to the professor, why was Abbott a good candidate for the FAP?

　　A She had already been documenting America.

　　B She had a fresh perspective due to her recent return.

　　C She was willing to change her approach to fit the FAP.

　　D She was a widely recognized figure in the art world.

19 Based on the lecture, what artistic characteristics did Abbott reject in her art?

　　(Choose two answers)

　　A use of softer focus

　　B depiction of older buildings

　　C meticulous composition

　　D rural settings and landscapes

20 What did Abbott do to "keep the life in her shots"?

　　A use a hand-held camera

　　B include random people in the frame

　　C frame scenes of urban activity

　　D juxtapose old and new buildings

21 Fill in the chart with events in the order that the professor discusses them.

1
2
3
4

　　A the Changing New York project

　　B Abbott's philosophy

　　C a description of the FAP

　　D the work of Doug Levere

22 What is the professor's attitude toward Levere's re-photography of Abbott's work?

　　A concerned

　　B unimpressed

　　C disappointed

　　D complimentary

Questions 23–28 are based on the following lecture.

Lecture 3 Synesthesia

2.26–2.34 Listen to part of a lecture in a psychology class.

grapheme-color synesthesia

axons

diffusion tensor imaging (DTI)

23 What does the professor mainly discuss?

   A the scholarly dispute over the cause of grapheme synesthesia

   B how a recent study focused on a physiological basis for synesthesia

   C how new technology caused researchers to alter their views on synesthesia

   D the discovery of a new type of synesthesia that enhances color perception

24 Why does the professor talk about a musical composer?

   A to introduce the general idea of synesthesia

   B to give an example of the most common form of synesthesia

   C to clear up a common misconception about synesthesia

   D to show how synesthesia enhances perception

25 According to the professor, what is the function of axons?

   A to assist in the flow of water molecules in the brain

   B to cover neural filaments in a protective coating

   C to receive neural messages between locations in the brain

   D to connect neurons in different parts of the brain

26 Why does the professor mention highways?

　A to stress the speed of neural connectivity

　B to describe how axons are formed in the brain

　C to illustrate how DTI scanning generates images

　D to show how blood flows through the brain

27 According to the professor, what can be concluded from the results?

　A There is a physical basis for grapheme-color synesthesia.

　B Neural connectivity explains individual differences.

　C More study is necessary before any conclusion can be reached.

　D The definition of synesthesia needs to be expanded.

28 Listen again to part of the lecture. Then answer the question.

　What does the professor indicate by saying this?

　A She is presenting a different perspective.

　B She is providing further support for her idea.

　C She has made a mistake and is correcting it.

　D She wants to return to a previous point.

Questions 29–34 are based on the following lecture:

Lecture 4　Galileo's experiment

2.35–2.40　Listen to part of a discussion in a physics class.

29 What is the main topic of this discussion?

  A recent discoveries in the physics of gravity

  B the development of a theory of gravity

  C the controversy surrounding an experiment on the moon

  D ideas about Galileo's experiment with falling bodies

30 What does the professor say about Galileo's biographer?

  A He is the source of the story about the Tower of Pisa.

  B He was present at the falling bodies experiment.

  C He was shocked by the results of the experiment.

  D He was wrong about Galileo's disagreement with Aristotle.

31 Listen again to part of the discussion. Then answer the question.

  Why does the professor say this?

  A to imply that Galileo was concerned with his reputation

  B to describe a drawing of the famous experiment

  C to explain the attractiveness of the story of the experiment

  D to suggest that the experiment was entertaining but flawed

32 Why does the professor mention scholars in the sixth century?

  A to support the point that Galileo was not the first person to doubt Aristotle

  B to demonstrate the influence of Aristotle's ideas

  C to prove that Galileo never performed the falling bodies experiment

  D to give an example of the resistance that Galileo encountered

33 According to the professor, what has been the most problematic factor in the falling bodies experiment?

  A the presence of air

  B inaccurate measurement

  C conflicting results

  D improper methods

34 What is most likely the professor's view of the experiment on the moon?

  A It was methodically flawed and therefore invalid.

  B It was an important step in our understanding of gravity.

  C It was an interesting show of respect for Galileo.

  D It was a necessary confirmation of Galileo's theories.

This is the end of the Listening section.

You should take a ten-minute break before beginning the Speaking section of the test.

SPEAKING approximately 20 minutes

In this section of the test, you will have the opportunity to demonstrate your ability to speak clearly and coherently on a variety of subjects. There are **six** tasks in this section with special directions for each task. You should answer each question as thoroughly as possible.

Tasks 1 and 2 are independent speaking tasks. After you hear and read each question you will have **15 seconds** to prepare your response and **45 seconds** to speak and record your response.

Tasks 3 and 4 are integrated speaking tasks. For these two tasks, you will read a short text and then hear part of a discussion or short lecture that is connected to the text. You will have **45 seconds** to read the text. After you play the listening track, you will see a question about what you have just read and heard. You will have **30 seconds** to plan your response and **60 seconds** in which to answer the question.

You will hear a tone on the CD indicating when your preparation time is up and you should begin your response. You may begin speaking when you hear the tone.

Tasks 5 and 6 are integrated speaking tasks. For these tasks, you will hear a short conversation or lecture. Then you will read a question related to what you have just heard. You will have **20 seconds** to plan your response and **60 seconds** in which to answer the question.

You will hear a tone on the CD indicating when your preparation time is up and you should begin your response. You may begin speaking when you hear the tone.

You should record all your responses on your computer or use a recording device. Then you can play back your responses and check them against the sample responses at the back of this book.

Speaking task 1

 What are the qualities of a good teacher? Use specific details and reasons to support your response.

Preparation time: 15 seconds   Response time: 45 seconds

Speaking task 2

 Would you rather see a new movie or go to a sporting event? Use details and examples to explain your choice.

Preparation time: 15 seconds   Response time: 45 seconds

Speaking task 3

Reading time: You have 45 seconds to read the passage. Set your timer and begin reading. You may take notes.

All-State University Campus Bookstore

Tired of paying a lot of money for your textbooks and not getting much back when you try to sell your used book? All-State University bookstore is now offering students a solution! Textbook rental!

BOOKS-2-RENT is a new system set up by the university to help you save money. Students can save almost half price off every book rental! It's easy.

With BOOKS-2-RENT you have the option of ordering your books online and having those heavy tomes shipped to your home, or, just bring your receipt and pick up your textbooks at the bookstore! Save even more with no shipping charges!

TEST 2 SPEAKING

🔊 2.43–2.45 Now listen to the conversation between two students. You may take notes as you listen.

Read the question. When you hear the tone, begin recording your answer.

> The woman expresses an opinion about the new rental system at the bookstore. State her opinion and explain the reasons that she gives to support it.

Preparation time: 30 seconds   Response time: 60 seconds

Speaking task 4

Reading time: You have 45 seconds to read the passage. Set your timer and begin reading. You may take notes.

> Hybrids were the focus of study by biologists such as Charles Darwin and Alfred Wallace. The hybrid, which is a cross between two subspecies within a species of animals, is found to differ greatly from both of its parents in aspects of its *phenotype*—that is, what the animal looks like. The mule is one example. Its mother is a horse and its father is a donkey. The mule is more like the donkey with its ears, its coloring and its temperament. On the other hand, if a female donkey breeds with a male horse, the result is called a hinny—which is not as large as the mule.

🔊 2.46–2.48 Listen to a professor giving a lecture in a zoology class. You may take notes as you listen.

Read the question. When you hear the tone, begin recording your answer.

> In the lecture, the professor describes the various hybrids that differ from those in the reading passage. Describe these animals and explain how they are examples of animal diversity.

Preparation time: 30 seconds   Response time: 60 seconds

Speaking task 5

 Listen to a conversation between two students. You may take notes as you listen.

The students discuss two possible solutions to the woman's problem. Describe her problem and explain which of the two solutions you prefer, and why.

Preparation time: 20 seconds   Response time: 60 seconds

Speaking task 6

 Listen to a professor in a history class giving a lecture about the Erie Canal. You may take notes as you listen.

Using points and examples from the talk, explain the benefits of Governor Clinton's idea for the Erie Canal.

Preparation time: 20 seconds   Response time: 60 seconds

This is the end of the Speaking section.

WRITING 50 minutes

This section measures your ability to write in an academic setting. There are two writing tasks.

Task 1 requires you to read a passage and listen to a lecture. Then you will answer a question based on what you have read and what you have heard. You will have **3 minutes** to read the passage and take notes on the passage. You will then listen to a lecture, which is also about **3 minutes** long. You may take notes. You have **20 minutes** to plan and write your response.

For **task 2**, you will answer a question based on your own knowledge and experience. You will read the question and then have **30 minutes** to plan and write your response.

Writing task 1

After you listen to the lecture, write a response to a question that asks you about the relationship between the reading and the lecture. Try to answer the question as completely as you can, based on what you have read and heard. Do not try to answer the question based on your own personal knowledge.

You will have **20 minutes** to plan and write your response.

Your essay will be judged on the basis of the quality of your writing and how well your response represents the points made in the lecture and their relationship to the passage.

You have **3 minutes** to read the passage. Set your timer for **3 minutes** and begin.

The origins of American theater are somewhat disputed by historians. Some scholars credit Englishmen Adam Hallam and his sons William and Lewis, with the establishment of the first theatrical company and theater house in the American colony. However, prior to the 1919 two-volume *A History of the Theatre in America*, by Arthur Hornblow, the Hallams' troupe is seldom mentioned in the historians' sources. In addition, even those scholars who did refer to the Hallams did so rather casually and without offering them their place of significance in the history of American theater. On the other hand, the earliest historian of American theater, William Dunlap, mistakenly bestows the title "Father of the American Stage," on William Hallam, even though William was not the first to actually introduce drama to America. Dunlap also claims that the first theater was established in 1752 in Williamsburg, Virginia. This however, is disputed by later scholars, who acknowledge Charles and Mary Stagg for constructing the first playhouse in Williamsburg, some 50 years before the arrival of the Hallams. Other theaters were erected in Charleston and Philadelphia, with these three towns being the main center of theatrical activity.

Despite the controversy, it would appear the Hallams do deserve credit for being the first to send an organized, fully outfitted theater production company to the States from England. According to Hornblow, the advent of the Hallams' arrival in the colonies was important because they were part of a troupe of talented actors, crew, and managers who brought a great repertoire of plays and performances to the stage.

 When you have finished reading, listen to part of a lecture in a history of theater class. You may take notes as you listen.

After the lecture has ended, set your timer for **20 minutes** and begin writing your response to the question below.

> Summarize the points in the lecture, being sure to discuss specifically how the speaker gives opposing information to the facts presented in the reading passage.

Writing task 2

For this writing task, you will write an essay in response to a question that asks you to explain and support your opinion on an issue. You have **30 minutes** to plan and write your response.

Read the question.

> Some people believe that human activity causes harm to the Earth and its environment. Others feel that human activity is necessary to make the Earth better for all.
>
> What is your opinion on this topic? Use specific reasons and examples to support your answer to the question.

Set your timer for **30 minutes** and begin writing your essay.

This is the end of Test 2.

Check your answers with the Key and explanations at the back of this book. Then, use the Further practice and guidance section to review your skills.

FURTHER PRACTICE AND GUIDANCE

BUILDING ACADEMIC SKILLS FOR THE TOEFL iBT™

READING

In the **Reading** section of the TOEFL iBT™ there are **ten** question types. In order to answer the questions efficiently and correctly, you can use several techniques to build your reading skills. In this section of the book, you will review sections of the tests and learn how to build your skills for each of the question types as well as your overall academic reading skills.

The following are the ten TOEFL iBT™ question types as organized by the skill area in which you are tested.

Reading for basic comprehension

- Understanding vocabulary in context
- Identifying pronoun references
- Making inferences
- Sentence simplification
- Sentence insertion
- Rhetorical purpose (author's purpose)

Reading to find information

- Facts and major details
- Negative facts

Reading to learn

- Understanding details as they relate to the main idea (schematic table)
- Summarizing information (summary information chart)

In this Further practice and guidance section, these ten TOEFL iBT™ reading question types have been organized by the number of each question type.

Vocabulary knowledge is necessary to answer successfully all question types. Therefore, **Understanding vocabulary in context** questions will be the first to appear in this practice section.

Vocabulary and fact or detail questions appear most frequently per passage, while you may only see one schematic table and summary question. You should note that some questions, such as rhetorical purpose, might not appear in every passage.

Examples of each section of the official test are available on the ETS website at www.toefl.org.

GENERAL READING TECHNIQUES

Though reading is a receptive skill, you can become an active reader. To improve your reading ability, you need to interact with the text. You can follow some basic steps toward becoming a better reader.

1. Before you read, you should try to predict vocabulary.
2. While you read, ask yourself questions about what the author says and why the author makes certain statements.
3. Try to evaluate what you have read.

IMPROVING YOUR SPEED ON THE TOEFL iBT™

How fast do you need to read?

The average educated native speaker of English can read silently at a rate of 250 words per minute, with about 60 percent accuracy in comprehension. Some people can read at a much higher rate. President John F. Kennedy claimed he could read at a rate of about 800 to 1,000 words per minute, with 50 to 60 percent accuracy in remembering information.

According to experts, most people read at a rate of **25 percent more slowly** on a **computer screen** than on paper. This is why it will be important for you to read books—novels or texts of interest to you, as well as magazines and newspapers—in order to improve your overall reading skills and increase your paper reading speed. It may take the average reader five minutes to read a 1,000-word article on a computer screen, while reading the same article in print would take the same person only four minutes.

If you read a 700-word TOEFL iBT™ passage in four minutes, your reading speed will be about 175 words per minute. TOEFL iBT™ passages may contain unknown vocabulary words, which may slow your reading rate down even more. That is why reading in "chunks" and trying to get the overall meaning will help you improve your reading pace.

Building vocabulary, note-taking, and using context clues will help you get through the reading passages more effectively.

On the test, you have **20 minutes** to read each passage and answer 13 to 14 questions. If you read the passage in four to five minutes, you have between 15 and 16 minutes to answer the questions.

Other ways to improve your timing on the TOEFL iBT™

Before the test, familiarize yourself with the technological aspects of the TOEFL iBT™, such as, reading texts on the computer screen, using the buttons and scroll bar to go to various parts of the text, paying attention to the clock, or adjusting the volume of the headphones, and speaking into the microphone.

SKILL BUILDER: SKIMMING AND SCANNING TECHNIQUES

Skimming and **scanning** are reading techniques we use every day. These are techniques that can help you move more quickly and efficiently through the reading passages to find the information you need in order to answer the questions.

- **Skimming** helps you determine the "big picture" or main idea. You may **skim** through a magazine or newspaper to find an article you want to read. You may skim the titles in a bookstore to find a book by a specific author.
- **Scanning** helps you find more specific information or details. You can **scan** a brochure to find the information you want. In the same way, you may scan a bus schedule or train timetable to find the specific information you want.

First, "glance" at the passage. **Skim** the text for headings, key words, dates, places, and names. This will help you determine what the passage is going to be about, and anticipate vocabulary. Skimming also helps you identify the main ideas of a text. You should skim a text at a speed of three to four times faster than you would normally read the text. When you read on the computer, you can skim quickly as you use the scroll bar to move down the page.

Read the first and last lines of each paragraph.

Take notes. Write down the key words that seem to be the most frequent. If there are illustrations, charts, or graphs, you can also skim over these to get information.

Next, scan the text for the specific technical terms, key words, dates, names, and places that you noted while skim reading. Do not read every word, but look line by line in each paragraph for the most important words. You can also scan for numbers, lists of items, bold or italicized words, or punctuation, such as dashes or colons. Write these in your notes. Look for pronoun references to these important words, such as *it*, *they*, *this*, *these* and phrases beginning with these pronouns.

FURTHER PRACTICE AND GUIDANCE | READING 67

PRACTICE FOR SKIMMING AND SCANNING TEXTS

Do these activities after you have completed Test 1.

A Use **Test 1**, **Passage 3**. Skim the text. Set your timer for 2 minutes. Write down the main idea or main topics from each paragraph. What is the paragraph about?

Main ideas or topics

Paragraph 1 ....
Paragraph 2 ....
Paragraph 3 ....
Paragraph 4 ....
Paragraph 5 ....
Paragraph 6 ....
Paragraph 7 ....

B Scan the text and look for *key words* and *phrases*. Set the timer for 3 minutes. Write down as many important facts, vocabulary, definitions, and phrases as you can. Then circle nouns and underline pronoun references.

Key words, terms, or phrases

Paragraph 1 ....
Paragraph 2 ....
Paragraph 3 ....
Paragraph 4 ....
Paragraph 5 ....
Paragraph 6 ....
Paragraph 7 ....

Do these activities after you have completed Test 2.

C Use **Test 2**, **Passage 2**. Skim the text. Set your timer for 2 minutes. Write down two or more key words and ideas from each paragraph.

Main ideas or topics

Paragraph 1 ....
Paragraph 2 ....
Paragraph 3 ....
Paragraph 4 ....
Paragraph 5 ....

D Scan the text and look for *key words* and *phrases.* Set your timer for 3 minutes. Write down as many important facts, vocabulary, definitions, and phrases as you can. Then circle nouns and underline pronoun references.

Key words, terms, or phrases

Paragraph 1 ....
Paragraph 2 ....
Paragraph 3 ....

Paragraph 4 ....
Paragraph 5 ....

VOCABULARY KNOWLEDGE AND GENERAL READING SKILLS

The most important step toward improving your overall academic reading is building your **vocabulary**. This will help you with all the other question types on the test. You can also learn to look at words in "chunks," which are set phrases that have a specific meaning. These techniques can help you read quickly and effectively.

There is an old expression, "repetition is the mother of learning." In language learning, this expression applies to building all your skills—reading, listening, writing and speaking. It might seem boring to read or hear a passage or lecture more than once, but this is actually the best way to acquire vocabulary, master pronunciation, and gain overall comprehension skills.

If you want to expand your vocabulary in a language, you must be able to understand and reproduce the words you have read in texts and use phrases and expressions you have heard. Through repetition, you can learn to do this correctly.

Vocabulary is the key to comprehension and fluency, but in order to acquire vocabulary in a new language, you must read, listen, and speak as much as possible. Building your vocabulary in English takes time. Vocabulary building helps you improve all your skills: reading and listening, and the active skills of writing and speaking.

What vocabulary do you need to know for the TOEFL iBT™?

Before you can answer the questions on the test, you need to know vocabulary.

Vocabulary words in English fall into three basic categories: general words, academic words, and technical or specialty terms. Linguists evaluated these word categories into groups by how frequently speakers use them or how frequently the words appear in texts. On the TOEFL iBT™, naturally you can expect more academic vocabulary than on other standardized tests.

- **General words** are the most frequent words used every day. Frequently used words are often called "sight words" because these words are among the first words that language learners recognize when learning to read.

- **Phrasal verbs** are two- or three-part verbs, usually a verb followed by one or two prepositions or an adverb. Phrasal verbs occur more frequently in speech than in texts. They also occur more commonly in informal texts than in formally written work. You might hear a speaker or lecturer use phrasal verbs such as, *go down*, *make up*, *put off*, *set up*, and *show up*. In a text, you are more likely to read the academic equivalents to these expressions: *go down = descend*; *make up = consist of*; *put off = delay*; *set up = establish*; *show up = appear*.

- **Idioms** are "fixed phrases" in a language that have a consistent connotative meaning. Idioms occur more in informal spoken and written English than in formal or academic contexts, but you will often hear and read these expressions. Phrasal verbs can be idiomatic. For example: *rides on* as an idiom means *depends upon*. In scientific and social science texts: *The funding of this research project rides on whether the experiments prove or disprove our theory.* Using English idioms fluently and accurately in the speaking and writing sections of the TOEFL iBT™ will help you achieve a higher score.

- **Academic words** Experts have determined that about 60 percent of all English words and 82 percent of academic words are from Greek and Latin. In the sciences and technology, the number of Latin and Greek words that appear in texts or in lectures rises to about 90 percent. Understanding and recognizing the roots, prefixes, and suffixes of words can help increase your academic vocabulary.

- **Technical/specialized terms (also known as *jargon*)** are specific to certain disciplines (like physics or art) and will appear more frequently in texts of a particular field. Technical terms are not common in daily conversation, though they may be heard more often in academic lectures. Journals and magazines that specialize in a particular field (like scientific journals or fashion magazines) will include technical terms. For example: *bioluminescence* of fish (Biology); *shards* of pottery (Archaeology), *a monopoly* in the market (Economics). Be aware that frequent vocabulary and general words are sometimes used in a technical or semi-technical way. For example, *wall* in biology usually refers to the wall of a microscopic cell; *demand* in economics refers to the specific need for a product. Though these are common words in English, they have a different meaning in the context of the fields in which they are used.

There are also many low-frequency words in each of the three categories that rarely occur in texts or lectures, although they might appear on standardized college entrance exams.

> **Did you know?** The most frequent word in the English language is the definite article *the*.

QUESTION TYPE 1 VOCABULARY IN CONTEXT

There are usually three to five questions on the TOEFL iBT™ that will test your understanding of vocabulary. Vocabulary questions may appear in this form:

- The word {X} is closest in meaning to …
- In stating {X} the author means that …

Some of the words or phrases in the answer choices may have a similar meaning to the word in the paragraph. However, the answer is usually a synonym closest to the meaning of the word in the context.

SKILL BUILDER 1 UNDERSTANDING CONTEXT CLUES

Authors will often explain technical terms or other more unfamiliar terms in the context of an academic passage. Some words will be defined in the **glossary**. On the actual TOEFL iBT™, you can click on the word and a definition will appear.

In most disciplines, but more often in social sciences, life sciences, and physical sciences, the author will define or explain a term which will then be repeated in the text. Context clues can define, explain, help the reader understand how the passage is organized, and often give contrasting information.

An author may use writing devices or techniques to illustrate or define a concept or a word. Some of these devices include the use of punctuation.

The long dash (also called the *em* dash) often appears in a sentence after a word or phrase to give an explanation, definition, or additional information about something that the author does not assume the reader knows.

A Read the excerpt from **Test 1**, **Passage 1**, **Paragraph 2** and answer the following questions.

> It has long been believed that they went to Croatoan Island—known today as Hatteras. Scholars speculated that the colonists may have gone to live with the Croatoans—a tribe of Native Americans with whom they had had very friendly relations.

1 Why does the author use the long dash after "Croatoan Island" in line 4?

   A to place the island in a historical context

   B to explain that the island once had a different name

   C to acknowledge that the reader is not familiar with the island

   D to provide more information about Croatoan Island's location

2 What is the significance of the author's use of the long dash in line 5?

   A The author provides a definition of Croatoan.

   B It is an explanation for why the settlers left the area.

   C It offers a more complete description of the Croatoan people.

   D It describes and explains the relationship between the settlers and the Croatoans.

Read an excerpt from **Test 1**, **Passage 1**, **Paragraph 3**. Then answer the question.

> The story upheld the angle that a few of the colonists had survived—among them, Governor John White's daughter Eleanor Dare, her husband Ananias, and their infant daughter Virginia.

3 Why does the author use the long dash after stating that "a few of the colonists had survived"?

   A to explain the story's angle about the survivors

   B to inform the reader of the birth of the colony's first child

   C to give examples of the survivors mentioned in the story

   D to support the theory that the settlers went to Croatoan Island

Appositive means "placed next to." An author will sometimes use a long dash or comma immediately after a term or phrase to define it or give an example of it, in order to facilitate the reader's understanding of the topic. This can often be an important detail to connect the reader to a major point in the passage or the main idea. Introductory phrases can also be used immediately before an appositive or definition, for example, *is*, *like*, *known as*, *called*, *such as*, *refers to*.

B

4 Read the line from **Test 1**, **Passage 2**, **Paragraph 1**. Circle the key word or phrase and underline its appositive.

> The concept of being environmentally conscious, or "green," has become more prevalent in twenty-first-century U.S. culture.

5 Read the excerpts from **Test 1**, **Passage 2**, **Paragraph 3**. Circle the key words or phrases and underline the appositives.

a

> A problem that has often arisen has been with how a site crew—whether it is demolition or construction crew—determines and sorts what is "waste" and what is recyclable.

b

> In new "green" construction, insulation that was once asbestos-based can be replaced with recycled denim or constructed with *cellulose*—a fibrous material found in paper products.

6 Read the excerpt from **Test 1**, **Passage 2**, **Paragraph 5**. Circle the key word or phrase and underline its appositive.

> In terms of energy and natural resources, sustainable architecture may incorporate many alternative energy sources—energy that is not harmful to the environment and does not rely on mineral-based fuels like coal or oil.

SKILL BUILDER 2 UNDERSTANDING DENOTATIVE vs. CONNOTATIVE MEANING

The vocabulary tested on the TOEFL iBT™ involves understanding a word or phrase as it occurs in written and spoken English. To answer questions that follow TOEFL iBT™ reading passages, you need to have a good understanding of the overall meaning of the text. To answer the vocabulary questions correctly, you must understand both **denotative** and **connotative** meanings of words.

A What is **denotation**? Can you guess the meaning from the context?

Example: The **denotation** of the word *comprehension* is *understanding*.

1 Which term best describes **denotative** meaning?

   A dictionary definition

   B figurative meaning

   C context

Denotation is the literal, explicit, or dictionary definition of a word.

B What is **connotation**? How do you think it differs from denotation?

Read the following sentences. What does **snake** mean?

1 He was a **snake** in business because he made deals that could hurt his competition.

   A reptile

   B flexible person

   C devious man

2 The long river **snakes** through the valley.

   A winds

   B slithers

   C is devious

Connotation is the meaning of the word in the context of the text. It applies to the imagery and emotional response connected with the word.

The denotative meaning of *snake* is *serpent* or *reptile*, but the man is clearly not a man who sells reptiles. You know that a man is not literally a *snake*, but his behavior may be potentially treacherous like a poisonous snake.

In sentence 2, a river behaves like a snake because it *winds* or *changes directions.*

SKILL BUILDER 3 STRATEGIES FOR LEARNING ACADEMIC WORDS

Academic words are hard to learn because their meanings are often *abstract* and refer to concepts, theories, and ideas about a particular field. However, it is possible to figure out the meanings of unknown academic words in the context of a TOEFL iBT™ passage (or texts from an academic coursebook).

First, use your skimming and scanning techniques and be aware of repetition in a text. As you have seen in the previous exercises, authors may define a term and then repeat it throughout the passage. Authors may also use general words and their synonyms in the context of an academic text and repeat those words. For example, words like *biologists* and *scientists* may appear in the same text to mean the same thing.

Many academic English words are French, Latin, or Greek in origin. **Analyzing the parts** of words—prefixes, suffixes, and roots—is one technique that can help you grasp the meaning of unfamiliar vocabulary on the TOEFL iBT™.

Prefixes come before a root to form adjectives, nouns, or verbs.

Examples are: *an-*, *de-*, *in-*, *pre-*, *pro-*, *re-*

Verbs with these prefixes are: **an**notate, **de**molish, **in**spire, **pre**cede, **pro**duce, and **re**consider.

Suffixes come at the end of the root and can form adverbs, adjectives, or some nouns.

Examples are: adjectives ending with *-ate*, *-ive*, *-al*; consider*ate*, product*ive*, classic*al*

 adverbs ending with *-ly*; historical*ly*, considerate*ly*, productive*ly*

 noun forms ending with *-y*, *-ism*, *-ist*, *–tion*; sociolog*ist*, histor*y*, demoli*tion*

Studying the **prefixes**, **suffixes**, and **roots** of Greek and Latin words will help you learn or identify words in the context of the reading and improve your overall academic vocabulary. As you read more, you will see patterns of written English with academic words that authors may use repeatedly. Academic words may have different meanings in different disciplines—so, pay attention to context clues.

A **Greek and Latin roots for disciplines**. Most of the "disciplines" that are part of a university curriculum are derived from Greek and Latin. *Logos*, in Greek, means *knowledge* or, *study of*.

Read each sentence and match the bolded part of the word with its meaning **a–l**. The first one has been done for you.

a	bird	e	primitive time	i	life
b	art, skill, craft	f	mind	j	growth, nature
c	soil, land formation	g	human	k	generation
d	atmosphere; high up in the sky	h	ancient	l	nation, people

1 General **anthropo**logy includes the understanding of biological and cultural systems over the entire world and through time. ..*g*...

2 The undertaking of salvage **archae**ology is a crucial step in protecting ruins and artefacts on a historical site before new construction begins. ......

3 Understanding organisms and their structure is an important component of **bio**logy. ......

4 **Ethno**musicology encompasses the areas of popular culture and sociology, while traditional musical scholarship focuses mainly on the history and literature of western music. ......

5 Charles Darwin began his career in the field of **geo**logy, taking particular interest in theories about Earth's origins. ......

6 **Genea**logy specialists at the Library in Salt Lake City, Utah have researched and documented the history of thousands of families. ......

7 The Greek philosopher Aristotle's book ***Meteor**ology* explained how the Earth and objects in the universe potentially affect weather patterns. ......

8 Leonardo Da Vinci's designs for flying machines called ornithopters were largely influenced by his interest in **ornitho**logy. ......

9 **Paleontolo**gy involves examining dinosaur bones and fossils as well as phenomena that occurred in Earth's past. ......

10 Scientists found that low levels of both classical and rock music had positive effects on the mood and **physi**ology of the listener. ......

11 Studies in sports **psych**ology help to determine the effects of an athlete's performance and level of pain when injured. ......

12 The older generation of writers has discarded the typewriter and embraced the tools of computer **techno**logy that have enabled them to produce work more quickly and publish online. ......

B Understanding meaning from roots. Fill in the sentences below with the appropriate word from the list. Many of these words are *low frequency*. These words appear in passages and lectures from both Test 1 and Test 2.

anthropomorphism	astro-biologists	geological	technological	archaic
biological	meteorological	archaeologists	ethnography	physiological

1 Historians and ……………………… alike have still not reached an agreement about this potential physical evidence of the Lost Colony.

2 The genealogical method, or, way of using symbols and diagrams to create a record of kinship connections, is an important technique of ……………………… .

3 Brain scientists have been wondering about whether there's a ……………………… basis for synesthesia for over a hundred years.

4 It's over the continent of Antarctica and even though there is a great deal of depletion to the ozone, ……………………… studies have found that there is still a significant amount of ozone there—even during times of extreme depletion.

5 One of the greatest mysteries in ……………………… science is why species of flowering plants began to rapidly dominate the earth around 100 million years ago.

6 John Smith's writing style was more like British English. … I saw one of his original texts in the library and it was, you know, a more ……………………… style of writing.

7 ……………………… advances in the nineteenth century helped improve the workers' ability to do things like clear tree stumps and move large amounts of dirt and rocks.

8 I'm looking for information on the way that animals behave like humans, or have human-like characteristics in movies and in cartoons. And I want to focus on live action films.

   Oh, you mean ……………………… ?

9 Analysis of meromictic lakes is important to the field of limnology—the study of inland waters—since the deep strata provide significant information about the formation of the lakes and its ……………………… record.

10 While many astrophysicists and ……………………… have argued the unlikelihood of life forms on other planets, the data from the Kepler Orbiting Telescope suggests the contrary.

PRACTICE FOR VOCABULARY QUESTIONS

Do these practice items after you have completed Test 1.

A Read the paragraph from **Test 1**, **Passage 4**. Then answer the questions.

> To social scientists, the field of genealogy is not typically considered a legitimate area of scholarly research. However, its relevance to cultural and historical anthropologists in understanding the connections among people in society is indisputable. The genealogical method, or, way of using symbols and diagrams to create a record of kinship connections, is an important technique of *ethnography*. Ethnography, therefore, is two things: a method that both cultural and historical anthropologists use to conduct research about a group of people, and, the written record of that research. Genealogy uses ethnographic tools because it includes both kinship connections and written records of the families. This is better known as a "family tree," which is a diagram of a person's ancestry.

1   The word **legitimate** in the paragraph is closest in meaning to
    A unlawful.
    B rightful.
    C valid.
    D legal.

2   The word **indisputable** in the paragraph is closest in meaning to
    A true.
    B arguable.
    C debatable.
    D undeniable.

3   The phrase **kinship connections** means
    A relationships.
    B relatives.
    C bindings.
    D ties.

4   The word **ancestry** in the paragraph is closest in meaning to
    A parents.
    B descent.
    C inheritance.
    D bequest.

B   Read the paragraph from **Test 1**, **Passage 4**. Then answer the questions.

> This cultural phenomenon may seem like a fad, but at the same time, its historical and more scholarly implications are not lost to cultural anthropologists and researchers in other disciplines. For archivists—the library science specialists who deal with documenting, preserving, and organizing old records—the field of genealogy and the needs of genealogical researchers are very important. There is no special credential or degree-bearing requirement for becoming a "professional" genealogist. Many people have become genealogists simply because of an interest in their own family history.

5   The word **phenomenon** in the paragraph is closest in meaning to
    A surprise.
    B prodigy.
    C incident.
    D occurrence.

6   The author uses the phrase **scholarly implications** in the passage to mean
    A references for research.
    B academic expectations.
    C educational ideals.
    D intellectual pursuits.

7 The word **archivists** in the paragraph is closest in meaning to
   A curators.
   B historians.
   C specialties.
   D documents.

8 The word **credential** in the paragraph is closest in meaning to
   A record.
   B permission.
   C official license.
   D documentation.

Do these practice items after you have completed Test 2.

C Read the paragraph from **Test 2**, **Passage 2**. Then answer the questions.

> In order to find planets that are light years from our own solar system, astronomers use two types of telescope, each with sensitive instruments that employ special techniques, to aid in the acquisition of data: ground-based and orbiting telescopes. A team of Swiss scientists discovered the first Earth-like planet outside of our solar system in 2007, *Gliese 581*, estimated to be approximately 50 percent bigger than Earth. Located about 20.5 light years from our world, Gliese 581 orbits a red dwarf star. To identify this new planet, the astronomy team used a *spectroscopic* instrument known as HARPS, which is linked to a 3.6-meter telescope at the European Southern Observatory in La Silla, Chile. Spectroscopic instruments use a Doppler, or "wobble" technique to identify *radial velocity*—how fast a star moves toward or away from the point of observation. By analyzing the wavelength of light emitted from a star, the instrument is therefore able to calibrate the mass of a planet in the star's orbit. With the wobble technique, astronomers are only able to perceive a planet that is less than 160 light years from Earth. Employing this technique can be slow, because astronomers must wait for the planet to make one complete orbit of its sun in order to confirm their data.

9 The word **sensitive** in the paragraph is closest in meaning to
   A soft.
   B insightful.
   C precise.
   D indifferent.

10 The word **acquisition** in the paragraph is closest in meaning to
   A deficit.
   B purchase.
   C gaining.
   D retention.

11 The word **velocity** in the paragraph is closest in meaning to
   A haste.
   B speed.
   C involvement.
   D determination.

12 The word **calibrate** in the paragraph is closest in meaning to
  A standardize.
  B regulate.
  C measure.
  D tune.

13 The word **perceive** in the paragraph is closest in meaning to
  A sense.
  B realize.
  C interpret.
  D identify.

D Read the paragraph from **Test 2**, **Passage 4**. Then answer the questions.

> In temperate climates, most lakes undergo a normal process where surface waters cyclically mix with waters from the lower layers. This process occurs in spring and fall, when water temperatures are uniformly the same from the surface of the lake to its bottom. A lake can be categorized according to the degree to which the upper and lower strata of its waters turn over and mix. This turnover of surface and bottom layers of water is closely related to seasonal temperatures as well as depth, elevation, and geographical latitude. In waters that are deep in proportion to their diameter, the water at the bottom of the lake does not mix with the surface waters, creating two distinct strata. In addition to temperature, other factors that affect mixing include the chemical and mineral composition of the lake, as well as wind.

14 The word **cyclically** in the paragraph is closest in meaning to
  A constantly.
  B irregularly.
  C seasonally.
  D continuously.

15 The word **proportion** in the paragraph is closest in meaning to
  A amount.
  B fraction.
  C quantity.
  D comparison.

16 The word **composition** in the paragraph is closest in meaning to
  A masterpiece.
  B arrangement.
  C structure.
  D form.

QUESTION TYPE 2 FACT AND DETAIL

On the TOEFL iBT™, reading passages and lectures require you to answer fact and detail questions. However, there is no directly stated "main idea" question in the Reading section, but there are questions phrased like fact questions that actually refer to the gist or main idea of the passage. Fact and detail questions are **Reading to understand information** questions. You need to understand the facts and major points in the passage in order to grasp the main idea. Questions that *indirectly* refer to the main idea may appear in this form:

- According to the passage, what is {X}?
- According to the passage, {X} is ...

Your understanding of the main idea of the passage will be tested when you answer fact questions, as well as when you do the **Reading to learn** summary chart question.

There are three to six **fact** and **detail** questions in each reading set. The author uses introductory phrases to state facts and details clearly. You should be able to recognize a fact or detail and differentiate them from an opinion.

Examples of fact and detail questions are:

- According to the paragraph, which is true about {X}?
- The author's description of {X} mentions which of the following?
- According to the paragraph, {X} happened because ...
- According to the paragraph, what is stated about {X}?

Facts and details can appear as definitions or statements about key words. Facts are often presented in the form of dates, events, or the names of people and places.

For example, from Test 1, Passage 1:

> In *1587*, the *explorer Sir Walter Raleigh* dispatched a ship bound for the *New World*, carrying a group of approximately 117 people—including their new governor, *John White*.

You can use skimming and scanning techniques to search for facts and details. You should also use the strategies you learned for Question type 1 to find important key words. These strategies will play an important role in helping you identify **main ideas**, **facts**, **details**, and **connecting information** throughout the text. You will also need these skills to answer the "prose summary" question and the "schematic table" question, which are **Reading to learn** questions.

Recognizing *nouns* that occur frequently in a history or science passage, or, *verbs* that authors use to refer to other scholars' research, can increase your vocabulary. Often, authors repeat specific academic vocabulary words or technical terms because they want to draw the reader's attention to certain facts and details.

SKILL BUILDER 1 RECOGNIZING SINGULAR AND PLURAL NOUNS AS KEY WORDS AND SUBJECTS

One way to identify nouns and noun phrases is to locate *definite and indefinite articles*. The author may frequently repeat nouns, adjective–noun, or noun–noun phrases to help the reader understand the subject or topic. This repetition is known as *redundancy*. Redundancy happens naturally in texts and lectures because the author or lecturer must repeatedly refer to the topic. In order to recognize these key words, especially nouns and noun phrases, you have to read or listen for signals such as indefinite or definite articles. Articles are also called "noun signals."

The, *a*, and *an* are among the 100 most frequent words in both spoken and written English. That means you are going to see these articles occur most frequently in any text and hear them most in conversations or lectures. Articles precede nouns and noun phrases, so they act as "signals" or "cues" to nouns and key words.

For the Reading section, you can quickly identify definite and indefinite articles that precede nouns or noun–adjective phrases by skimming and scanning. Identifying these "chunks" of language will help you understand the **main idea** and answer **vocabulary**, **fact and detail**, or **negative fact** questions.

In many cases, the first time a general idea or subject is mentioned, the author will use the indefinite articles *a* or *an* before the noun. This can indicate that the noun is "one of many things," or, that the author doesn't expect the reader to already be familiar with the idea or thing.

SKILL BUILDER 2 IDENTIFYING FACTS AND DETAILS

Phrases containing *article + noun* or a noun phrase often appear in *introductions* or *topic sentences* as well as in definitions given in both reading passages and in lectures.

Read the excerpt from **Test 1, Passage 1**.

> In 1991, Robert White published <u>a book</u> about **the mystery** of **the Lost Colony** that re-examined **the hoax** from 1940.

This is the first time the author mentions Robert White's book. The reader does not know how many books White has written or how many books on the mystery exist, therefore, *a* book means *one* book. The definite article is used with *the* mystery, *the* Lost Colony and *the* hoax, to signify that the author has already mentioned these nouns as topics. The author assumes that the reader knows these specific things or ideas already mentioned in the text.

Do these practice items after you have completed Test 1.

A Read the paragraph from **Test 1, Passage 1** and <u>underline</u> each noun or phrase beginning with the indefinite article ***a***. Then, circle nouns or noun phrases beginning with the definite article ***the***.

> Settled by English colonists in the late sixteenth century, Roanoke Island lies off the coast of what is now the state of North Carolina. It is best known as the home of "the Lost Colony." In 1587, the explorer Sir Walter Raleigh dispatched a ship bound for the New World, carrying a group of approximately 117 people—including their new governor, John White. The captain was supposed to take them farther north, to Chesapeake Bay near Massachusetts, but instead dropped the passengers at Roanoke Island—the site of the first, unsuccessful English colony. Governor White realized that supplies were low and sailed back to England to acquire more food, promising to return in three months. However, the war between England and Spain prevented White from voyaging back to the island for three years. When White finally returned to Roanoke in 1590, he found that the settlers had disappeared. The entire site had been abandoned without a trace of the colonists having been there. The only clue that White found was the word "CROATOAN" carved into a fence post, and the letters CRO etched into a tree trunk. There was nothing else to indicate where the colonists had gone or the manner in which they had left.

B Find six nouns or key words from the passage and write them in the chart below. Then make a check [✓] if the author has mentioned this idea previously. In the last column of the chart, write whether the noun refers to *what, when, where,* or *who*.

	The + noun, plural noun, noun phrase or *a/an* + noun or noun phrase	First time mentioned or non-specific	Previously mentioned or specific	What, when, where, or who
1				
2				
3				
4				
5				
6				

C Read the paragraph from **Test 1**, **Passage 1** again. Write full sentences to answer each of the questions.

1   Where is Roanoke Island?

    ....

2   When was Roanoke Island settled?

    ....

3   What was Roanoke Island known as?

    ....

4   What did Sir Walter Raleigh dispatch from England?

    ....

5   Who was supposed to take the colonists to Chesapeake Bay?

    ....

6   What prevented Governor John White from returning for three years?

    ....

7   What was carved into a fence post and etched into a tree trunk?

    ....

D Read the paragraph from **Test 1**, **Passage 2** and <u>underline</u> each noun or phrase beginning with the indefinite article **a**. Then, circle nouns or noun phrases beginning with the definite article **the**.

> A problem that has often arisen has been with how a site crew—whether it is demolition or construction crew—determines and sorts what is "waste" and what is recyclable. Architects and environmental scientists have to decide whether or not a material is appropriate for use in new construction and how it will impact the environment. They must evaluate the materials from the demolition and determine what those materials contain, and if they meet the standards set by the U.S. government's Environmental Protection Agency (the EPA). If the debris from the demolition contains hazardous materials that are harmful to the environment or to the consumer, such as asbestos, then the material is not salvageable. Use of asbestos for insulation and as a form of fire retardation in buildings and fabrics was common in the nineteenth century. Asbestos was once used in shingles on the sides of old buildings, as well as in the insulation in the interior walls of home or other construction. In new "green" construction, insulation that was once asbestos-based can be replaced with recycled denim or constructed with cellulose—a fibrous material found in paper products. The same assessment applies to wood or wallboard painted with toxic lead-based paints. In addition, gas-flow regulators and meters on both water and gas heating systems constructed prior to 1961 must be carefully evaluated to determine that they do not contain dangerous substances such as mercury. Mercury can be harmful to humans and the environment if it is spilled during the removal of these devices.

E Find six nouns or key words from the passage and write them in the chart overleaf. Then make a check [✓] if the author has mentioned this idea previously. In the last column of the chart, write whether the noun refers to *what*, *when*, *where*, or *who*.

	The + noun, plural noun, noun phrase or *a/an* + noun or noun phrase	First time mentioned or non-specific	Previously mentioned or specific	What, when, where, or who
1				
2				
3				
4				
5				
6				

F Read the paragraph from **Test 1, Passage 2** again. Then write full sentences to answer each of the questions.

1 What problem often occurs during a demolition?

....

2 Who is responsible for determining and sorting waste?

....

3 What happens if debris contains hazardous material?

....

4 What materials might be harmful to people and the environment?

....

5 What is important to evaluate about devices used with water or gas heaters manufactured before 1961?

....

SKILL BUILDER 3 INTRODUCTORY PHRASES

Authors often use introductory phrases to define a term or give examples. Introductory phrases can also help you find **facts** and **details** as well as **negative facts**. They may also use colons or lists, as well as phrases like these: *refers to, is, are, such as, for example.* These phrases may also include vocabulary word definitions, such as, *means, can be defined as, is a term that, is typically used to mean.* These are not only vocabulary statements, but also statements of fact. These statements of fact and supporting details will connect you to information in the rest of the passage.

A Read the excerpt from **Test 1, Passage 2, Paragraph 1**. Underline the subject. Circle the introductory phrase. Then answer the question.

> Sustainable buildings are those that do not impose on the environment or rely on the over-utilization of energy or natural resources.

1 The author uses the introductory phrase to

  A describe the buildings.

  B give a definition of the word "sustainable."

  C introduce the reader to a new concept.

  D explain how buildings may utilize too many resources.

FURTHER PRACTICE AND GUIDANCE   READING   **81**

Read the excerpt from **Test 1**, **Passage 2**, **Paragraph 3**. Circle the introductory phrase. Then answer the question.

> If the debris from the demolition contains hazardous materials that are harmful to the environment or to the consumer, such as asbestos, then the material is not salvageable.

2 The author uses an introductory phrase in this sentence to give the reader

    A an example of debris that could be hazardous.

    B a definition of how sorting decisions are made.

    C more information about salvageable materials.

    D an example of what happens on a demolition site.

Parentheses. An author can also use parentheses ( ) to explain an idea, give a range of dates, or sometimes, provide the reader with additional information about a word or phrase. Parentheses can also provide the reader with a shortened version of other information, such as an acronym (letters that stand for a name or title).

B Read the excerpt from **Test 1**, **Passage 2**, **Paragraph 3**.

> They must evaluate the materials from the demolition and determine what those materials contain, and if they meet the standards set by the U.S. government's Environmental Protection Agency (the EPA).

3 What is the purpose of the parentheses with (EPA) following the phrase "Environmental Protection Agency?"

    A to offer a further explanation of the phrase

    B to give a definition of the government agency

    C to give the reader additional information about the government

    D to provide the reader with the agency's commonly known acronym

PRACTICE FOR FACT AND DETAIL QUESTIONS

Do these practice items after you have completed Test 1.

A Read the paragraph from **Test 1**, **Passage 2**. Then answer the questions.

> These factors contribute to the use of sustainable materials and construction practices in commercial buildings as well as residential homes. When the intended construction is a new home, the owners themselves may now participate in deciding what recycled materials go into building their homes. Homeowners may also decide on aspects such as the indoor air quality, sources of energy and water efficiency, and the consistency of the soil on which to build the home. About two percent of all homes built in the U.S. in 2005 were deemed "green." Some reports predict that this number will increase in the next five to ten years, so that the number of "green" buildings may surpass ten percent of the number of newly constructed homes.

1 According to the paragraph, what does the author mention as an aspect of building a "green" home?

    A Where to build the house.

    B How the location will affect air quality.

    C The kind of energy that will be used.

    D How to dispose of material that is non-recyclable.

2 According to the paragraph, what is true about "green" building since 2005?

    A It may rise to more than ten percent of all new homes in the next decade.

    B It may cut down on the amount of recycling in new home construction.

    C The decisions for homeowners may focus more on energy and water.

    D Eight percent of newly constructed homes will be green in the next ten years.

B Read the paragraphs from **Test 1**, **Passage 3**. Then answer the questions.

> Colossal squid (*mesonychoteuthis hamiltoni*) were once only imagined as the sea-monsters of myths, like those portrayed in author Jules Verne's eighteenth-century novel *Twenty Thousand Leagues Under the Sea*, or illustrated in other works of science fiction. Today, the existence of colossal squid has been validated. Even larger than the giant squid, the aptly named colossal squid is also a much heavier creature. However, despite its daunting size, recent research has speculated that it may not be such an aggressive predator as was previously thought. Instead of hunting its prey, the colossal squid may be a "sit and float" predator that waits for fish to swim by, unaware of its presence, before ambushing its prey.

3 According to the paragraph, what did scientists once believe about the *mesonychoteuthis hamiltoni*?

    A They did not believe it was a sea monster.

    B They thought it was the same as the giant squid.

    C They thought that it was a passive creature.

    D They believed that it was a very aggressive hunter.

4 What is the colossal squid's method of catching its food?

    A It aggressively hunts its prey.

    B It sits quietly until it sees its prey, then attacks.

    C It attempts to catch fish while floating on top of the water.

    D It swims quickly through the water chasing its prey.

> All squid are scientifically classified in the *cephalopoda* class of animals. The term is derived from Greek roots meaning *head* and *foot*. Cephalopods are invertebrates, lacking a backbone or spinal column. Squid, like octopus and cuttlefish, belong to the same subclass of cephalopods called *Coleoidea*. Squid have a distinct head, a mantle and eight arms, two fins, and two pairs of tentacles. The colossal squid differs from the giant squid in that it has hooks on the tentacles. Another difference is in the distribution of giant squid in the oceans surrounding New Zealand whereas the colossal squid seem to prefer colder, deeper waters. Colossal squid are more likely to inhabit the Ross Sea in the region near Antarctica. Another notable difference is that the colossal squid can weigh over a thousand pounds and may be up to 40 feet long. These squid can move through the water to a submerged depth of about 6,560 feet.

5 According to paragraph 3, what is true about giant squid?

    A They have hooks on their tentacles.

    B They inhabit the deep waters near Antarctica.

    C They are in a different subclass from octopus and cuttlefish.

    D They inhabit the oceans near the island of New Zealand.

6   The author states that colossal squid differ from giant squid because
    A they are invertebrates.
    B they have sharp hooks.
    C they prefer warm shallow waters.
    D they have eight arms and a mantle.

Do these practice items after you have completed Test 2.

C   Read the paragraph from **Test 2**, **Passage 1**. Then answer the questions.

> Scholars have claimed that it is difficult to reconstruct these musical instruments because so few musical instruments from the Renaissance era have survived. In addition, some of the pages of the notebooks were missing, leaving potential instrument-makers at a loss. It was not until 2008 that some Italian instrument makers created the first functional model of da Vinci's "harpsichord viola." For the first time in history, people were able to hear how the instrument would sound. Listeners claimed that it sounded somewhat like a violin, but that the wooden mechanism by which it worked was grating and noisy.

7   According to the paragraph, what factor prevented da Vinci's instruments from being built?
    A Not enough pages of the designs had survived.
    B There was a lack of efficient instrument-makers.
    C No instruments existed with which to compare the designs.
    D Their complex design made them too difficult to build correctly.

8   Based on information from the paragraph, what is true about the reproduction of da Vinci's harpsichord viola?
    A The device used to operate it interfered with the musical tone.
    B The reproduction sounded more like a keyboard than a violin.
    C It was not a true model of da Vinci's instrument.
    D It did not function properly.

D   Read the paragraph from **Test 2**, **Passage 4**. Then answer the questions.

> In a *meromictic* lake, stratification of the water exists permanently, whereby surface and bottom waters never mix completely. The upper to surface water, known as the *mixolimnion*, is most affected by wind. Water in the top layers may mix when the temperatures rise above four degrees and the water warms. Mild to moderate winds may cause the waters to mix. A transitional layer, called the *chemocline*, separates the top layer from the sedimentary bottom layer, known as the *monimolimnion*. The sedimentary layers do not physically mix with the other layers, so, the deepest layers of water remain unoxygenated. Because of this, few plants or animals are able to survive in the deeper strata.

9   According to the paragraph, mixing of water occurs in a meromictic lake when
    A the middle layer reaches a temperature of above four degrees.
    B there is a combination of warmed water and air movement.
    C the bottom layer becomes oxygenated.
    D the top layer is disturbed by wind.

10 What is true about the sedimentary layer of meromictic lake water?
   A It may mix with the mixolimnion layer.
   B It is controlled by wind and air temperatures.
   C Some life could exist there with very little oxygen.
   D It is isolated from the chemocline layer by another layer.

QUESTION TYPE 3 NEGATIVE FACTS

On the TOEFL iBT™, reading passages also require you to answer **Negative fact** questions. This type of question requires you to find information that the author does not mention, to make sure you understand the facts presented in the passage. There are usually one to two negative fact questions on the test.

Examples of negative fact questions are:

- Which of the following is NOT mentioned about {X}?
- All of the following are true about {X} EXCEPT
- The author mentions the following details about {X} EXCEPT
- Which of the following is NOT discussed about {X}?

Negative fact questions can be more difficult to answer than fact and detail questions because you have to understand what has been clearly stated in the passage in order to eliminate incorrect answer choices. The correct answer often states something opposite (contradictory) to what was presented in the passage.

SKILL BUILDER: USING THE PROCESS OF ELIMINATION

Use your skimming and scanning techniques to check the passage and make sure that information in the answer choice is NOT in the passage. You can use the skill building strategies for vocabulary and fact/detail questions to find answers to negative facts. Pay attention to introductory phrases, key words (articles and nouns), *italicized words* and punctuation. You can also use the process of elimination to find the right answer by identifying information that is clearly stated, then selecting the answer that contains the contradiction or false information.

PRACTICE FOR NEGATIVE FACT QUESTIONS

Do these practice items after you have completed Test 1.

A Read the paragraph from **Test 1**, **Passage 2**. Then answer the questions.

> Sustainable architecture consists of environmentally conscious design techniques. In the past, the demolition of an old building meant that all or most of the debris of the building would end up in a landfill or a waste disposal site. Today, architects can plan and design a building that uses recycled materials, such as wood, concrete, stone, or metal. These materials are salvaged from the demolition of an older building and can be appropriately incorporated into a new construction. Architects and construction supervisors may also choose to recycle more organic parts of demolished buildings, such as wooden doors, windows and other glass, ceramics, paper, and textiles.

1 Which of the following is NOT true about building demolition in the past?
   A Almost all of the building would be taken to a landfill.
   B Most of the material in the building was salvageable.
   C Organic parts of demolished buildings were recycled.
   D Old buildings could be constructed of wood, stone, and metal.

2 According to the paragraph, all of the following could be examples of recycled materials used in construction EXCEPT

  A wooden doors.

  B cement blocks.

  C broken china dishes.

  D plastic bottles.

B Read the paragraph from **Test 1**, **Passage 4**. Then answer the questions.

> The genealogist must learn how to reconstruct family trees based on the information provided by an individual, as well as have a deep knowledge and understanding of the sources, in order to reconstruct another person's family tree. Other skills include understanding how to work with a variety of records: registers from religious institutions, population census reports, deeds to land, immigration and emigration records, as well as other primary sources. Anyone conducting genealogical research must know how to read these documents and interpret the data. Often, the researcher must also be able to decipher script or handwriting on records from different eras and from various regions of the world.

3 According to the paragraph, what is NOT true about the genealogist's skills?

  A They must have a deep understanding of how to do research.

  B They have to be familiar with many types of documents.

  C They should be able to interpret various styles of handwriting.

  D They have to be a family member in order to reconstruct a family tree.

4 According to the paragraph, genealogical documents include all of the following EXCEPT

  A deciphering handwriting.

  B records from churches.

  C deeds to property.

  D citizenship papers.

Do these practice items after you have completed Test 2.

C Read the paragraph from **Test 2**, **Passage 2**. Then answer the questions.

> Though earth-bound telescopic systems like HARPS at La Silla play a prominent role in space exploration, orbiting telescopes, like the Hubble Space Telescope and the Kepler Orbiting Telescope, can provide astrophysicists with different data. Circling 380 miles above the Earth, the Hubble Space Telescope (HST) is about the size of a yellow school bus. Soon after its launch in 1990, astronomers were shocked to find that images sent back by the Hubble were slightly blurry due to a defective mirror. To remedy this problem, NASA created a special lens for the Hubble, similar to the way eyeglasses correct human eyesight. In a special mission, a team of astronauts serviced the Hubble by mounting this corrective lens. They also added several other specialized instruments, including an infrared camera and a spectrograph, which is used to analyze light. Among the Hubble's discoveries are new planets, newly born stars, various nebulae, and even collisions of asteroids on the planet Jupiter. In joint observation with several ground-based telescopes, the Hubble found several exoplanets that exist in a habitable zone from their stars. It is also credited with the discovery of a molecule of methane in the atmosphere of a Jupiter-sized exoplanet, supporting the theory of life forms in space.

5 All of the following instruments were new to the Hubble telescope during a special servicing mission EXCEPT

    A a mirror.

    B a special camera.

    C a corrective lens.

    D an instrument used for light analysis.

6 Which of the following is NOT included among the Hubble's discoveries?

    A significant types of chemicals in a planet's atmosphere

    B astronomical objects colliding with planets

    C clusters of dust clouds known as nebulae

    D newly formed moons

D Read the paragraphs from **Test 2**, **Passage 3**. Then answer the questions.

> John Maynard Keynes, (1883–1946) was born in Cambridge, England. His parents were a well-educated, middle-class couple, which undoubtedly influenced his intellectual development. His mother was a social reformer and his father was an economist and lecturer at the University of Cambridge. Keynes's interest and adeptness in a vast range of subjects were most noticeable during his studies at Eton College. Keynes gained early acceptance at King's College, Cambridge where he earned his bachelor's degree. At both institutions, Keynes had been offered academic scholarships. He excelled in mathematics and took his first BA in that field. He worked briefly as a clerk in the India Office, having passed the service exams by 1906. In his post-baccalaureate pursuits, his inclination was to study philosophy, but with encouragement and persuasion from one of his mentors, he finally decided on economics.

7 According to paragraph 2, which of the following statements is NOT true about Keynes's academic pursuits?

    A He was very interested in philosophy.

    B He was educated at two different universities.

    C He studied economics after he had completed his BA.

    D He was encouraged to pursue economics by his professor.

> Keynes's knowledge and excellence in the field of economics served him well in his appointment as editor of the *Economic Journal*, in 1911. He chose to remain in Cambridge at King's College as a lecturer, where he taught several economics courses such as Theory of Money, the Stock Exchange, and the Money Market; Principles of Economics, and Currency and Banking, as well as two courses specializing in the economics of India: The Currency and Finances of India, and, The Monetary Affairs of India. It was from the combination of his teaching these two latter courses and his position at the India Office that he was inspired to develop the idea for his first book, *Indian Currency and Finance*, published in 1913.

8 According to paragraph 3, all of the following are mentioned as courses taught by Keynes EXCEPT

    A Principles of Economics.

    B Theory of Money in India.

    C Currency and Banking.

    D The Currency and Finances of India.

QUESTION TYPE 4 IDENTIFYING PRONOUN REFERENCES

Reference questions require you to find relationships between words or phrases in the passage. You must be able to identify a pronoun, such as, *it*, *its*, *they*, *this*, *these*, or *which*, and the word to which the pronoun refers. The pronoun or phrase will be highlighted in the passage. There may be two reference questions in each reading set on the TOEFL iBT™. Some reading sets on the test have only one or no reference questions.

Reference questions typically appear in this form:

- The word **it** in the paragraph refers to …
- The word **they** in the passage refers to …
- The word **which** in the passage refers to …
- The phrase {**X**} in the passage refers to …

SKILL BUILDER 1 DIFFERENTIATING BETWEEN ANTICIPATORY *IT* AND REPEATED REFERENCE

Reference pronouns are important to recognize for your overall comprehension of the passage. The author uses a reference pronoun to *refer back to* the subject in the previous line, or, to a previous noun or noun phrase in the same sentence. This is another form of *redundancy*, which you read about in the Skill builder for fact and detail questions. In written texts, the pronoun might appear before the subject, while in lectures, it is more likely to follow the subject for better clarity.

Anticipatory *it* introduces a subject or topic. The anticipatory *it* may distract you from a pronoun reference. In this case, the pronoun *it* takes the place of the subject and is sometimes unnecessary. These phrases occur in all disciplines, but are most commonly found in life science passages, such as, *it is important to*, *it is possible that*, *it was found that*, and *it should be noted that*.

Recognizing anticipatory *it*, and phrases like *there is/there are*, can help you identify the main idea or a statement of fact, as well as make inferences. You can differentiate between anticipatory *it* and *it* as a reference by identifying the verb form immediately after the pronoun *it*.

Demonstrative pronouns, such as *this*, *that*, *these*, *those*, and *which*, may also be used as reference pronouns. When a sentence begins with a phrase such as, *this refers to*, *this means that*, *this suggests that*, *this is one of the*, or *these are factors in*, you will likely find the *antecedent*—the word or phrase to which the pronoun refers—in the **previous sentence**. The demonstrative pronoun may also refer to a main idea or statement of fact in the passage.

When you find the noun or noun phrase that the reference pronoun refers to, try to substitute that noun for the pronoun. Think about whether the noun is singular or plural, and whether it is the same number as the reference pronoun.

A Differentiate between the *anticipatory* pronoun *it* and *it* as a reference pronoun. Read each sentence. Circle the pronoun *it*. If the pronoun *it* is being used as anticipatory *it*, write A on the line. If you believe *it* is a reference pronoun, write R on the line and underline the noun or noun phrase in the sentence to which *it* refers.

1 It has long been believed that they went to Croatoan Island—known today as Hatteras—and assimilated with the tribe of Native Americans with whom they had very friendly relations.   ……..

2 Architects and environmental scientists have to decide whether or not a material is appropriate for use in new construction and how it will impact the environment.   ……..

3 Mercury can be harmful to humans and the environment if it is spilled during the removal of these devices.   ……..

4 It is rare that a colossal squid is ever seen.   ……..

5 The fishermen who caught it also got the squid on video.   ……..

88 READING   FURTHER PRACTICE AND GUIDANCE

6 The colossal squid differs from the giant squid in that it has hooks on the tentacles.   ……..

7 It was from the combination of his teaching these two latter courses and his position at the India Office that he was inspired to develop the idea for his first book, *Indian Currency and Finance*, published in 1913.   ……..

B **Practice with pronouns** as they relate to ideas in the paragraph.

Read the paragraph from **Test 1, Passage 4**. Find reference pronouns and underline them. Next, circle the demonstrative pronouns that refer to a fact or main idea. Then answer the questions.

> To social scientists, the field of genealogy is not typically considered a legitimate area of scholarly research. However, its relevance to cultural and historical anthropologists in understanding the connections among people in society is indisputable. The genealogical method, or, way of using symbols and diagrams to create a record of kinship connections, is an important technique of *ethnography*. Ethnography, therefore, is two things: a method that both cultural and historical anthropologists use to conduct research about a group of people, and, the written record of that research. Genealogy uses ethnographic tools because it includes both kinship connections and written records of the families. This is better known as a "family tree," which is a diagram of a person's ancestry.

8 The word **its** in line 2 of the paragraph refers to
   A understanding connections.
   B the field of genealogy.
   C scholarly research.
   D society.

9 The word **This** in the last line of the paragraph refers to
   A the concept of ethnographical research.
   B the idea that genealogy is not a legitimate field.
   C the link between a family and its written records.
   D the written research conducted by cultural anthropologists.

PRACTICE FOR REFERENCE QUESTIONS

Do these practice items after you have completed Test 1.

A Read the paragraphs from **Test 1, Passage 2**. Then answer the questions.

> The concept of being environmentally conscious, or "green," has become more prevalent in twenty-first-century U.S. culture. It has begun to affect the manufacturing of everything from non-toxic household cleaning products to motor vehicles powered by alternative sources of energy.

1 The word **It** in the paragraph refers to
   A manufacturing.
   B alternative sources of energy.
   C twenty-first century U.S. culture.
   D the concept of being environmentally conscious.

FURTHER PRACTICE AND GUIDANCE — READING — 89

> The same assessment applies to wood or wallboard painted with toxic lead-based paints. In addition, gas-flow regulators and meters on both water and gas heating systems constructed prior to 1961 must be carefully evaluated to determine that they do not contain dangerous substances such as mercury. Mercury can be harmful to humans and the environment if it is spilled during the removal of these devices.
>
> These factors contribute to the use of sustainable materials and construction practices in commercial buildings as well as residential homes. When the intended construction is a new home, the owners themselves may now participate in deciding on what recycled materials go into building their homes.

2. The phrase **These factors** in the paragraph refers to
   A evaluating dangerous substances.
   B the use of sustainable materials.
   C the removal of water and gas heating devices.
   D the evaluation of wallboard and water or gas heating systems.

B Read the paragraph from **Test 1**, **Passage 4**. Then answer the questions.

> Genealogists often find that researching a family tree is a multi-faceted task. The family tree then becomes much more than a list of names and dates on a diagram. It reaches a deeper level—one that explores the personality, character, lifestyle, and humanity of the individuals it represents. This is perhaps the desired result of genealogical research: to create a more holistic and realistic picture of families and kinship ties, and in turn, societies, as they change and grow over time.

3. The word **it** in the paragraph refers to
   A a diagram.
   B lifestyle.
   C the family tree.
   D the character.

4. The word **this** in the paragraph refers to
   A a deeper level of exploration of the family.
   B the humanity of the individuals represented.
   C societies changing and growing over time.
   D creating a more holistic and realistic picture of kinship.

Do these practice items after you have completed Test 2.

C Read the paragraphs from **Test 2**, **Passage 1**. Then answer the questions.

> Of his many skills, his abilities as a musician have often been disputed. However, among his top talents, he notably listed "engineer" as well as "inventor of instruments" in a letter of introduction he wrote to the Duke of Milan, Italy. Da Vinci described himself as "as capable as any man," in these areas. According to Vasari, da Vinci's biographer, he constructed a silver *lyre*—an ancient stringed instrument—in the shape of a horse's head, which he gave to the duke as a gift. Some historians claimed that da Vinci played it with great skill, comparable to any musician at his patron's court.

5 In the paragraph, the phrase **these areas** refers to

　A his musical abilities.

　B his talent as a writer.

　C his ability to design instruments.

　D his skills as an engineer and inventor of instruments.

> One of two, lesser-known notebooks (the *Madrid I*) housed at the Madrid National Library, contained sketches of two other instruments: a bell with a damper system, and, a pipe-like wind instrument. This wind instrument was designed to operate by pumping air through a bag attached to the pipes. Da Vinci called this a *pipa*. Scholars have also disagreed on this instrument's true appellation. Some believe it resembled a bagpipe due to the pumping of air and the mouthpiece, while others designated it to be a "triple trumpet" because it looked more like a horn than a bagpipe.

6 The word **it** in the paragraph refers to

　A the instrument's true appellation.

　B the mouthpiece.

　C a bagpipe.

　D the *pipa*.

D Read the paragraph from **Test 2**, **Passage 2**. Then answer the questions.

> In 2009, NASA launched the Kepler Orbiting Telescope. Its primary task is to focus on or, "stare at" the stars. Instead of orbiting the Earth like the Hubble, it "trails" the Earth, meaning it travels behind the Earth's orbit around the Sun. The Kepler's mission is to observe about 150,000 stars and determine if these stars contain planetary systems, most particularly, habitable planets. Unlike the La Silla and the Hubble telescopes, the Kepler Orbiting Telescope uses a *photometric* instrument to measure light emanating from a star. When a planet passes in front of a star (similar to an observation of Mercury or Venus crossing in front of the Sun), the Kepler telescope analyzes a change in the intensity of light emitted by that star. This process allows astronomers to evaluate and examine the data further to determine if one or more planets may orbit the star.

7 The word **it** in the paragraph refers to

　A NASA.

　B the Sun.

　C the Hubble Space Telescope.

　D the Kepler Orbiting Telescope.

8 The phrase **This process** in the paragraph refers to

　A a planet passing in front of a star.

　B the photometric instrument on the telescope.

　C the telescope's analysis of light emanating from a star.

　D an observation of Mercury or Venus crossing in front of the Sun.

E Read the paragraph from **Test 2**, **Passage 3**. Then answer the question.

> Despite its flaws, the effects of this book were long lasting. In it, Keynes clearly laid out a foundation for how a government should "run deficits" to manage or end a recession. The government creates a budget deficit by borrowing capital and purchasing goods from a world market. The government must then bolster demand and increase taxation and consumption in an effort to stabilize its workforce. During an economic downturn, private individuals do not invest or spend. This creates a cycle where businesses also reduce investments resulting in fewer jobs and less investment. Keynes's idea was that the government should take the place of businesses by investing in public works while simultaneously creating jobs for the unemployed.

9 The word **This**, in the paragraph refers to

   A the downturn of an economy.

   B the budget deficit created by the government.

   C the lack of spending and investment by people.

   D the demand and increase of taxation and consumption.

QUESTION TYPE 5 RHETORICAL PURPOSE

The **Rhetorical purpose** question on the TOEFL iBT™ requires you to understand the purpose or organization of the essay. There may be one or no rhetorical purpose questions in a reading set.

To answer fact and detail questions, you have to think about the passage in terms of *who*, *what*, *where*, and *when*. To answer rhetorical purpose questions, you need to consider *why* the author presents material in a certain way and ask yourself questions about the facts and details. What does the author want the reader to know? How does the author present the material?

Rhetorical purpose questions usually appear in the following forms:

- In the paragraph, the author mentions {X} in order to ...
- Why does the author say {X}?
- The author mentions {X} as an example of ...
- The author discusses {X} in order to ...

SKILL BUILDER 1 FINDING THE AUTHOR'S PURPOSE

The **Rhetorical purpose** questions may require you to relate one statement in the passage to another, or to determine the reason why the author has made a particular statement of fact. Does the author want to compare or contrast certain points? Does the author want to illustrate an idea? Is the author attempting to offer a solution to a problem? You should ask yourself these questions as you read. You should also try to eliminate wrong answer choices that are too general or do not include information that is specific to the structure of the passage.

Familiarize yourself with the *infinitive* phrases used in the answer choices. Each infinitive phrase is connected to the author's intention and how the author links information in one paragraph to the rest of the passage. The rhetorical purpose question may require you to understand how a statement in one paragraph relates to information in a previous paragraph.

The following are some of the infinitive phrases used in the answer choices. Look up the meaning of any unfamiliar words in your dictionary.

To argue	To clarify	To compare	To contradict
To contrast	To criticize	To demonstrate	To describe
To illustrate	To indicate	To inform	To introduce
To note	To offer	To provide	To show

A Read the following excerpt from **Test 1**, **Passage 1**. Then answer the questions.

> Fifty years later, Robert W. White's book *A Witness for Eleanor Dare* revisited the story of the Dare stones. White raised the question of the stones' authenticity by stating that Sparkes had created the controversy in order to get publicity about the mystery of the Lost Colony, but moreover, to seek monetary gain for himself. White's examination of the evidence reintroduced the possibility that the stones were not fake. However, historians and archaeologists alike have still not reached an agreement about this potential physical evidence of the Lost Colony. Despite the controversy, one of the infamous Dare stones is now on exhibit at the Lost Colony Center for Science and Research in Williamston, North Carolina.

1 Why does the author introduce the book by Robert W. White?

....

2 Why does the author discuss Sparkes's motives?

....

3 In the paragraph, why does the author mention the disagreement between historians and archaeologists?

....

B Read the following paragraphs from **Test 1**, **Passage 3**. Then fill in the blanks with an infinitive phrase that best fits the sentence. Not all the infinitive phrases will be used.

> In 2003, fishermen in the Ross Sea caught a colossal squid of almost 20 feet in length with enormous eyes and razor-sharp hooks on its tentacles. From examining the physiology of this specimen, scientists realized that because of *dimorphism*—a difference in size between the genders, the female of the species are atypically much larger than the males. Thus, the discovery of an enormous male colossal squid indicates the possible existence of even larger female squid.
> Scientists proved this theory in 2007 when fishermen in the Ross Sea captured a colossal squid that was feeding on toothfish. This female squid weighed over a ton and was nearly 33 feet long. The fishermen also filmed the squid on video. This enabled scientists to examine it, to some extent, as a live specimen. They were unable to contain the live squid, but preserved it in ice and took it to New Zealand for further study. In spring of 2008, scientists thawed the squid and began a thorough examination, which allowed them to obtain much more information on the lethal hooks of its tentacles.

to describe	to inform	to support	to offer an example of

4 The author discusses the idea of *dimorphism* .... the claim that the female squid could be larger its male counterpart.

5 The author mentions that fishermen filmed the squid on video .... one way that scientists were able to examine a live squid.

6 The author states that the scientists preserved the squid in ice .... how they transported the squid to New Zealand for further study.

PRACTICE FOR RHETORICAL PURPOSE QUESTIONS

Do these practice items after you have completed Test 1.

A Read the paragraph from **Test 1**, **Passage 1**. Then answer the question.

> Questions about the colonists' fate still exist: Did they assimilate with the Croatoan Indians? Did they attempt to sail back to England and were they lost at sea? Did they all succumb to disease or harsh weather? These questions and the authenticity of the Dare stones continue to be one of the most enduring unsolved mysteries of early American history.

1. Why does the author raise questions about the colonists' fate?
   A to contradict the theories that the stones are real
   B to introduce new ideas about the colonists
   C to offer other possible theories for the reader to consider
   D to provide the reader with more information about the colonists' fate

B Read the paragraph from **Test 1**, **Passage 2**. Then answer the question.

> The concept of being environmentally conscious, or "green," has become more prevalent in twenty-first-century U.S. culture. It has begun to affect the manufacturing of everything from non-toxic household cleaning products to motor vehicles powered by alternative sources of energy. However, one way of being "green" that is perhaps not as apparent to the viewer but of equal importance in being environmentally conscious, is the construction of buildings that are considered "sustainable." Sustainable buildings are those that do not impose on the environment or rely on the over-utilization of energy or natural resources. There are four main principles of sustainability, which include consideration of the health and stability of all living things and their environmental diversity, as well as the economic opportunities of humanity.

2. In the paragraph, why does the author list the principles of sustainability?
   A to clarify the concept of sustainable building
   B to demonstrate the seriousness of environmental issues
   C to illustrate the rationale behind the concept of being "green"
   D to define the underlying concepts of how sustainability works

C Read the paragraph from **Test 1**, **Passage 4**. Then answer the questions.

> The American public's fascination with genealogy may have started in 1976 with the publication and television mini-series of author Alex Hailey's acclaimed book, *Roots*, the story of his eighteenth-century African ancestors from the time of their enslavement to the emancipation proclamation in the U.S. The popularity of genealogy as a "cultural phenomenon" has grown to a point where people worldwide are subscribing to various ancestry websites, becoming members of genealogical societies, and even having their DNA tested, all in order to trace their family trees. In addition to a recent rise in the number of Internet-based genealogical research companies, genealogy has also generated commercial appeal by way of television broadcasting. Today, programs on television about "finding your roots" are ubiquitous in several countries. The premise of one show, for example, is investigating the family trees of American celebrities. These features, combined with a celebrity factor, have boosted the interest in genealogy in the U.S. and Canada by nearly half a million people.

3. Why does the author mention Alex Hailey's book *Roots*?
   A to offer an example of a book about U.S. history
   B to connect the story of a family to the media
   C to explain why the American public became interested in genealogy
   D to provide a possible event that inspired Americans to research their own roots

4. In the paragraph, why does the author mention television broadcasting?
   A to show that genealogy is primarily a commercial field
   B to demonstrate how people obtain genealogical information
   C to offer an example of how the media influences Americans
   D to support his statement about genealogy as a cultural phenomenon

Do these practice items after you have completed Test 2.

D Read the paragraph from **Test 2, Passage 2**. Then answer the questions.

> In order to find planets that are light years from our own solar system, astronomers use two types of telescope, each with sensitive instruments that employ special techniques, to aid in the acquisition of data: ground-based and orbiting telescopes. In 2007, a team of Swiss scientists discovered the first Earth-like planet outside of our solar system, *Gliese 581*, estimated to be approximately 50 percent bigger than Earth. Located about 20.5 light years from our world, *Gliese 581* orbits a red dwarf star. To identify this new planet, the astronomy team used a *spectroscopic* instrument known as HARPS, which is linked to a 3.6-meter telescope at the European Southern Observatory in La Silla, Chile. Spectroscopic instruments use a Doppler, or "wobble" technique to identify *radial velocity*—how fast a star moves toward or away from the point of observation. By analyzing the wavelength of light emitted from a star, the instrument is therefore able to calibrate the mass of a planet in the star's orbit. With the wobble technique, astronomers are only able to perceive a planet that is less than 160 light years from Earth. Employing this technique can be slow, because astronomers must wait for the planet to make one complete orbit of its sun in order to confirm their data.

5 Why does the author mention *Gliese 581* in the paragraph?
  A to offer an example of a possibly habitable exoplanet
  B to demonstrate the technology of the telescopes
  C to define a planet outside our solar system
  D to illustrate the work of the scientists

6 In the paragraph, why does the author explain *radial velocity*?
  A to define the wobble technique
  B to elaborate on the techniques of spectrometric instruments
  C to describe how astronomers were able to locate *Gliese 581*
  D to support the idea that Earth-like planets can be located

E Read the paragraphs from **Test 2, Passage 4**. Then answer the questions.

> In a meromictic lake, stratification of the water exists permanently, whereby surface and bottom waters never mix completely. The upper to surface water, known as the mixolimnion, is most affected by wind. Water in the top layers may mix when the temperatures rise above 4°C and the water warms. Mild to moderate winds may cause the waters to mix. A transitional layer, called the *chemocline*, separates the top layer from the sedimentary bottom layer, known as the *monimolimnion*. Because the sedimentary layers do not physically mix with the other layers, the deepest layers of water remain unoxygenated. Because of this, few plants or animals are able to survive in the deeper strata.
>
> In most cases, meromictic lakes are extremely deep, with static, undisturbed layers throughout the bottom. This creates an actual historical stratification system, in which scientists are able to take samplings of layers of water from particular points in time.

7 In the first paragraph, why does the author discuss the transitional layer in the lake?
  A to provide more information about the mixolimnion
  B to further explain the stratification of the lake water
  C to describe how the waters only mix in certain layers
  D to give another reason why the top and bottom waters do not mix

8   In the second paragraph, why does the author mention the undisturbed layers at the bottom of meromictic lakes?

   A   to explain why the lake water does not mix

   B   to illustrate the condition of the lake bottom

   C   to provide facts and details about meromictic lakes

   D   to introduce the idea that scientists can obtain information on the lake's history

QUESTION TYPE 6   MAKING INFERENCES

Inference questions require you to think about information which is not explicitly or directly stated in the passage. You must think about the facts and details presented, then draw conclusions. This question may take you more time to answer than vocabulary or fact questions.

There are one or two inference questions per reading set on the TOEFL iBT™. Inference questions include words like *imply*, *infer*, or *suggest*, and usually appear in the following form.

- What can be inferred about {X}?
- The author implies that {X} …
- The author suggests that {X} …

SKILL BUILDER 1   INFERENCE QUESTIONS

To answer **Inference questions**, you will need to read the answer choices very carefully. You can take the following steps to build your skills at answering this type of question and improve your overall comprehension of the passage.

- Read the four answer choices carefully to eliminate choices that might be true but do not have enough information to be the correct answer.
- Skim the paragraph to which the inference question refers and read the first and last sentence.
- Scan for key words and think about the author's choice of words.
- Scan for details and think carefully about the facts and details that the author has presented and why the author chose to include them.
- Think about the author's purpose and how the purpose might influence the answer choice.

A   Read the paragraph from **Test 1**, **Passage 1**. Read the sentences and make a check ✓ next to the statements that are inferences drawn from the paragraph.

> However, any scholarly inquiries regarding this 350-year-old mystery nearly came to a halt in 1940 when the *Saturday Evening Post* newspaper published a story claiming that it was "solved." The story upheld the angle that a few of the colonists had survived—among them, Governor John White's daughter Eleanor Dare, her husband Ananias, and their infant daughter Virginia. Eleanor had allegedly inscribed her story on a series of 48 stones so that her father would know what had happened to them. The article included photographs of some of the stones that the reporter said had been found in swamps and various other places in North and South Carolina, as well as Georgia, all within a 400-mile radius of each other. The stones were given to Dr. Haywood Pearce, a professor of American History at the University of Atlanta, who examined them and took his story to the media. The text on the stones was simple, but written in what appeared to be sixteenth-century Roman letters. Pearce thought that the stones were authentic and the *Post* printed the story.

1   The *Saturday Evening Post*'s article about the Dare stones almost prevented further research about the stones' authenticity.   ....

2   The members of the Dare family were the only survivors.   ....

3   By 1940, people were no longer curious about the mystery of the Lost Colony.   ....

4   The story about the Dare Stones offered a solution to the mystery.   ....

5   The photographs of the stones were probably fakes.   ....

6   There was proof that Eleanor carved messages into the stones.   ....

7   The text on the stones was not modern.   ....

PRACTICE FOR INFERENCE QUESTIONS

Do these practice items after you have completed Test 1.

A   Read the paragraph from **Test 1, Passage 1**. Then answer the question.

> However, any scholarly inquiries regarding this 350-year-old mystery nearly came to a halt in 1940 when the *Saturday Evening Post* newspaper published a story claiming that it was "solved." The story upheld the angle that a few of the colonists had survived—among them, Governor John White's daughter Eleanor Dare, her husband Ananias, and their infant daughter Virginia. Eleanor had allegedly inscribed her story on a series of 48 stones so that her father would know what had happened to them. The article included photographs of some of the stones that the reporter said had been found in swamps and various other places in North and South Carolina, as well as Georgia, all within a 400-mile radius of each other. The stones were given to Dr. Haywood Pearce, a professor of American History at the University of Atlanta, who examined them and took his story to the media. The text on the stones was simple, but written in what appeared to be sixteenth-century Roman letters. Pearce thought that the stones were authentic and the *Post* printed the story.

1   According to the paragraph, what can be inferred about who found the stones?
   A   They were found in Georgia by Haywood Pearce.
   B   Governor John White was the first to discover the stones.
   C   They were found by a reporter at the *Saturday Evening Post*.
   D   An unknown source discovered them and gave them to a reporter.

2   Based on information about where the stones were located, what can be inferred about where the survivors had gone?
   A   The colonists had stayed in a very isolated area.
   B   The colonists might have travelled through at least three states.
   C   The survivors from the colonies tried to get back to Roanoke Island.
   D   Most of the settlers had left and only the Dare family remained.

B   Read the paragraph from **Test 1, Passage 2**. Then answer the questions.

> In terms of energy and natural resources, sustainable architecture may incorporate many alternative energy sources—energy that is not harmful to the environment and does not rely on mineral-based fuels like coal or oil. Some utility companies around the world are offering wind and solar power as alternatives to electricity. In the U.S. today, these options are available to homeowners and commercial building management. Along with the capability to use recyclable materials in residential or commercial constructions, as well as options for generating power from renewable energy sources, society can contribute to the concept of a greener way of life.

3   What does the author imply about mineral-based fuels?
    A They are not harmful to the environment.
    B They are considered alternative energy sources.
    C They are present in existing buildings today.
    D They are preferred sources of energy for sustainable building.

4   In the paragraph, the author suggests that
    A society will benefit from using alternative and renewable energy.
    B there are few options for homeowners to use in building.
    C commercial constructions are less likely to be green.
    D wind and solar power are not available in the U.S.

Do these practice items after you have completed Test 2.

C   Read the paragraph from **Test 2**, **Passage 4**. Then answer the questions.

> In the 1950s, Hutchinson and Loffler classified lakes into six categories. However, experts now agree that there are eight types of lakes. In addition to deep-water lakes, this new classification system also includes shallow-water lakes. Thus, lakes are categorized by depth, temperature, and the pattern by which their waters mix. The two main types are *holomictic* and *meromictic*. These types are further sub-categorized based on the water's temperature and the pattern of mixing that occurs in the lake during the year. For example, some lakes are *animictic*, meaning that they remain ice-covered for the entire year. The distinction of *mixis* (mixing) ranges from lakes with temperatures that rise above 4 degrees Celcius /39 degrees Fahrenheit, and mix once annually, to lakes in tropical climates where the waters may mix several times during the year.

5   What does the author imply about the previous classification of lakes?
    A It did not include holomictic and meromictic lakes.
    B It did not categorize lakes based on water depth.
    C Shallow lakes were not part of the classification system.
    D Ice-covered lakes had not been incorporated into a specific category.

6   What can be inferred about *animictic* lakes?
    A Their waters probably never mix.
    B The water mixes once per year.
    C The ice melts once annually.
    D They are not true lakes.

7   What does the author suggest about lakes in tropical climates?
    A The waters mix once annually.
    B Climate change is not a factor in the water's frequent mixing.
    C It is difficult to determine how many times per year the waters will mix.
    D Temperature is more important than depth in the mixing of tropical waters.

D Read the paragraph from **Test 2**, **Passage 1**. Then answer the questions.

> Da Vinci's designs for percussion instruments were also quite unusual. Unlike his concepts for string and wind instruments, these designs were more detailed. Intended for use in processions, da Vinci's motorized drums were set on a cart that had a crank mechanism containing several rows of curved mallets on either side. The musician could "program" the mechanism by using movable pegs that were inserted into rows of holes on rollers. The player then adjusted the mechanism to a desired rhythm. When the player pulled the cart behind him, the beat could sound continuously as long as the player kept the speed of the cart constant.

8   What does the author imply about da Vinci's motorized drum?
   A It was probably played in parades along with other instruments.
   B The player was not able to change the rhythm of the drum.
   C The designs for the percussion instruments were incomplete.
   D The player had to keep the beat of the motorized drum continuous.

9   What does the author suggest about the crank mechanism?
   A It was dependent on the speed of the cart.
   B Its parts were fixed and could not be changed.
   C The player was able to set its rhythmic pattern in advance.
   D The player had to turn the crank mechanism so the drum would move.

QUESTION TYPE 7 SENTENCE INSERTION

The TOEFL iBT™ requires you to understand the organization of the passage and make logical connections between sentences in the passage. The **Sentence insertion** question presents a new sentence that can be added to the passage. To answer this type of question, you will read the sentence and choose among four places in the passage where the sentence could be added.

On the TOEFL iBT™, you will see four squares in the paragraph, or near the end of one paragraph and the beginning of the next paragraph. You will click on one of the squares to indicate where the sentence should be added. Sentence insertion questions appear in this form:

   Look at the four squares ■ that indicate where the following sentence could be added to the passage.
   Then you read a sentence in bold.
   Where would the sentence best fit?

For the tests in this book, you will choose among four bracketed letters, **[A]**, **[B]**, **[C]**, or **[D]**, and mark the correct answer on the answer sheet. There is usually one **Sentence insertion** question per set, but some sets do not have this question type.

SKILL BUILDER 1 UNDERSTANDING TRANSITIONAL PHRASES

Transitional phrases and **cohesive devices** can help you understand the organization and logic of a passage. These phrases are cues in both text and speech to aid the reader or listener in understanding how certain information connects.

Some transitional phrases show connections in time, such as, *first*, *next*, *then*, *finally*, *as a result*. Other connecting words may show rhetorical functions. For example, the phrases, *similarly*, *like*, *in other words*, *in the same way*, show comparison. Phrases such as, *On the other hand*, *in contrast*, *on the contrary*, show contrast.

Among the disciplines, some transitional phrases occur more frequently than in other disciplines. This has to do with the rhetorical function of the passage, or the author's purpose for writing. For example, the following lists are organized by how frequently these phrases occur:

FURTHER PRACTICE AND GUIDANCE READING 99

Life sciences: *in the presence of, on the other hand, at the beginning of, as well as, in the case of, at the same time, the results of the, in addition to the*

Social sciences: *on the other hand, at the same time, in the case of, as well as, the results of the, in terms of, in the sense that, can be seen, for example*

Organization of transitional phrases and cohesive devices	
Example or illustration	*by way of, for example, for instance, one way, such as, to illustrate*
Numbering in importance	*First, second, third, next, last, another, finally*
Cause/effect and purpose	*because, because of, consequently, in order to, since, therefore, thus*
Comparison	*in the same way, like, likewise, similarly*
Addition/continuation	*also, combined with, in addition to, and, further, another*
Contrast	*in contrast, on the contrary, on the other hand, however, more importantly*

A Transitional phrases. Read the following paragraphs. Find **seven** transitional phrases and underline them.

> The popularity of genealogy as a "cultural phenomenon" has grown to a point where people worldwide are subscribing to various ancestry websites, becoming members of genealogical societies, and even having their DNA tested, all in order to trace their family trees. In addition to a recent rise in the number of Internet-based genealogical research companies, genealogy has also generated commercial appeal by way of television broadcasting. Today, programs on television about "finding your roots" are ubiquitous in several countries. The premise of one show, for example, is investigating the family trees of American celebrities. These features, combined with a celebrity factor, have boosted the interest in genealogy in the U.S. and Canada by nearly half a million people.
>
> This cultural phenomenon may seem like a fad, but at the same time, its historical and more scholarly implications are not lost to cultural anthropologists and researchers in other disciplines. For archivists—the library science specialists who deal with documenting, preserving, and organizing old records—the field of genealogy and the needs of genealogical researchers are very important.

B Read the paragraphs again. Write the transitional phrases you found in the "Phrase" column. Then choose the correct rhetorical mode for each phrase and make a check ✓ in the correct column.

	Phrase	Addition or continuation	Contrast	Example or illustration	Cause–effect or purpose
1					
2					
3					
4					
5					
6					
7					

SKILL BUILDER 2 UNDERSTANDING THE ORGANIZATION OF A PARAGRAPH

Reference words (see the Practice for reference questions section for more information) are important for making connections in the text. Reference words create links to aid in the reader's comprehension of the text because they are directly connected to key words or phrases within the context.

A Organize the paragraph. Put the sentences in order from 1–6 to form a coherent paragraph from **Test 1, Passage 4**. Look for reference words, transitional phrases, and cohesive devices to help you understand the logic of the paragraph.

.... These principles are the social building blocks of many nonindustrial-based societies: societies that are "kin based."

.... For example, genealogical records were perhaps most important to the aristocracy of Europe.

.... For example, there was no barrier to Charles, Prince of Wales and Lady Diana Spencer marrying because of her impeccable lineage.

.... Throughout history and even today, in upper-class families, one's pedigree determined whether a couple could wed.

.... Genealogical research reveals significant facts that can be analyzed in order to see how descent, marriage, and kinship ties play a role in the development of a given society over time.

.... Similarly, in the U.S., one's lineage often played a role in uniting families of a particular socio-economic level—such as the marriage between President John F. Kennedy and Jacqueline Bouvier.

PRACTICE FOR SENTENCE INSERTION QUESTIONS

Do these practice items after you have completed Test 1.

A Read the paragraph from **Test 1, Passage 1**. Then answer the question.

1 The following sentence can be added to the paragraph. Look at the four letters that indicate where the sentence could fit the paragraph. Circle the letter **A**, **B**, **C**, or **D**.

Consequently, White's work also further implicated Sparkes's involvement in a conspiracy to benefit from the development of a Roanoke tourist attraction.

Fifty years later, Robert W. White's book *A Witness for Eleanor Dare* revisited the story of the Dare stones. **[A]** White raised the question of the stones' authenticity by stating that Sparkes had created the controversy in order to get publicity about the mystery of the Lost Colony, but moreover, to seek monetary gain for himself. **[B]** White's examination of the evidence reintroduced the possibility that the stones were not fake. **[C]** However, historians and archaeologists alike have still not reached an agreement about this potential physical evidence of the Lost Colony. **[D]** Despite the controversy, one of the infamous Dare stones is now on exhibit at the Lost Colony Center for Science and Research in Williamston, North Carolina.

B Read the paragraph from **Test 1, Passage 3**. Then answer the question.

2 The following sentence can be added to the paragraph. Look at the four letters that indicate where the sentence could fit the paragraph. Circle the letter **A**, **B**, **C**, or **D**.

However, the squid's size does not hinder its ability to move quickly.

[A] Another factor that may cause gigantism is the frigid temperature of the deep sea. **[B]** Biologists believe there is a correlation between the body temperature and size of the colossal squid. **[C]** Their larger size enables the colossal squid to conserve body heat in a frigid environment, thus giving them another edge over their competition. **[D]**

FURTHER PRACTICE AND GUIDANCE · READING · 101

Do these practice items after you have completed Test 2.

C Read the paragraph from **Test 2**, **Passage 3**. Then answer the question.

3 The following sentence can be added to the paragraph. Look at the four letters that indicate where the sentence could fit the paragraph. Circle the letter **A**, **B**, **C**, or **D**.

Despite its flaws, the effects of this book were long lasting.

> In the next decade, Keynes published several treatises and tracts on subjects such as probability and monetary reform. He completed and published his most important text, *The General Theory of Employment, Interest and Money* during a time when most of the nations of the world were suffering in the grips of the Great Depression. **[A]** In this work, published in 1936, Keynes established his theories on the world's economy, which became known as the *Keynesian model*, and sought to explain fluctuations in aggregate business. **[B]** The book was widely criticized for being poorly organized and for presenting ideas that were so complicated that they were often incomprehensible to its readers. **[C]** In it, Keynes clearly laid out a foundation for how a government should "run deficits" to manage or end a recession. **[D]** The government creates a budget deficit by borrowing capital and purchasing goods from a world market.

D Read the paragraph from **Test 2**, **Passage 4**. Then answer the question.

4 The following sentence can be added to the paragraph. Look at the four letters that indicate where the sentence could fit the paragraph. Circle the letter **A**, **B**, **C**, or **D**.

A lake can be categorized according to the degree to which the upper and lower strata of its waters turn over and mix.

> In temperate climates, most lakes undergo a normal process where surface waters cyclically mix with waters from the lower layers. **[A]** This process occurs in spring and fall, when water temperatures are uniformly the same from the surface of the lake to its bottom. **[B]** This turnover of surface and bottom layers of water is closely related to seasonal temperatures as well as depth, elevation, and geographical latitude. **[C]** In waters that are deep in proportion to their diameter, the water at the bottom of the lake does not mix with the surface waters, creating two distinct strata. **[D]** Other factors that affect mixing include the chemical and mineral composition of the lake, as well as wind.

QUESTION TYPE 8 SENTENCE SIMPLIFICATION

The **Sentence simplification** question tests your ability to understand a paraphrase of one sentence from the passage. Paraphrasing is an important skill that you will also use in the speaking and writing section of the test. To paraphrase means to put something into your own words. To answer this type of question, you will read four answer choices that are a paraphrase of one sentence in the passage. These are paraphrased sentences, one of which captures the essential information in the highlighted sentence. There can be one or none of these questions on the TOEFL iBT™ reading section.

Sentence simplification questions appear in the following form:

> First, one sentence in the passage will be highlighted. You then read this question:
> Which of the following best expresses the essential information in the highlighted sentence? Incorrect answer choices change the meaning or leave out essential information.

SKILL BUILDER 1 PARAPHRASING

Sentence simplification questions require you to have a good overall understanding of a paragraph or sentence and to be able to break the sentence down into parts. When you paraphrase, you need to remember to put the sentence in your own words. The answer choices on the TOEFL iBT™ provide examples of one correct and three incorrect paraphrases.

To help you answer this type of question you should:

- Look for **punctuation** and **transitional phrases**.
- Find **synonyms** or key words in the sentence.
- Read the context in which the highlighted sentence occurs.

Punctuation review. As you read in the Skill builder for facts and details, punctuation is often a useful tool in making connections in comprehension of the passage. Find punctuation such as, colons, commas, long dashes, and parentheses. Look at the key words and phrases within, before, or after those punctuation marks.

Look at the examples below. If you need further review, go back to the Skill builders for facts and details starting on page 76.

Colon. Often follows phrases like, *such as, for example, as follows*. Colons may begin a list of information or offer facts.

Commas. May surround an *appositive*, or be a restricted adjective clause, or separate words in a series or list.

Long dash. Precedes an appositive or more information about the previous key words or phrase.

Parentheses. Surround more information about an idea; can enclose an acronym, explanation, definition, or date range.

A   Using synonyms. Read each sentence. Then match a synonym or similar phrase from the box to the key words or phrases in **bold**. Rewrite the sentence using the new words. Make sure the word or phrase is grammatically correct in the sentence.

recreate	is constructed by using	methods	falsely created
verified proof	in the past	ancestral line	
believed	intimidating	showed	

1 He systematically **proved**, with **supporting evidence** from experts, that the words written on the rocks in an Elizabethan-era Roman script had been **fabricated**, and the dates on the rocks could not be scientifically proven.

....

2 Sustainable architecture **consists of** environmentally conscious design **techniques**.

....

3 However, despite its **daunting** size, recent research has speculated that it may not be such an aggressive predator as was **previously thought**.

....

4 The genealogist must learn how to **reconstruct** family trees based on the information provided by an individual, as well as have a deep knowledge and understanding of the sources, in order to create another person's **family tree**.

....

B   Read each sentence again. Then rewrite the sentence in your own words to capture the essential meaning.

1 ....
2 ....
3 ....
4 ....

PRACTICE FOR SENTENCE SIMPLIFICATION QUESTIONS

Do these practice items after you have completed Test 1.

A Read the paragraph from **Test 1**, **Passage 2**. Then answer the question.

> Sustainable architecture consists of environmentally conscious design techniques. In the past, the demolition of an old building meant that all or most of the debris of the building would end up in a landfill or a waste disposal site. Today, architects can plan and design a building that uses recycled materials, such as wood, concrete, stone, or metal. These materials are salvaged from the demolition of an older building and can be appropriately incorporated into a new construction. Architects and construction supervisors may also choose to recycle more organic parts of demolished buildings, such as wooden doors, windows and other glass, ceramics, paper, and textiles.

1. Which of the following best expresses the essential information in the highlighted sentence? Incorrect answer choices change the meaning or leave out essential information.
    - A The decision to use organic materials like doors, glass and paper products is the responsibility of the architects and supervisors of the construction site.
    - B The choice of architects and construction site personnel is to use the material collected from a demolished building, like glass, wood, and paper.
    - C Architects and supervisors have decided to use more parts from the ruins of destroyed buildings, such as doors and windows.
    - D The use of natural recyclable materials, such as glass or ceramics, may be the preferred method of construction in an architect's or site supervisor's approach to dealing with the remains of a demolished building.

B Read the last line from paragraph 3 and part of paragraph 4 from **Test 1**, **Passage 4**. Then answer the question.

> These features, combined with a celebrity factor, have boosted the interest in genealogy in the U.S. and Canada by nearly half a million people.
> This cultural phenomenon may seem like a fad, but at the same time, its historical and more scholarly implications are not lost to cultural anthropologists and researchers in other disciplines. For archivists—the library science specialists who deal with documenting, preserving, and organizing old records—the field of genealogy and the needs of genealogical researchers are very important. There is no special credential or degree-bearing requirement for becoming a "professional" genealogist. Many people have become genealogists simply because of an interest in their own family history.

2. Which of the following best expresses the essential information in the highlighted sentence? Incorrect answer choices change the meaning or leave out essential information.
    - A Though it is just a trend, the importance of genealogy is easily uncovered by historians and anthropologists.
    - B To scholars in anthropology, genealogy is a phenomenon, but to scholars in other fields, it is merely a popular trend that will not last.
    - C Cultural anthropologists and researchers do not lose the validity of their work by understanding the phenomenon of genealogy.
    - D The importance of genealogy to the pursuit of scholarship in cultural anthropology and history is evident even though it might appear to be a trend.

Do these practice items after you have completed Test 2.

C Read an excerpt from **Test 2**, **Passage 1**, **Paragraph 3**. Then answer the question.

> To operate the harpsichord-viola, air would be forced through a bellows attached to the keyboard and powered by the player's leg when he marched or walked. Designs for this instrument show that it could be easily carried by use of shoulder straps and a belt placed around the waist of the player.

3 Which of the following best expresses the essential information in the highlighted sentence? Incorrect answer choices change the meaning or leave out essential information.

- **A** The harpsichord-viola player can adjust the instrument by use of straps placed on the shoulders.
- **B** It is possible to carry the harpsichord-viola if the player fastens the instrument to his shoulders and waist.
- **C** The diagrams for the harpsichord-viola reveal that it was intended to be carried by its player by use of a belt and shoulder straps.
- **D** The instrument was moved with ease because the player could belt it to his waist and shoulders.

D Read an excerpt from **Test 2**, **Passage 2**, **Paragraph 3**. Then answer the question.

> Soon after its launch in 1990, astronomers were shocked to find that images sent back by the Hubble were slightly blurry due to a defective mirror. To remedy this problem, NASA created a special lens for the Hubble, similar to the way eyeglasses correct human eyesight. In a special mission, a team of astronauts serviced the Hubble by mounting this corrective lens.

4 Which of the following best expresses the essential information in the highlighted sentence? Incorrect answer choices change the meaning or leave out essential information.

- **A** NASA's solution to the mirror problem was to make a lens for the Hubble that would correct its vision.
- **B** In order to fix the mirror, NASA made a lens that worked like eyeglasses.
- **C** The Hubble was repaired with a new lens that fixed its visual problem.
- **D** NASA solved the Hubble's mirror problem by inventing a corrective lens.

QUESTION TYPE 9 PROSE SUMMARY

There are two **Reading to learn** type questions on the TOEFL iBT™: **Prose summary** and **Schematic table**. Both of these questions test your ability to understand the major ideas in a passage and make connections between the paragraphs to understand those ideas.

The **Prose summary** question requires you to understand the connections between different parts of the passage. You have to distinguish between major and minor ideas in the passage. You need to be able to locate major ideas and other information in the passage and organize it into a cohesive summary. The **Prose summary** question usually appears in this form:

> An introductory sentence for a brief summary of the passage is provided below. Complete the summary by selecting **three** answer choices that express the most important ideas in the passage. Some sentences do not belong because they express ideas that are not presented in the passage or are minor ideas.

The introductory sentence appears in **bold** font.

FURTHER PRACTICE AND GUIDANCE   READING   105

SKILL BUILDER 1 UNDERSTANDING SUMMARY

Like paraphrasing, summarizing is a skill that you will use when you write. In a paraphrase, you use your own words to quote or reiterate something stated by an author or speaker. In a summary, you have to understand the passage or lecture in its entirety, and discuss it using your own words. These are important tools that you may also apply to the Speaking and Writing sections of the test.

A summary is the shortened version of a written text, which includes the major points. For the **Prose summary** question, you will have to reread the entire passage and choose which points best represent the essential information from the passage.

- Use your **notes**, which should include: **key words**, dates, important names or places, **major ideas**, **facts**, and the author's purpose.
- Create an outline or a chart to help you organize the information.

A Create a summary. Read the following paragraph. Circle key words and underline the main ideas of the paragraph. Then write a short summary of the paragraph in your own words, focusing on the major ideas and essential information. You should try to paraphrase important points and summarize the paragraph in three to four short sentences.

> There are essentially three roles a computer can play in computer crime. It can be the target of the crime, it can be the instrument used to commit the crime, or it can be a source of evidence concerning the crime. It can also have multiple roles. If someone uses a computer to steal information or hack into a system, and then they store that information on the same computer, computer forensic experts must tailor their investigation to the multiple roles of the computer in the crime. There are many factors to take into consideration, such as, illegally recovering the data or destroying important evidence. It is also possible to waste valuable time if one merely dives into the work without carefully considering the possible multiple roles of the computer in the crime.

....
....
....
....
....

PRACTICE FOR PROSE SUMMARY QUESTIONS

Do these practice items after you have completed Test 1.

A Reread **Test 1, Passage 1**. Then answer the question.

1 An introductory sentence for a brief summary of the passage is provided below. Complete the summary by selecting **three** answer choices that express the most important ideas in the passage. Some sentences do not belong because they express ideas that are not presented in the passage or are minor ideas.

In 1587, a ship carrying a group of English settlers unintentionally landed at Roanoke Island off the coast of North Carolina.

  A When the war between England and Spain broke out, their governor decided to travel back to England to get supplies but could not return for many years.

  B The fate of the settlers has been shrouded in mystery for more than four hundred years because no one has been able to determine why they left the colony, where they went, or ultimately, if the letters CRO were a clue.

  C When the investigative reporter Boyden Sparkes declared the Dare stones to be a hoax, he damaged Pearce's reputation and precluded historians and archaeologists from actually determining the authenticity of the stones.

D Dr. Pearce vanished because Boyden Sparkes published a story that proved the writing on the stones was not really Elizabethan script and that Pearce was a fraud.

E The settlers must have found conditions in this area to be so harsh that they were compelled to abandon the area.

F Though there were possible clues to the colonists' whereabouts, no one was able to authenticate the alleged 48 Dare stones that were described in the 1940 newspaper article by Dr. Haywood Pearce.

B Reread **Test 1, Passage 2**. Then answer the question.

2 An introductory sentence for a brief summary of the passage is provided below. Complete the summary by selecting **three** answer choices that express the most important ideas in the passage. Some sentences do not belong because they express ideas that are not presented in the passage or are minor ideas.

The idea of "green" living is an important part of twenty-first-century culture that includes everything from how products are designed and manufactured to the use of energy sources.

A Architects can save materials from demolished sites or buildings and use the organic parts in new construction sites if those parts meet predetermined safety levels.

B People have a difficult time distinguishing waste from recyclable material and this has to be determined by standards that the EPA sets.

C After regarding the EPA standards for the disposal of hazardous materials and determining what materials are salvageable, architects and construction crews can begin to use those materials for sustainable building.

D There are many residential homes and commercial buildings that have been labelled "green" because they use only recycled materials in their construction and are powered by alternative energy sources.

E If people want to be green they have to use sustainable materials in their homes and find alternative energy sources, such as wind or sun, to power their residences.

F Giving people options in their choice of building materials and power sources—whether for residential or commercial use—will allow the opportunity for more sustainable homes and lifestyles to increase in the next decade.

Do these practice items after you have completed Test 2.

C Reread **Test 2, Passage 2**. Then answer the question.

3 An introductory sentence for a brief summary of the passage is provided below. Complete the summary by selecting three answer choices that express the most important ideas in the passage. Some sentences do not belong because they express ideas that are not presented in the passage or are minor ideas.

Astronomers and astrophysicists worldwide use a variety of telescopes and other instruments in their quest to find exoplanets, or, planets beyond our solar system.

A There is little likelihood the exoplanets that the telescopes can identify are actually habitable, but many scientists believe that they might find life forms in small molecules or the existence of water.

B Ground telescopes and orbiting telescopes have enabled astrophysicists to collect data on distant planets by using special instruments that can measure a star's movement and the light it emits.

C Both the Hubble and the Kepler telescopes can identify masses in space like asteroids or dust clouds, but their primary mission is to find planets that might sustain life because they are located near a Sun-like star.

FURTHER PRACTICE AND GUIDANCE — READING — 107

    D The Hubble telescope differs from the Kepler telescope in that it orbits around the Earth and uses spectrographic imagery to analyze the wobble of a distant star.

    E The goal of the La Silla, Kepler and Hubble telescopes is to find habitable planets, stars, and potential life forms, though they use various types of astronomical instruments to carry out their missions.

    F Whether telescopes are Earth-bound or orbiting, their primary function is to provide astrophysicists with data on new phenomena, potential Earth-like exoplanets or stars.

D Reread **Test 2**, **Passage 4**. Then answer the question.

4 An introductory sentence for a brief summary of the passage is provided below. Complete the summary by selecting three answer choices that express the most important ideas in the passage. Some sentences do not belong because they express ideas that are not presented in the passage or are minor ideas.

Most lakes experience cyclical mixing, whereby water from the top and water from the bottom strata will turn over and are combined.

    A Depending on their geographical locations, depth, and water temperature, lakes have mixing patterns that can be classified into different types: those that mix annually, seasonally, or never at all.

    B Meromictic lakes are unusual because unlike holomictic lakes, their surface and bottom layers never turn over.

    C Holomictic and meromictic lakes differ in that the waters of the holomictic lake may turn over from bottom to top because of warm water temperatures, whereas the layers of the meromictic lake will only mix if wind or temperature affect the surface water.

    D In a meromictic lake, the top layer, called the mixolimnion, is mostly affected by wind and may mix; however, the bottom layer, known as the monimolimnion, never turns over and has little to no oxygen.

    E The bottom layer of water (the monimolimnion) in a meromictic lake will remain without oxygen and supports very few life forms because its cold temperatures prevent it from mixing with the layers of water above it.

    F One example of the world's rare meromictic lakes is Green Lake, in New York State, which has a blue-green color due to its depth, the unusual bacteria in the lake, and the prevalence of calcium carbonate in its water.

QUESTION TYPE 10 SCHEMATIC TABLE

On the TOEFL iBT™, the second type of **Reading to learn** question requires you to understand the organization and purpose of the passage and be able to recognize the structure or framework of the text. To do this, you must be able to make connections between ideas, and remember major ideas and other important facts. Note that there is only one **Reading to learn** (Type 9 or Type 10) question on the TOEFL iBT™.

The **Schematic table** (Fill in a table) question measures your ability to organize major ideas and other important information in a text, then put those ideas into appropriate categories in a chart.

Schematic table questions can appear in the following ways:

- Complete the table below to organize information about the two types of {X} discussed in the passage.
- Complete the table below by matching five or six answer choices with the {X} to {Y} that they exemplify.
- Complete the table below by indicating which of the answer choices describe the characteristics of {X} and which describe the characteristics of {Y}.

On the actual TOEFL iBT™, a chart appears on the computer screen. You will then drag the appropriate answer choices to the table. For the purpose of the tests and practice exercises in this book, you will choose from among a number of answer choices and mark the appropriate letters on your answer sheet.

For a table requiring you to choose **five** correct answers, the question is worth **three** points. For a table requiring you to choose **seven** correct answers, the question is worth **four** points.

SKILL BUILDER 1 RECOGNIZING THE ORGANIZATION OF THE READING PASSAGE

The types of passages on the TOEFL iBT™ are examples found in introductory material from college textbooks or other academic texts. Often, you can connect the type of passage that you will encounter with a specific *discipline*, or field of study.

The passages on the TOEFL iBT™ reading section are taken from four major academic disciplines, including **fields of study** such as:

- **Arts and humanities**: art, design, history, literature, philosophy, photography.
- **Social science**: anthropology, economics, psychology, sociology.
- **Life sciences**: anatomy, biology, botany, ecology, physiology.
- **Physical sciences**: astronomy, climatology, computer science, geology, meteorology, physics, technological sciences.

Understanding the organization and purpose of the passage will help you understand the main idea of the passage as well as the author's focus. On the TOEFL iBT™, the structure or purpose of each passage falls into one of the following **categories:**

- **Expository**: an expository passage gives an explanation and description of a topic.
- **Argumentation**: argumentative writing takes an argument by presenting a point of view and giving evidence to support the topic.
- **Historical**: a historical passage will provide history and background information of the topic with supporting facts and evidence.

In a passage, the author presents a point of view or an "angle." This point of view is the way in which the author organizes the passage in order to present the facts and evidence to support his or her ideas. There are many ways to express these ideas called, "**rhetorical modes**." The most common modes used in TOEFL iBT™ reading passages are: cause/effect, classification, compare/contrast, definition, description, and problem/solution.

In certain disciplines, particular rhetorical modes occur more often than in others. On the TOEFL iBT™ (and in academic reading) you may find the following correspondances of modes and areas of academic study.

- Classification, cause/effect, problem/solution—Physical sciences, Life sciences

Physical science and life science passages may attempt to classify things that occur in nature or the universe; they may present an event in nature and its causes and the effect on the environment or the body; the passage may ask a question about a problem that exists and offer a solution to the problem.

- Compare/contrast, cause/effect—Social sciences, Life sciences

In social sciences, you may read about two sides to an issue about society or a problem, action, or behavior. The author may show the cause of a problem and its effects on society or a group of people in present times or in history.

- Definition, description, compare/contrast—Arts, Humanities

Authors of history will describe events that happened or important people who initiated that event. In art, history, and philosophy passages you will find more descriptive writing than in science texts. Although texts in all disciplines (physical sciences, social sciences, arts, and humanities) contain definitions of terms, arts and humanities passages are likely to be more expository than science texts.

FURTHER PRACTICE AND GUIDANCE   READING

A   **Rhetorical patterns**. Read the following excerpts from passages on **Test 1**. Then choose the letter corresponding to the type of essay you believe each excerpt **best reflects** and write it on the line.

    A Cause/effect

    B Classification

    C Definition

    D Problem/solution

    E Description

1. Both scientists and observers of the colossal squid have investigated how these squid came to be "colossal" and how this benefits the animal's survival. This is a phenomenon known as *deep-sea gigantism*. Deep-sea gigantism is a tendency where invertebrates, such as squid and octopus, or crustaceans such as lobsters, grow much larger than invertebrates that swim in shallow waters. ....

2. To social scientists, the field of genealogy is not typically considered a legitimate area of scholarly research. However, its relevance to cultural and historical anthropologists in understanding the connections among people in society is indisputable. ....

3. Squid, like octopus and cuttlefish, belong to the same subclass of cephalopods called *Coleoidea*. Squid have a distinct head, a mantle and eight arms, two fins, and two pairs of tentacles. ....

4. This centuries-old case of the Lost Colony has long puzzled scholars who have tried to reconstruct the events that led to the colonists' vanishing act. Both historians and archaeologists have been unable to piece together exactly what happened to the colonists. ....

5. A problem that has often arisen has been with how a site crew—whether it is demolition or construction crew—determines and sorts what is "waste" and what is recyclable. ....

B   Look at the title of each passage on **Test 1**. Use your skimming and scanning techniques as you read the passage and see if you can determine the topic of the passage. This will help you understand and anticipate the **organizational structure** and **framework** of the passage.

Write the title of the passage, then decide what field of study it relates to, and which rhetorical pattern it is, according to the patterns presented in activity A.

Passage	Title	Field of study	Pattern
1			
2			
3			
4			

SKILL BUILDER 2 REVIEW OF COHESIVE DEVICES

You read about the importance of **cohesive devices** and **transitional phrases** in the practice sections for **Rhetorical purpose** and **Sentence insertion** questions. In both cases, you need to understand the organization of the passage and why the author has structured the passage in a certain way. You also need to be aware of the connections—the cohesive devices and transitions—that the author uses to make the paragraph logical.

In addition, **synonyms** and **antonyms** can play a very important role in alerting the reader to a change in the direction of the passage. **Antonyms** are the opposite meaning of a word, and are often used to show *contrast* in a text.

Find **key words**, **synonyms**, **antonyms**, and **cohesive devices** or **transitional phrases**. Ask yourself: What is the author's purpose? Is the author comparing and contrasting? Showing cause and effect? Describing or illustrating an event? Putting information into a classification system? Describing a problem and offering a solution?

A Read the paragraph from **Test 1, Passage 2** and organize the information in the T-chart. Look for **synonyms**, **antonyms**, **punctuation**, **transitional phrases**, and **cohesive devices** to find the major ideas.

> A problem that has often arisen has been with how a site crew—whether it is demolition or construction crew—determines and sorts what is "waste" and what is recyclable. Architects and environmental scientists have to decide whether or not a material is appropriate for use in new construction and how it will impact the environment. They must evaluate the materials from the demolition and determine what those materials contain, and if they meet the standards set by the U.S. government's Environmental Protection Agency (the EPA). If the debris from the demolition contains hazardous materials that are harmful to the environment or to the consumer, such as asbestos, then the material is not salvageable. Use of asbestos for insulation and as a form of fire retardation in buildings and fabrics was common in the nineteenth century. Asbestos was once used in shingles on the sides of old buildings, as well as in the insulation in the interior walls of homes or other construction. In new "green" construction, insulation that was once asbestos-based can be replaced with recycled denim or constructed with *cellulose*—a fibrous material found in paper products. The same assessment applies to wood or wallboard painted with toxic lead-based paints. In addition, gas-flow regulators and meters on both water and gas heating systems constructed prior to 1961 must be carefully evaluated to determine that they do not contain dangerous substances such as mercury. Mercury can be harmful to humans and the environment if it is spilled during the removal of these devices.

Identify the types of toxic and non-toxic materials discussed in the passage. How do these types of materials affect the environment? Make notes in the chart to organize this information.

Toxic materials	Non-toxic materials

PRACTICE FOR SCHEMATIC TABLE QUESTIONS

Do these practice items after you have completed Test 1.

A Refer back to **Test 1, Passage 3**. Then answer the question.

1 Complete the table below by indicating **six** statements that describe the behavioral or physical characteristics of the colossal squid.

Physical	*Select three*
Behavioral	*Select three*

A has lethal hooks

B displays *dimorphism*

C is elusive

D is similar to crustaceans

E has a very slow metabolism

F preys on sleeper shark

G waits patiently for its prey

H prefers frigid water temperatures

B Refer back to **Test 1, Passage 4**. Then answer the question.

2 Complete the table below to organize information about the **two** types of genealogical research materials discussed in the passage.

| Media resources | Select two |
| Printed resources | Select four |

A research companies on the web

B the book *Roots*

C property documentation

D DNA testing

E ancestry-themed TV shows

F old passports

G oral family histories

H court records

Do these practice items after you have completed Test 2.

C Reread **Test 2, Passage 1**. Then answer the question.

3 Complete the table below to organize design information about **two** types of instruments discussed in the passage.

| Viola-organista | Select two |
| Motorized drum | Select three |

A could be preset by the player

B played by using a mouthpiece

C was attached to the player

D was played with sticks

E relied on air movement

F used a crank mechanism

G could be played in a stationary position

D Reread **Test 2, Passage 3**. Then answer the question.

4 Complete the table below by matching **six** descriptions of Keynes's work to the appropriate categories.

Economics courses	*Select three*
Written work	*Select three*

    A dealt with the repercussions of the Treaty of Versailles

    B discussed theories on money and the stock exchange

    C incorporated the theories of his father and mentor

    D included knowledge gained from his experience at the India office

    E created out of the effects on World War I on Keynes and his family

    F proposed different theories on money, profit and the stock market

    G focused on the financial aspects of one country

    H contributed to students' knowledge of economic principles

LISTENING

In this section, you will build your skills for each of the eight **Listening** question types on the TOEFL iBT™. The questions are divided into **three** categories of listening skills: *listening for basic comprehension*, *listening for pragmatic understanding* (function and attitude), and *listening to connect information*.

Listening for basic comprehension
- Listening for gist (overall comprehension)
- Listening for purpose
- Listening for details

Listening for pragmatic understanding
- Understanding the function
- Understanding the attitude of the speaker

Listening to connect information
- Understanding organization
- Listening for inferences
- Listening to connect content

The listening stimuli on the TOEFL iBT™ are in the form of **conversations** and **lectures**.

TOEFL iBT™ **conversations** exemplify consultations between a student and a professor, or, a service encounter between a university administrator or staff member and a student. You may also hear a conversation between two students. Both the consultations and service encounters focus on a problem that needs to be solved or an issue that the two speakers must address. Conversations last for **three to five** minutes and are followed by **five** questions.

Lectures on the TOEFL iBT™ characterize the way spoken English occurs in a university classroom setting. You will hear a professor give a lecture on a topic, or you will hear an *interactive* lecture where one or more students may ask questions or make comments. Each lecture is between **four and five minutes** long, followed by **six** questions. Like the Reading passages, the topics of the lectures are drawn from the four major disciplines in a university setting: **Arts/Humanities**, **Life sciences**, **Physical sciences**, and **Social sciences**. You do not need any background information on these subjects to be able to answer the questions on the test: all the information you need is presented in the lecture.

Question types on the test appear in several formats. The majority of questions are multiple choice with **four** answers. There are also multiple-choice questions that require you to choose **two** to **four** answers. For some questions, part of the conversation or lecture will be repeated. The organization question type requires you to select (drag or click on) information in a chart.

SKILL BUILDER: NOTE TAKING

You may take notes on the listening section of the TOEFL iBT™. Be prepared to make an outline of the lecture, or, create a framework that you find easy to follow. Pay attention to the topic statement provided by the narrator.

- **Before you listen** write down the following categories: *topic*, *main idea*, *major points*, *key words*, and *details*.
- **As you listen** focus on the speaker's intonation pattern and word stress. Words that are more important usually get more stress. Note down key words and phrases, dates, names and other details in the categories you have written down. Listen for connections between words and phrases during the lecture or conversation.

- **Notice the visuals on screen.** On the actual TOEFL iBT™, there will be one or more visual cues on the screen. This might be an image of two people, a professor in front of a class, or, it may be a visual connected to a word or idea presented in the lecture.

SKILL BUILDER: HOW FAST DO WE LISTEN AND SPEAK?

The average person spends about 75 percent of the day just listening. Regardless of native language, people speak and listen at a much slower rate than they are able to read. The average native speaker of English can speak at a rate of 125 to 150 words per minute in normal conversation, and can comprehend at a much faster rate—about 175 to 200 words per minute. Of course, this can vary among individuals. As a learner of English, you may listen and speak at a much slower rate. However, with practice and strategies, you can improve your overall listening skills for the TOEFL iBT™.

In an academic lecture, it is possible that the professor will speak more slowly than the normal rate of speed. The professor may pause to ask questions, make sure the students are following, allow students to take notes, spell a technical term, or pause to write information on the board.

SKILL BUILDER: VOCABULARY IS THE KEY

Native speakers of any language need a vocabulary of approximately 3,000 word families to understand everything in a conversation. Unfamiliar or infrequently used words can often interfere with the listener's comprehension. Listeners need to recognize almost 95 percent of the content words in order to have a significant understanding of a conversation. If you want to improve your English language skills, **vocabulary is the key**. Active listening is a complex process. When we listen, we must be able to do many things at the same time: organize information, comprehend information, interpret the information, and then respond to the information.

> **Did you know?** Academic lectures often raise more questions than they answer.

QUESTION TYPE 1 LISTENING FOR GIST—CONTENT

Gist is another word for "main idea." This means you have to understand the general meaning of the lecture or the discussion. Main idea or gist questions appear in the following format:

- What are the speakers mainly discussing?
- What problem does the man (woman) have?
- What is the lecture mainly about?
- What is the main topic of the lecture?
- What aspect of {X} does the professor mainly discuss?

SKILL BUILDER 1 LISTENING FOR TOPIC INTRODUCTION

A speaker will use phrases of introduction to start the conversation or lecture. If the conversation is a consultation between a student and professor or campus staff member, you often hear a service-oriented phrase like, "How can I help you?" You will also hear the exchange of normal greetings and salutations between the speakers.

In a lecture, there are certain phrases that professors use to introduce a topic and which will help you focus on the main idea or gist of the lecture. These are oral cues and they are typically followed by a noun or noun phrase. These cues are important when you listen for **key words**.

FURTHER PRACTICE AND GUIDANCE — LISTENING

Phrases of introduction to a topic or major idea

We're going to look at …
I'm going to talk about …
What I want to do is …
I want you to know something about …
We've been discussing …
But the way they did that was …
So we're going to focus on …
The purpose of this is to …

I'm going to talk a bit about …
I wanted to ask about …
So we were talking about …
By that I mean …
Now, you have to realize that …
You could say that …
This was the beginning of …
As far as I know …

Remember also that definite and indefinite articles are cues to help you understand the topic or details about a lecture, that is, who, what, when, and where.

A Topic introductions. Match the sentence starters with the grammatically appropriate clause.

1 … We're going to look more closely
2 … I'm going to try
3 … What I want to do is
4 … So what I'm going to focus on
5 … We've been discussing
6 … I want you to know a bit

A to give you a clear definition of *dimorphism*.
B elaborate on his ideas, so write this down …
C about the reason behind the economic downturn.
D angiosperms and how they basically took over …
E at the research the scientists presented.
F is how these theories have evolved over time.

B 🎧 1.16 Listen to the following excerpt from **Test 1**, **Lecture 1**. Fill in the text with the missing **phrases of introduction**.

So, last week ………………………… bookmaking and the different types of paper. I want ………………………… printing—and ………………………… the production of multiple copies of an image on paper or some other medium. Now, China … China has a long tradition of woodblock printing that goes back to at least the 800s and well, a lot of these images included written words, or Chinese language characters. So, ………………………… the Chinese are credited with being the first to actually print words on paper. But ………………………… was to carve words into a block of wood, spread ink over it and transfer that to paper. Now, you ………………………… carving words into wood is a slow process. And eventually, someone came up with the idea of carving individual characters into separate blocks of wood, so that of course they could move these around into any combination. ………………………… what is called movable type.

PRACTICE FOR LISTENING FOR GIST QUESTIONS

Do these practice items after you have completed Test 1.

A 🎧 1.3 Listen to part of **Test 1**, **Conversation 1**. Then answer question 1. Listen again, and answer question 2.

1 What are the speakers mainly discussing?

   A two chapters in the book
   B how to review the information
   C how the student can connect information
   D which chapters the student should study

2 What is the woman's problem?
   A She doesn't understand the book.
   B She's not sure what the teaching assistant means.
   C She is not sure what she should focus on for her test.
   D She is having difficulty making time to study for the test.

B 🔊 1.31 Listen to part of **Test 1, Lecture 3**. Then answer question 3. Listen again, and answer question 4.

3 What is the professor mainly discussing?
   A theories about the fossil records
   B the population shift in the size of dinosaurs
   C the puzzling details of the probable environment
   D the hypotheses about the evolution of angiosperms

4 What aspect of angiosperms does the professor discuss?
   A theories about their development
   B how they developed
   C how they spread
   D their environment

Do these practice items after you have completed Test 2.

C 🔊 2.2 Listen to part of **Test 2, Conversation 1**. Then answer question 5. Listen again, and answer question 6.

5 What is the man's problem?
   A He is concerned about his low grade.
   B He does not want to take the final exam.
   C He wants to withdraw from the class.
   D He has to move out of his apartment.

6 What is the professor mainly concerned about?
   A the student's grades
   B the student's last exam score
   C filling out a change of grade form
   D the student not completing the course

D 🔊 2.36 Listen to part of **Test 2, Lecture 4**. Then answer question 7. Listen again, and answer question 8.

7 What is the professor mainly discussing?
   A Galileo's theories
   B famous film footage
   C an astronaut's experiment
   D whether Galileo's theories were correct

8 What aspect of Galileo's work are the speakers discussing?
  A Galileo's experiment at the Leaning Tower of Pisa
  B Galileo's theories of gravity and bodies in motion
  C how Galileo dropped a hammer and a feather
  D an astronaut's experiment on Galileo's theories

QUESTION TYPE 2 LISTENING FOR A SPEAKER'S PURPOSE

When you listen for the speaker's purpose, you need to understand why the professor gives the lecture, or why the conversation between two speakers occurs. Purpose questions are typically phrased in the following form:

- Why does the student visit the {X's} office?
- Why does the professor explain {X}?
- Why did the student go to see the professor?
- Why are the speakers discussing {X}?

SKILL BUILDER 1 PURPOSE

Listening for purpose is another aspect of listening for the main idea. This means you have to understand *why* the speaker is discussing something in a lecture, or perhaps why the student is meeting with a professor, or going to talk to a university administrator.

Listen for the overall structure of the lecture. The framework of the professor's talk may be designed to compare and contrast two ideas or points, show cause and effect, discuss a problem and offer a solution, describe a historical event or a person who had an effect on an event, or, define a technical term and explain it.

Be aware of distracting answer choices. There may be answer choices that are too general, or contain ideas that are minor to the author's purpose. Look for antonyms or opposite information in the answer choices.

A **Phrases to introduce purpose.** Match the phrases in the right column with the phrases in the left column that introduce the speaker's purpose.

1	... First, I want to call your attention	**A**	about the point that the author was trying to make, do I?
2	... OK, I want to remind you	**B**	you a bit of background on this subject.
3	... Next, I'll get into	**C**	to cover everything I want you to know in today's session.
4	... There's not enough time	**D**	to the differences between American and British literature.
5	... I don't need to go into details	**E**	the second chapter of the book by our next class.
6	... I expect you to read	**F**	you've got this down correctly ...
7	... So now I'm going to give	**G**	that the next reading is posted on the class website.
8	... OK, so, I'll go over this again to make sure	**H**	the specifics on this topic, which is pretty complicated ...

B After you have matched the phrases above, write the full sentences on the lines below. Then, think about the speaker's purpose and write it on the line next to your new sentence. Choose from the list below.

Purpose	Sentence

Purposes

	to justify a reason	to compare/contrast
to define	to offer an explanation	to clarify instructions
to elaborate	to confirm understanding	to give instructions

C Fill in the blanks with the correct infinitive.

to clarify	to discuss	to focus	to illustrate	to put

1 I want ………………………… now on printing—and by that, I mean the production of multiple copies of an image on paper or some other medium.

2 Remember, I'm going ………………………… the notes from today's lecture and your writing assignment on the class website so you can refer to those documents.

3 By saying this, I'm trying ………………………… a few of the points that the author tried to make in his book.

4 I would agree with that statement, but then, we'd have ………………………… the whole idea about letters and script.

5 So, just ………………………… what we were talking about … you need to file a change of grade form, right?

PRACTICE FOR LISTENING FOR PURPOSE QUESTIONS

Do these practice items after you have completed Test 1.

A 1.9–1.10 Listen to part of **Test 1**, **Conversation 2**. Then answer question 1. Listen again, and answer question 2.

1 Why does the student visit the registrar's office?

    A to discuss his schedule

    B to declare his major

    C to get permission to take a class

    D to make up a semester he spent abroad

2 Why are the speakers discussing the student's major?
   A to clarify his course prerequisites
   B to make sure he has done all his coursework
   C to elaborate on the details of his classes
   D to review the classes he has already taken

B 🎧 1.24 Listen to part of **Test 1, Lecture 2**. Then answer question 3. Listen again, and answer question 4.

3 Why does the professor mention the United States Constitution?
   A to offer an example of how the law protects people
   B to demonstrate the effectiveness of the law
   C to exemplify illegal search and seizure
   D to state a problem about computer crime

4 Why does the professor discuss computer forensics?
   A to explain the difference between legally and illegally retrieving data
   B to inform the students about legal methods of acquiring data
   C to illustrate the methods of capturing computer criminals
   D to present information that is admissible in court

Do these practice items after you have completed Test 2.

C 🎧 2.13 Listen to part of **Test 2, Conversation 2**. Then answer question 5. Listen again, and answer question 6.

5 Why does the tutor say that the presentation software program is intuitive?
   A to make sure the student uses it
   B to convince the student to use it
   C to demonstrate the way it works
   D to reassure the student that it's easy to use

6 Why does the student mention her schedule?
   A to review the problem with the tutor
   B to ensure that she will have an appointment
   C to make sure she has enough time to learn the program
   D to find out if she can bring her laptop to the tutoring session

D 🎧 2.28 Listen to part of **Test 2, Lecture 3**. Then answer question 7. Listen again and answer question 8.

7 Why does the professor mention a theory about the cause of synesthesia?
   A to elaborate on various parts of the brain
   B to review what the class discussed last week
   C to illustrate an example of grapheme-color synesthesia
   D to find connections in the brains of people with synesthesia

8 Why does the professor discuss the brain and color perception?

  A to support the theory about connections in the brain

  B to give an example of grapheme-color synesthesia

  C to offer information about a recent study

  D to prove that the theory is correct

QUESTION TYPE 3 LISTENING FOR DETAILS

The TOEFL iBT™ **Listening** section tests your ability to understand the overall meaning. However, you also need to be able to understand some of the details that are mentioned in a conversation or lecture. The details are the significant facts or important information about the topic that the speaker mentions. When a speaker provides important, major details, this is called *elaboration.* You will not be asked about *minor* details on the test. So, it is important that you take very concise notes and pay attention to key words, facts, and examples. Detail questions are usually presented in the following forms:

- According to the professor, what is {X}?
- What is one way that {X} can affect {Y}?
- According to the professor, what is one problem with the theory about {X}?
- What resulted from {X}?

SKILL BUILDER 1 LISTENING FOR DETAILS AND ELABORATION

If you want to understand details in a conversation or lecture, you should listen for cues or signals that precede key words or phrases. Speakers use signal phrases to let the listener know that they are planning to elaborate on a topic.

Signal phrases for elaboration

Signal phrases or cues indicate that specific information is going to follow. This information will add to the elaboration by the speaker, or offer examples.

On the other hand	in a sense	That's not what I mean, I mean …
As well as the …	at the same time	You might say …
Here's the key	in addition to	As far as I know …
We can think of …	for instance	I'll tell you what …
As long as the …	for example	This has to do with …

A **Take notes.** Listen to part of **Test 1**, **Conversation 1**. As you listen, write down the student's problems and the solutions offered by the teaching assistant. What signal words or clues did you hear that helped you identify the problems and solutions?

Student's problem	Teaching assistant's solution

FURTHER PRACTICE AND GUIDANCE — LISTENING 121

B 🔊 1.33 **Listen for signal phrases.** Listen to part of **Test 1**, **Lecture 3** and fill in the blanks with signal phrases from the list above. Then, underline the details that follow them.

> Gymnosperms, ... , are built to last. They live longer, grow slower and their leaves are thicker and store nutrients within them. Angiosperms require more nutrition from the soil than gymnosperms. They also grow much faster. Now .... : they tend to shed their leaves onto the ground in much higher quantities. And what is it that puts more nutrients into the soil? Leaves. Decomposing leaves deposit nutrients like nitrogen into the soil. So .... angiosperms create their own food by shedding leaves. .... , gymnosperms and ferns shed their leaves at a much slower rate. And their leaves don't decompose the same way—they really keep the soil low in nutrients. And so it's very difficult for angiosperms to compete in the same area as gymnosperms. There aren't enough nutrients in the soil to give them a foothold.

PRACTICE FOR LISTENING FOR DETAIL QUESTIONS

Do these practice items after you have completed Test 1.

A 🔊 1.4 Listen to part of **Test 1**, **Conversation 1**. Then answer question 1. Listen again, and answer question 2.

1 According to the teaching assistant, what did the professor assign? (Choose two answers)
   A sections of the test in advance
   B parts of the book about distributions
   C information about using percentiles
   D about one hundred pages of reading

2 What does the student say about *quartiles*?
   A that they are odd
   B that they are difficult
   C that she doesn't know what they mean
   D that they are very difficult to remember

B 🔊 1.43 Listen to part of **Test 1**, **Lecture 4**. Then answer question 3. Listen again, and answer question 4.

3 What does the student say about Captain John Smith?
   A that he was a British writer
   B that he was not the first American writer
   C that his writing style seemed very old-fashioned
   D that his work was not accepted by American authors

4 What does the student mention about Captain Smith's style? (Choose two answers)
   A that it used an unknown form of English
   B that it was not developed in the U.S.
   C that it was from the seventeenth century
   D that it had vocabulary and spelling similar to British English

Do these practice items after you have completed Test 2.

C 🔘 2.10–2.12 Listen to part of **Test 2**, **Conversation 2**. Then answer question 5. Listen again, and answer question 6.

5 According to the tutor, what are ways to make the presentation look good? (Choose two answers)
   A to use bells and whistles
   B to include graphics and animations
   C to get a colorful screen that moves
   D to put visuals and sounds in the presentation

6 According to the conversation, what are examples of visuals? (Choose two answers)
   A graphics   **C** sounds
   B whistles   **D** video

D 🔘 2.21 Listen to part of **Test 2**, **Lecture 2**. Then answer question 7. Listen again, and answer question 8.

7 According to the lecture, what is the FAP?
   A a government organization to end the Depression
   B a project that the school systems took on
   C a smaller division of the WPA that was only for artists
   D a federal project that enlisted the skills of unique photographers

8 What was the WPA's main purpose? (Choose two answers)
   A to support the building of schools
   B to employ artists
   C to maintain parks
   D to find highways

QUESTION TYPE 4 LISTENING TO UNDERSTAND RHETORICAL FUNCTION

The **Listening** section of the TOEFL iBT™ includes questions on *Pragmatic understanding*. When you listen for pragmatic understanding, you have to comprehend the reason *why* a speaker mentions something as well as the *manner in which* the speaker delivers the information. There are two types of questions in the listening section that test pragmatic understanding: **Rhetorical function** questions and **Attitude** questions.

The first type, **Rhetorical function**, tests your ability to understand *why* a speaker mentions an issue or what the speaker feels about the topic. Often, the speaker does not directly state this information. You have to listen for ideas or information implied by the speaker.

Rhetorical function questions usually include a replay of spoken text from a lecture or conversation. The rhetorical function question usually takes the following form, with part of the lecture or conversation replayed for you:

- What does the professor imply when he says this: {X}?
- What can be inferred from the professor's response to the student?
- What does the professor mean when he says this: {X}?
- What is the purpose of the student's response?

FURTHER PRACTICE AND GUIDANCE — LISTENING

SKILL BUILDER 1 LISTENING FOR THE FUNCTION OF WHAT IS SAID

Speaking, like writing, is a productive skill. A speaker organizes the speech for a lecture in the same way an author organizes a passage. The language used in an academic lecture is usually less formal than the language used in a textbook. However, the structure of a lecture is more formal than that of a consultation or conversation. As a listener, you should be aware of these features of language usage.

Regardless of the level of formality, the rhetorical functions of a spoken or written text exist in its structure. As you listen to a lecture, the speaker will use specific cues to indicate the purpose or function of the spoken text, such as phrases that introduce topics, lists, give summaries or give concessions.

The following is a partial list of the **cohesive devices** that appear in speech and writing. They are cue phrases used to determine the type of information the speaker wants to convey.

Adding ideas	Cause/effect	Compare/contrast	Concession	Summary
besides	accordingly	at the same time	admittedly	as a result
for example	and so	conversely	although	in summary
for instance	and that's why	despite	but of course	therefore
furthermore	as a consequence	however	certainly	thus
in addition	as a result	in spite of	doubtless	
in fact	as might be expected	nevertheless	granted that	
indeed	consequently	nonetheless	it's true that	
likewise	for this reason	notwithstanding	of course	
moreover	hence	not at all	though	
once more	since	on the contrary	to be sure	
similarly	then	on the other hand	to doubt that	
that is (i.e.)	therefore	still		
then, too	thus	unlike		
		whereas		
		while		
		yet		

A 🔊 1.33 **Practice with cohesive devices.** Listen to the following excerpt from **Test 1, Lecture 3**. As you listen, fill in the missing cohesive devices.

> Gymnosperms, ... are built to last. They live longer, grow slower and their leaves are thicker and store nutrients within them. Angiosperms require more nutrition from the soil than gymnosperms. They also grow much faster. .... : they tend to shed their leaves onto the ground in much higher quantities. .... puts more nutrients into the soil? Leaves. Decomposing leaves deposit nutrients like nitrogen into the soil. .... , angiosperms create their own food by shedding leaves.
>
> .... , gymnosperms and ferns shed their leaves at a much slower rate. And their leaves don't decompose the same way—they really keep the soil low in nutrients. .... it's very difficult for angiosperms to compete in the same area as gymnosperms. There aren't enough nutrients in the soil to give them a foothold.

B 🔊 1.33 Listen to the track again. Then, write each of the cohesive devices you heard into the correct category below.

Adding ideas	Compare/contrast	Cause/effect	Concession

C **Grammatical patterns are clues to rhetorical function**. Read the script from the lecture extract in A above. Circle the comparative forms that you find. Then use the T-chart to organize information about the angiosperms and gymnosperms.

Angiosperms	Gymnosperms

SKILL BUILDER 2 RHETORICAL QUESTIONS, INTERROGATIVES AND TAG QUESTIONS

Speakers may ask different types of questions in a lecture or conversation, with specific functions or intentions behind each question.

1 A **rhetorical question** is a question that does not need to be answered. This type of question can also indicate a person's tone.

Example: *I don't need to spell that out for you, do I?* This is formed like a tag question but the speaker either rarely expects, or assumes, the answer.

Do you really need me to answer that? This is formed like a direct question, but the speaker either does not expect, or assumes, the answer.

2 An **interrogative question** is a question that a speaker asks directly.

Example: *Where are you from?* This is a direct question. The speaker expects a response from the listener. When a person is not sure about an answer, it is possible to respond with a negative interrogative question: "Isn't that [quarantine] what happens when doctors think someone has a contagious illness?"

3 A **tag question** is used frequently in speech and rarely in academic texts. The tag question is a modal or auxiliary followed by a pronoun, and comes at the end of a statement. The speaker sometimes expects a response, but not always.

Example: *It's hot out today, isn't it?* This is a conversation starter. The speaker usually expects agreement.

A 🔊 1.10–1.11 **Practice with rhetorical, interrogative, and tag questions**. Listen to the excerpt from **Test 1, Conversation 2**. Play the tracks again. Fill in the speaker's questions with the correct phrases.

1 So, ………………………… your major?

2 ………………………… ? That's quite an undertaking.

3 And … which ancient languages ………………………… ? I'm just asking because undergraduate students need special permission to take those classes.

4 Oh, ………………………… ?

5 Wait … I thought you were in your first year … sorry, ………………………… ?

FURTHER PRACTICE AND GUIDANCE LISTENING **125**

B 🔊 1.10–1.11 **Listen again.** Play the tracks again and check your answers. Then check the type of question that the speaker asks and write yes/no to indicate whether the speaker expects a response.

	Rhetorical	Interrogative	Tag	Does the speaker expect a response? (write *yes* or *no*)
1				
2				
3				
4				
5				

PRACTICE FOR LISTENING FOR RHETORICAL FUNCTION QUESTIONS

Do these practice items after you have completed Test 1.

A 🔊 1.12 Listen to part of **Test 1, Conversation 2**. Then answer question 1.

1 What is the woman trying to find out from the student?
   A whether the student is aware of the system there
   B whether the student has the right prerequisites
   C whether the student took archaeology
   D when the student was in Cairo

2 🔊 1.12 Listen again to part of the conversation. Then answer question 2.

What does the woman mean when she says this: "OK, OK, so let me get this straight"?
   A The student's transfer credits did not get him very far.
   B She wants to revise the information in his transcript.
   C She wants to make sure she understood him.
   D She wants to straighten out his records.

B 🔊 1.41 Listen to part of **Test 1, Lecture 4**. Then answer question 3.

3 What is the purpose of the student's statement?
   A He wants to assert an opinion.
   B He does not completely agree with the professor.
   C He is positioning a counterargument to the professor.
   D He believes that the professor will disagree with him.

4 🔊 1.42 Listen again to part of the lecture. Then answer question 4.

What does the professor imply when he says this: "It would appear that way, wouldn't it"?
   A He is disagreeing with the student.
   B He wants to know what the student thinks.
   C He believes what the student said is true.
   D He is not able to determine the accuracy of the student's statement.

Do these practice items after you have completed Test 2.

C 🔘 2.4   Listen to part of **Test 2**, **Conversation 1**. Then answer the questions.

5 🔘 2.4   Listen again to part of the conversation. Then answer question 5.

What does the student imply when he says this: "Oh, wow … that's …"?

  A He changed his mind about writing the paper.

  B He is not sure he has to write the paper.

  C He did not expect to write a paper.

  D He does not want to change his grade.

6 🔘 2.4   Listen again to part of the conversation. Then answer question 6.

Why does the professor say this: "You want to get that change of grade, right"?

  A to find out if the student has corrected his work

  B to let the student know that she will sign the form

  C to make sure the student will write a paper on Shakespeare

  D to determine whether the student will change the grade in the right way

D 🔘 2.23   Listen to part of **Test 2**, **Lecture 2**. Then answer the questions.

7 🔘 2.23   Listen again to part of the lecture. Then answer question 7.

Why does the professor say this: "He reframed Abbott's shots exactly as possible. Why would someone do that"?

  A because he doesn't understand Abbott's work

  B because he is questioning the rationale behind Levere's photos

  C because he found that the photographs were complete copies

  D because he now understands why Levere took the photographs

8 🔘 2.23   Listen again to part of the lecture. Then answer question 8.

What does the professor imply when he says this: "I have to admit, when I first heard about this I was skeptical about one artist copying another so completely"?

  A He wants to show that he changed his mind about Levere's work.

  B He is trying to explain why he is skeptical about the work.

  C He wants to see if students will agree with him.

  D He is uncertain of Levere's reasons.

QUESTION TYPE 5   LISTENING TO UNDERSTAND the SPEAKER'S ATTITUDE

Listening to understand the speaker's attitude is the second type of pragmatic understanding question. This question tests your ability to understand a speaker's feelings about a subject and the reasons *why* the speaker has a preference or opinion about the topic. Like the **Listening for rhetorical function** question, this type of question requires you to understand purpose and make an inference about something that is not directly stated. In addition to cohesive devices, the speaker's intonation can also act as a clue to help you understand the purpose or motivation behind the speaker's statement.

Listening to understand attitude questions take the following form:

- What can be inferred about the student/professor?
- What is the professor's attitude toward {X}?
- What is the professor's opinion of {X}?
- What does the professor mean when she says this: {X}?
- What can be inferred about the student when he says this: {X}?

SKILL BUILDER 1 HEDGING

Speakers, like writers, may indicate an attitude about a topic. This attitude ranges from "speculating with uncertainty" to "believing with certainty." In a lecture as well as in a conversation, the speaker will deliver information in the speech that indicates feelings about the topic. Sometimes, when speakers want to soften a statement or feel uncertain about a statement, they use a device called *hedging*.

Hedging is a strategy to make a statement sound more polite, to distance oneself from an assertion, or, to reduce embarrassment if the speaker is not confident about what he said. There are many ways to use the language of hedging.

- **Verbs**: *appear, guess, seem, indicate, suppose, suggest, tend to*
- **Modals**: *can, could, may, might*
- **Adjectives and adverbs**: *basically, essentially, for the most part, generally, kind of, sort of*
- **Conditionals**: *if we judge by, if we assume that*
- **Phrases**: *based on these results, judging from this appearance, there is evidence to suggest that*

SKILL BUILDER 2 MENTAL VERBS

Verbs are classified into groups according to the action they represent. **Mental verbs** represent a state of mind. Speakers can use these verbs to make a claim or assertion about a subject. Using a mental verb demonstrates not only how strongly the speaker feels about the statement, but also influences how the listener evaluates the statement.

Mental verbs may indicate a level of certainty in the following way:

doubt	imagine	speculate	assume	think	believe	know
Least certain		←	→			Most certain

On the other hand, the negative of *know* (don't know) represents feeling uncertain about something.

SKILL BUILDER 3 ADJECTIVES AND ADVERBS OF ATTITUDE AND CERTAINTY

You will also hear speakers use adjective phrases to represent their level of certainty.

Uncertain	→	Certain
I'm not sure	→	*I'm sure*
I think so	→	*I'm certain*
It's doubtful	→	*I'm positive*

Adjectives that are an indication of **feelings or emotions** are: *afraid, authoritative, concerned, critical, disappointed, embarrassed, happy, objective, optimistic, pleased, puzzled, questioning, surprised, worried*.

Adjective phrases that speakers use to show their evaluation of a subject: *good/better/best, essential, important, interesting, necessary, surprising, useful, wrong*.

Adverbs are often used by the speaker to express various levels of attitude, their belief in the likelihood of the subject, or certainty about a subject.

Attitude: *amazingly, astonishingly, curiously, fortunately, importantly, ironically, surprisingly.*

Certainty: *actually, admittedly, allegedly, apparently, incredibly, unfortunately.*

Likelihood: *always, apparently, evidently, kind of, maybe, in most cases, perhaps, possibly, probably, sort of.*

A Listen to the following excerpt from **Test 1, Conversation 1**. As you listen, fill in the blanks with the missing adjective phrase or adverb.

M Hi. Can I help you?

W Hi … um, ………………………… . Professor McGee isn't in his office today and I missed the last class … so now I'm ………………………… what I should study for the test on Friday.

M ………………………… I can help … Uh, have you looked at the course syllabus?

W Oh, no. … Um, ………………………… idea. I ………………………… forget to refer to that.

B Listen to the excerpt from **Test 1, Lecture 3**. As you listen, circle the language that indicates certainty, likelihood, or attitude. Then listen again and answer the questions by circling T for true or F for false.

Recently, two researchers took an entirely different approach. Reasoning that none of these theories in itself constitutes a complete answer, they took another look at the available information, looking for common factors. One intriguing factor was that early angiosperms always grew in areas where there was no competition by gymnosperms and ferns. Why would that be? Now it gets interesting.

1	Ferns and gymnosperms competed with each other.	T F
2	The professor is certain about the growth of early angiosperms.	T F
3	Gymnosperms could be more abundant than angiosperms.	T F
4	The professor is skeptical about the competition between the plants.	T F

SKILL BUILDER 4 LISTENING FOR INTONATION AND STRESS

A speaker's intonation and stress pattern can affect the listener's understanding of attitude. Intonation rises at the end of an interrogative or tag question. However, the intonation for a rhetorical question falls. After an adverb or adjective of certainty, likelihood, or attitude, the stress may fall on the following verb or noun phrase.

A **Intonation.** Listen to the excerpts from some **Test 1 Conversations**. Listen to the speaker's stress and intonation. Then choose the adjective that best represents the speaker's attitude.

1	critical	friendly	sarcastic
2	embarrassed	disappointed	disinterested
3	critical	surprised	discouraged
4	impressed	sarcastic	surprised
5	annoyed	authoritative	indifferent

FURTHER PRACTICE AND GUIDANCE — LISTENING — 129

PRACTICE FOR LISTENING FOR SPEAKER'S ATTITUDE QUESTIONS

Do these practice items after you have completed Test 1.

A 🎧 1.13 Listen to part of **Test 1**, **Conversation 2**. Then answer question 1.

1 What is the speaker's attitude toward the student?

   A questioning

   B authoritative

   C disappointed

   D neutral

2 🎧 1.13 Listen again to part of the conversation. Then answer question 2.

   What does the speaker mean when she says this: "But you do realize that there are several prerequisites, right"?

   A She wants to be sure the student understands the requirements.

   B She thinks the student has not prepared for this class.

   C She is not sure that the student knows the rules.

   D She is uncertain about the student's credentials.

B 🎧 1.20 Listen to part of **Test 1**, **Lecture 1**. Then answer question 3.

3 What is the professor's attitude toward the topic?

   A argumentative

   B impressed

   C indifferent

   D amused

4 🎧 1.20 Listen again to part of the lecture. Then answer question 4.

   What does the professor mean when she says this: "I mean, I think you could really argue that the greatest advancement in communication after the invention of writing was the invention of moveable type"?

   A She thinks scholars argue about great advancements in communication.

   B She believes that moveable type is second in importance only to writing.

   C She is not sure if movable type happened at the same time as writing.

   D She sees similarities between writing and type.

Do these practice items after you have completed Test 2.

C 🎧 2.10–2.12 Listen to part of **Test 2**, **Conversation 2**. Then answer question 5.

5 What is the man's attitude toward the woman?

   A He is bored with her presentation.

   B He is puzzled by her lack of knowledge.

   C He is determined to give her important information.

   D He is not interested in finding out what she already knows.

6 ▶ 2.12 Listen again to part of the conversation. Then answer question 6.

What does the woman imply when she says this: "Um, you mean like images and graphics that move around the screen"?

　A She's not really sure what he meant.

　B She is not confident about using bells and whistles.

　C She is embarrassed that she never used the program.

　D She is curious about what the images will look like on screen.

D ▶ 2.33 Listen to part of **Test 2**, **Lecture 3**. Then answer question 7.

7 What is the professor's attitude toward synesthesia?

　A curious

　B objective

　C sympathetic

　D disinterested

8 ▶ 2.33 Listen again to part of the lecture. Then answer question 8.

What does the professor mean when she says this: "But let's not get ahead of ourselves. There's certainly a lot more to learn about synesthesia in relation to neural connectivity before we can comfortably generalize that far"?

　A She is eager to cover more information right now.

　B She is unsure about the information she gave the class.

　C She is generalizing about synesthesia and neural connectivity.

　D She wants to make certain that the class understands all the information.

QUESTION TYPE 6 LISTENING TO UNDERSTAND ORGANIZATION

Listening to understand organization questions require you to connect information by listening for general ideas, relationships, or details in the lecture or conversation. This question type requires you to integrate information you have heard from different parts of the lecture or conversation. You will have to focus on specific details from the lecture such as, the introduction, review of previous information, the presentation of new material, a summary, or the conclusion. You may be required to organize information from the lecture into a chart and click on the correct answer choices within the chart to indicate how the speaker organized the information.

The **Listening to understand organization** question may appear in the following forms:

- How does the professor organize the information in the lecture?
- How does the professor clarify points about {X}?
- The professor categorizes {X} by …
- How is the discussion organized?
- Why does the professor mention {X}?
- Why does the professor discuss {X}?

SKILL BUILDER 1 LISTENING FOR ORGANIZATION THROUGH RHETORICAL FUNCTION

TOEFL iBT™ questions that require you to listen to understand organization will often follow a lecture. When you listen for organization, you are listening for rhetorical function on a deeper level. Think about the speaker's main point. What is the speaker discussing and how is the speaker presenting the information? As you take notes, ask yourself questions that will help you determine the rhetorical structure of the lecture.

- Is the speaker comparing and contrasting issues or subjects?
- Is the speaker describing a problem and offering a solution?
- Is the purpose of the lecture to explain the cause and effect of an issue?
- Is the speaker defining a term and giving examples?
- Is the speaker describing a process and listing steps?

Use a T-Chart (graphic organizer) to include details that can help you organize the topic.

A 1.20 **Listen for contrast and comparison**. Listen to part of **Test 1, Lecture 1**. First time listening, fill in the blanks with the key words or phrases that signal a comparison. Then listen again and fill in the remaining blanks. Then fill in the T-chart to compare and contrast the facts.

> Well, OK, let's just stop here for a second, because … well, this is really interesting. Remember I said that the Jikji document ………………………… ? Well, ………………………… and halfway across the world, the first movable type document in the western world was printed by a man named Gutenberg, in Germany. I mean, if you think about the span of human history, 75 years is a very short time, and ………………………… basically made ………………………… in communication within a very short period of time. There are, of course, ………………………… between Gutenberg's methods and the methods of the creators of Jikji. ………………………… , the kind of metal they used. ………………………… , the Korean type was made of copper ………………………… the German type was ………………………… . And the … the kind of paper they used was ………………………… . Korean paper was made from the bark of mulberry trees and the German paper was ………………………… . It was parchment … made of sheepskin. But you know, ………………………… are really ………………………… .
>
> I mean, I think you could really argue that the greatest advancement in communication ………………………… the invention of writing was the invention of movable type. And it happened in ………………………… at relatively ………………………… .

Now write down the facts you learned about Jikji to organize the information from the lecture.

Jikji	Gutenberg

B 1.27 **Listening for steps in a process**. Listen to part of **Test 1, Lecture 2**. Then put the steps in order.

……. Recover files that are accessed by a password or are hidden.

……. Isolate all computer files.

……. Take steps to find files that were temporarily stored or lost.

……. Locate files that have been sent to the computer's trash.

……. Take precautions to ensure that files do not get damaged.

C 1.45 **Listen to categorize information**. Listen to part of **Test 1**, **Lecture 4**.
Listen and make a check ✓ in the correct column.

	Washington Irving	James Fenimore Cooper
Born in 1789		
Born in New Jersey		
Named for a U.S. president		
Was born and died in New York		
The elder of the two authors		

PRACTICE FOR LISTENING FOR ORGANIZATION QUESTIONS

Do these practice items after you have completed Test 1.

A 1.30–1.31 Listen to part of **Test 1**, **Lecture 3**. Then answer the questions.

1 The professor organizes the lecture by

   A outlining the growth processes of the angiosperm.

   B describing the evolutionary history of two types of plants.

   C defining two plant types and discussing their evolutionary differences.

   D introducing two plant types and listing theories of how they evolved.

2 The professor categorizes information about the plants. Indicate whether the phrases below describe a gymnosperm or an angiosperm. Make a check in the correct box for each sentence.

	Angiosperms	Gymnosperms
are similar to modern pine trees		
were originally segregated but then spread into larger areas		
are flowering plants		
may have been spread by animals		
were dominant more than 125 million years ago		

Do these practice items after you have completed Test 2.

B 2.31 Listen to part of **Test 2**, **Lecture 3**. Then answer question 3.

3 How does the professor organize information in this lecture?

   A by comparing the synesthetes to non-synesthetes

   B by discussing several techniques for identifying synesthesia

   C by using research to illustrate examples of different detection techniques

   D by identifying traits of synesthesia with the DTI scanning process

4 2.32 Listen to the next part of the lecture. The professor mentions how researchers used the DTI technique. Put the processes of the DTI study in order.

.... The DTI scan revealed connections between two areas of the brain.

.... Researchers found evidence of the physical basis of synesthesia.

.... Water molecules move through the brain along the coating of the axon.

.... The DTI generates an image of the brain's nerve pathways.

.... The molecules in the brain are tracked by the DTI scan.

QUESTION TYPE 7 LISTENING FOR INFERENCES

The next type of **Listening to connect information** question focuses on **inferences**. When you listen for inferences or implications made by a speaker, you listen for information that is not directly stated. This is "listening between the lines," and it is a skill similar to *reading for inferences*. You must be able to identify the speaker's purpose, understand the speaker's point of view, and recognize the speaker's tone. These factors can influence the implication made by the speaker or what can be inferred from the talk. To answer inference questions, you need to connect parts of the lectures, discussions, or conversations, such as, the speaker's introduction or opening statements, any review of previously presented information, the presentation of new material, a summary of the information, and/or the conclusion.

Inference questions appear in the following formats:

- What can be inferred about {X}?
- What does the speaker imply about {X}?
- What will the student probably do next?
- What does the professor imply when he says {X}? [replay]

SKILL BUILDER 1 LISTENING FOR KEY VOCABULARY, FACTS AND DETAILS

It is important that you write down key words, facts, and details in your notes. When you take notes, circle or underline repeated vocabulary. Pay attention to the rhetorical structure of the lecture and ask yourself questions as you listen. Understanding the structure can also help you answer inference questions correctly. Determine if the professor is discussing a problem and solution, making a comparison or contrast, or discussing a cause and effect before you answer a question about the implications made by the speaker.

SKILL BUILDER 2 LISTENING FOR VOCABULARY CLUES

When you listen for inferences, try to make connections between details and facts stated in the lecture that may be presented differently in the answer choices. Often, you may hear the speaker use idioms or less formal vocabulary, including verbs like *get, make, take*. Speakers may also use phrasal verbs (verb + preposition) more often in a conversation or lecture, while more formal or academic vocabulary may be used in the answer choice.

The following lists are examples of phrasal verbs or multi-part verbs used in lectures of all disciplines and have formal, often Latin-root, equivalents. Though professors speak more formally during a lecture, the number of phrasal verbs used in speech is much higher than the number used in a written text.

Formal	Phrasal verb or multi-part verb
convey	get across
imply	get at
communicate	put across
explain	tell [someone] about, get into
explore, access	get into
focus	pay attention to
suggest, propose	put forward
raise (a question)	bring up
examine, observe	take a look at
write, record, note	take down
compose, reconcile	make up
discuss	talk about
exhibit	hold up
create, invent	come up with
examine	look at
mention	bring up

A **Phrasal verbs**. Read the sentences and fill in the blanks with the correct multi-part verbs. Make sure to use the right grammatical form and tense of the verb.

| get into | talk about | focus on | come up with | go back |

1 So last week we were .... bookmaking and the different types of paper.

2 I want to .... printing—and by that I mean the production of multiple copies of an image on paper or some other medium.

3 Now, China ... China has a long tradition of woodblock printing that .... at least the 800s.

4 Eventually, someone .... the idea of carving individual characters into separate blocks of wood, so that of course they could move these around into any combination.

5 Um ... I don't want to .... the specifics of that right now.

FURTHER PRACTICE AND GUIDANCE   LISTENING   **135**

PRACTICE FOR LISTENING FOR INFERENCES QUESTIONS

Do these practice items after you have completed Test 1.

A 🎧 1.6   Listen to part of **Test 1**, **Conversation 1**. Then answer the questions.

1 What does the man imply about the other students in the class?
   A There may be more students who need to join the study group.
   B He has scheduled sessions with each student individually.
   C The other students in class understand the information.
   D The other students already decided which sections of the book they will present.

2 What can be inferred about the woman's participation in the study group?
   A She is unsure about the subjects on the exam.
   B She will not contribute very much to the study group.
   C She will focus on the other students' presentations.
   D She will confidently present information on many topics.

B 🎧 1.30   Listen to part of **Test 1**, **Lecture 3**. Then answer the questions.

3 What can be inferred about gymnosperms?
   A They dominated until 125 million years ago.
   B They are the same as ferns.
   C They are flowering plants.
   D They were near the poles.

4 What does the professor imply about angiosperms?
   A They were dominant before gymnosperms.
   B They began to surpass the gymnosperms about 125 million years ago.
   C Until 125 million years ago, they were the most common plant type.
   D They caused the gymnosperms to die out about 100 million years ago.

Do these practice items after you have completed Test 2.

C 🎧 2.7   Listen to part of **Test 2**, **Conversation 1**. Then answer the questions.

5 What does the man imply about the semester break? (Choose two answers)
   A He believes he can get a higher grade on his paper.
   B He will spend most of his time at the library.
   C He is not planning to visit the library.
   D He does not know what will happen.

6 What will the professor probably do? (Choose two answers)
   A She will process the change of grade.
   B She will reconsider the student's transcript.
   C She will change the student's grade in several weeks.
   D She will wait to see if the student improves his paper.

D 🔘 **2.17** Listen to part of **Test 2**, **Lecture 1**. Then answer the questions.

7 What does the professor imply when he says this: "You have to look at the context of the market at the time"?

   A It is important to look at the context of the market rather than only the price of the stock.

   B The viewers probably bought Crunchy brand stock after seeing the film.

   C Because Crunchy brand potato chips were in a scene, the stock rose.

   D Crunchy brand potato chip stocks rose in price because the chips were in a movie.

8 What can be inferred about the price of Crunchy brand potato chip stock?

   A The Crunchy brand stock was less valuable after the film's release.

   B It may possibly have risen in value because of the product placement.

   C It is difficult to determine the market value of the potato chips at that time.

   D The Crunchy brand stock could not be evaluated in the context of the film.

QUESTION TYPE 8 LISTENING TO CONNECT CONTENT

The last type of **Listening to connect information** question requires you to connect content from various parts of the lecture or conversation. This means that you will be listening for gist, details, facts, organization, and implications, and combining those skills. To answer this question you will listen to understand relationships between ideas mentioned in the conversation or lecture.

Listening to connect content questions appear in the following forms:

- What does the professor say about {X}?
- What information does the lecture provide about {X}?
- What is the outcome of doing {X}?
- What does the professor imply about {X}?
- What will the woman probably do next?

These types of questions are usually accompanied by a chart or table, in which you must identify information from the conversation or lecture.

SKILL BUILDER 1 LISTENING TO CONNECT CONTENT

Take notes and pay attention to important key words and phrases. Remember that the organization of conversations usually includes the presentation of a problem and a solution. You should also review skill building tips from question types one through seven.

Remember that the organization of lectures can be problem/solution, cause/effect, compare/contrast, illustration, description, etc. Follow some basic steps in structuring your notes.

- Recognize the rhetorical feature of the lecture.
- Outline the major points the speaker makes.
- Note repeated key words, facts, dates, or names.
- Listen for key words to indicate a process or sequence of events.
- Underline or circle important information in your notes to help you locate the answers more quickly.

FURTHER PRACTICE AND GUIDANCE — LISTENING

A 🎧 2.4–2.5 Listen to part of **Test 2**, **Conversation 1**. Then answer the question.

1 Check ✓ all the information that the professor suggests or implies.

.... Read five of Shakespeare's plays.

.... Write an essay on Shakespeare's plays.

.... Write an opinion essay describing Shakespeare's worst play.

.... Turn in the paper in two weeks.

.... Receive a change of grade after your paper has been submitted.

B 🎧 1.19 Listen to part of **Test 1**, **Lecture 1**. Then answer the question.

2 The professor describes several steps in the process of creating the metal type. Put the steps in order.

.... Spread clay over the shaped wax.

.... Pour hot molten metal into the mold.

.... Separate the metal from the clay and trim it.

.... Form the wax into the proper shape.

.... Let the metal cool.

.... Bake the formed clay.

PRACTICE FOR LISTENING TO CONNECT CONTENT QUESTIONS

Do these practice items after you have completed Test 1.

A 🎧 1.13 Listen to part of **Test 1**, **Conversation 2**. Then answer the question.

1 What will the student probably do next?

   A Make an appointment with his undergraduate advisor.

   B Return to the office to find out about the woman's progress.

   C Get special permission from the course professor.

   D Fill out the permission form after 3 p.m.

B 🎧 1.46 Listen to part of **Test 1**, **Lecture 4**. Then answer the question.

2 What information about each author does the professor mention in the lecture? For each statement below, make a check ✓ in the correct column.

	James Fenimore Cooper	Washington Irving	Both authors
wrote non-fiction books			
wrote novels			
wrote a biography of a U.S. President			
was popular in Europe			
wrote the *Last of the Mohicans*			
had a story made into a film			

Do these practice items after you have completed Test 2.

C 2.10–2.13 Listen to **Test 2**, **Conversation 2**. Let the conversation play in its entirety. Then answer the question.

3 Based on the discussion, what steps should the student take? Put the steps that were mentioned in the conversation in order.

.... Decide on an appropriate type of presentation program.

.... Make an outline of the presentation.

.... Schedule a tutorial to learn how to use the program.

.... Bring a laptop to the next appointment.

.... Identify if graphics, images, and sound effects are necessary.

D 2.21–2.24 Listen to **Test 2**, **Lecture 2**. Let the lecture play in its entirety. Then answer the questions.

4 What does the professor imply about Abbott's decision to use a large format camera? (Choose two answers)

 A It was based on her experience of photographing large cities.

 B It enabled her to capture large modern buildings structures without destroying the essence of older buildings.

 C It was the result of her experimentation with the hand-held camera in Paris.

 D It was not as easy to use but gave her more realistic shots of the city.

5 According to the professor, what is true about Berenice Abbott's work? Make a check ✓ in the box next to each true statement that the professor mentions.

	True
a Used a hand-held camera to photograph urban activity.	
b Re-photographed the same locations as Doug Levere.	
c Appreciated the sentimentality of pastoral scenes.	
d Wanted to depict people in a modern, urban setting.	
e Used a large-format camera to make sure small buildings were not overshadowed by skyscrapers.	
f Would not have done her "Changing New York" project without funding from the FAP.	

SPEAKING

In the **Speaking** section of the TOEFL iBT™ there are **two** independent tasks and **four** integrated tasks. The total time of the Speaking section of the test is about **20 minutes**. The response time ranges from **45 seconds** for tasks 1 and 2 to **60 seconds** for tasks 3, 4, 5, and 6. The format of the speaking questions will vary depending on the type of speaking task.

Independent tasks

- State an opinion
- State a preference

Integrated tasks

- **Read** a bulletin or announcement—**Listen** to a conversation—**Speak**
- **Read** a passage—**Listen** to a lecture—**Speak**
- **Listen** to a conversation—**Speak**
- **Listen** to a lecture—**Speak**

On the speaking section of the TOEFL iBT™, you must demonstrate your proficiency in several areas of spoken language:

- **Clarity** in conveying ideas: your response should be coherent and fully answer the question.
- **Effectively** convey your response: there are no "right" or "wrong" answers on the speaking section. However, your score reflects how well you answer the question and whether your response contains supporting details, reasons, and examples.
- **Vocal variety**: use intonation, stress patterns, pacing, and pronunciation to make your response clear.
- **Organization**: raters evaluate your response on how well you organize your ideas. It is important to use an introductory phrase, main idea, supporting details or examples, paraphrases, summary, and conclusion to demonstrate an effective response.

GRAMMAR AND WORD CHOICE

In spoken language, as in written language, grammar plays an important role in getting the message across. Vocabulary is important, but without correct **grammar**, comprehension of the message may not be clear to the listener. However, you should not spend time translating from your native language into English or trying to speak so accurately that you run out of time to answer the question. It is much more important to sound fluent—that means that your response is clear and comprehensible to the listener.

Word choice plays an important role in how the raters score your response. You should try to use academic vocabulary and repeat key words from the independent speaking prompts or the reading text, conversations or lectures.

INDEPENDENT TASK 1 STATE AN OPINION

Speaking task 1 is an independent task. This task requires you to base your response on personal opinion or experience. The question or prompt has been constructed in a way that will guide your response and give you clues on how to plan your answer. **Speaking task 1** allows 15 seconds to prepare and 45 seconds to respond to the prompt. Your response will be between 80 to 100 words, depending on how quickly you speak.

SKILL BUILDER 1 INTRODUCTORY PHRASES TO BUILD A TOPIC SENTENCE

Stating an opinion usually requires an introductory phrase. This phrase signals to the listener that you are about to state your opinion. The most common phrases are:

In my opinion …	It's my opinion that …	I think that …
I believe …	As I see it …	To me …

SKILL BUILDER 2 BRAINSTORMING

Listen and read along as the narrator reads the task question. You will have 15 seconds to prepare your response. Do the following activities to help you prepare your response.

State an opinion questions can appear in the following form:

> What are the characteristics of a good language learner? Use reasons and details to support your response.

A Brainstorm 1. Rewrite the example sentence below with three adjective phrases that describe a good language learner.

Example: A good language learner should be ..*enthusiastic about language*..........

1 ....
2 ....
3 ....

B Brainstorm 2. Rewrite the example sentence with two **verb phrases** that represent actions which a good language learner must do well.

Example: A good language learner ..*practices every day*.................................

1 ....
2 ....

C Introductory phrases. Fill in the blanks with an adjective or verb phrase you wrote above.

1 I believe that a good language learner has to be ....
2 I think that in order to be a good language learner, a person should be ....
3 In my opinion, a good language learner is someone who is ....
4 I think a good language learner ....
5 It's my opinion that a good language learner ....

D Connect ideas. Use the introductory phrases, adjectives, verbs, and connectors to fill in the sample response below.

In my opinion	because	feels	hear
takes chances	to me	grammar	I think that
repeat	brave	pronunciation	afraid

.... , a good language learner has to be .... I mean, someone who is not .... of making mistakes in speaking or writing. .... , a good language learner .... with vocabulary and tries to make sure the listener understands them. .... my friend Maria is a good language learner .... she can .... the sounds of language and .... them accurately. She is very good at .... and .... She also .... comfortable in conversations with native speakers.

PRACTICE FOR INDEPENDENT SPEAKING TASK 1

Do this practice item after you have completed Test 1.

A *What famous person in history would you like to meet? Use reasons and details to support your response.*

Set your timer for one minute. Estimate about 15 seconds and make an outline of your response. Then record your answer. When one minute is up, play track 74 on CD1. Compare your answer to the answer you hear. Take notes. Play your recorded response again.

Do this practice item after you have completed Test 2.

B *What place in the world would you most like to visit? Use reasons and details to support your response.*

Set your timer for one minute. Estimate about 15 seconds and make an outline of your response. Then record your answer. When one minute is up, play track 64 on CD2. Compare your answer to the answer you hear. Take notes. Play your recorded response again.

INDEPENDENT SPEAKING TASK 2 STATING A PREFERENCE

The second **Speaking task** on the TOEFL iBT™ is a paired-choice or **State a preference** task. You will read and listen to a question that requires you to choose between two possible situations or actions. Like Independent task 1, you have **15 seconds** to prepare and **45 seconds** to respond.

You may be presented with two opposing ideas or opinions. You must state your preference for one of the two opinions and explain your answer with details and reasons or examples.

SKILL BUILDER 1 INTRODUCTORY PHRASES FOR PREFERENCE QUESTIONS

You can use some of the introductory phrases for stating an opinion. Also, you may use phrases for stating a preference.

The following is the "grammatical formula" for using these types of phrases.

Introductory phrase	Followed by ...
I'd rather ...	the base form of the verb *I'd rather live in a dormitory.*
I would prefer ... I'd prefer ...	the *-ing* form (gerund) *I'd prefer living at home with my family.*
If it were up to me, I would ... If it were up to me, I'd ...	the base form of the verb *If it were up to me, I would live in an apartment.*

SKILL BUILDER 2 PLANNING YOUR RESPONSE

You have 15 seconds to plan your response so be prepared for this task by keeping a mental outline in your head that you can easily note on paper.

A **Choose and plan**. Read the question. Make your selection between the two situations. Then write **three reasons** why you have chosen {X} or {Y}.

Question example: Some people think living in the city is the best experience. Others prefer to live in the suburbs. Which would you prefer? Use reasons to support your response.

1 ....
2 ....
3 ....

SKILL BUILDER 3 SUPPORTING DETAILS AND EXAMPLES

You can use certain phrases to signal that you are going to give additional information, examples, reasons, or details to support your answer.

Elaboration and addition: *in addition, also, but …, so.*

Giving an example: *for example, such as, for instance, to give you an example …*

Giving a reason: *Here's why I think so …, This is because …, This is why:, One reason is …, another reason is …*

A **Support your preference**. Listen to the response from **Test 1, Task 2**. Fill in the missing introductory phrases and cohesive devices to elaborate and give examples, and reasons. You may play the track more than once.

> …………………………… communicate with my friends in person … um,
> …………………………… : I don't like to spend too much time on the Internet or computer …
> you know, playing games or just chatting with instant message. ……………………………
> I think, uh, I use my cell phone a lot every day and I'm texting …………………………… too often.
> …………………………… , …………………………… could be that ……………………………
> our society is now more technological. …………………………… , it's easy to do. But
> I …………………………… it's more important to see family or friends face-to-face
> …………………………… when you're in person you can see someone's reaction and body
> language. …………………………… I …………………………… speak in person.

PRACTICE FOR INDEPENDENT SPEAKING TASK 2

Do this practice item after you have completed Test 1.

A *Many American students take out loans to pay for a four-year college education. Some students work part time while they attend school, which may cause them to take longer to complete their degree. Which do you think is better? Use reasons and details to support your answer.*

Set your timer for one minute. Estimate about 15 seconds and make an outline of your response. Then record your answer. When one minute is up play track 75 on CD1. Compare your answer to the answer you hear. Take notes. Play your recorded response again.

Do this practice item after you have completed Test 2.

B *Some people think strenuous exercise, such as running or cycling, is the best way to relieve stress. Others prefer a quiet activity, such as reading, taking a walk, or meditation. Which do you prefer? Use reasons and examples to support your answer.*

Set your timer for one minute. Estimate about 15 seconds and make an outline of your response. Then record your answer. When one minute is up play track 65 on CD2. Compare your answer to the answer you hear. Take notes. Play your recorded response again.

INTEGRATED SPEAKING TASK 3 LISTEN, READ, SPEAK

The first integrated task is task 3, which is a campus situation type of task. You will read a notice or bulletin similar to one you might see on a university campus. The text is usually short—about 75 to 100 words long. You will have **45 seconds** to read the text. You should take notes as you read. Then, you will hear a short conversation between two people—two students, a professor and a student, or a university staff member or administrator and a student. The conversation is **60 to 80 seconds** long. You can take notes as you listen to the conversation. When the conversation stops, the narrator will read the question aloud. You have **30 seconds** to plan your response and **60 seconds** to answer.

Use the note-taking and preparation skills you learned for tasks 1 and 2 to prepare an outline and brainstorm your response.

SKILL BUILDER 1 READING AND LISTENING FOR GRAMMATICAL STRUCTURES

Grammar of institutional texts

The writing style of institutional texts—those texts found in university catalogs, bulletins, or announcements—generally uses a specific grammatical structure. It is often in the form of a directive to the reader. This means that a person is expected to follow a rule or a directive after reading the message.

Institutional texts often use the passive voice with these verbs: *allowed*, *asked*, *authorized*, *encouraged*, *expected*, *intended*, *permitted*, or *required*. For example, *Students are **expected** to report to their academic advisors at the beginning of the semester.*

In contrast to the passive voice, the stative passive is used as an adjective, often in a neutral tone: ***Interested** students should ... The university is **pleased** to announce ...*

Another structure often found in institutional texts is the noun + infinitive clause: *If you have **plans to attend** the graduation ceremony, please return the response card by April 23.*

The language of institutional texts is also usually impersonal and written in the third person singular or plural.

Grammar of conversation

The speakers will respond to the directive in the bulletin or notice. They will state their opinions about what they have both read. The speakers will focus on the key points from the notice or bulletin and usually disagree with something that they have read. The grammatical structures of verbs in the conversation will be in active voice. Pay attention to the speaker's attitude, tone of voice, intonation, and word choice. These factors will help you in taking notes as well as in making your response.

A Passive voice vs. stative adjectives. Read a similar notice to the one in **Test 1**, **Speaking Task 3** from a university institute regarding their summer internships. Underline the passive verbs. Circle the stative passive adjectives.

> The Office of Academic and Research Programs of the World Cultural Institute is pleased to announce the Summer Internship Program. Students who are interested in the program may apply for full-time summer internships within one of the many divisions of the World Cultural Institute. Internships are offered to both undergraduate and graduate students and all positions are paid. Please note that only current students of All-State University are eligible. Applicants are expected to be in good academic standing with a grade point average of 3.5 or above. Applicants should submit a résumé that details their relevant work and educational experiences, along with a cover letter stating their interests and qualifications. If responding by e-mail, please specify the name of the internship in the subject line of the e-mail.

B Evaluate the spoken grammar. Read the script and underline all the active verbs (present tense, progressive, past tense).

> **M** Hey, did you see that the Institute is offering internships this summer?
>
> **W** Yeah. I really want to apply but, I'm not sure if I'm qualified ...
>
> **M** Why not? What do you mean?
>
> **W** Well, uh, I'm not sure how I did in one of my history classes.
>
> **M** Oh ... yeah, it says they expect you to be in good academic standing. I guess that means you gotta get good grades in all your classes. ... But how's your grade point average?
>
> **W** Well ... I think I have a 3.4 ... and this semester I sort of think I did OK, except for that one class. So I'm not sure I will get a 3.5 ... Anyway, these internships are pretty competitive.
>
> **M** OK, but if you have a strong résumé and cover letter, I don't think they're going to hold one grade against you. Maybe you should send an e-mail and ask for more specific information about academic standing ... like what your grade has to be or something like that.
>
> **W** As much as I'd like to ... I'm not sure I should. I'll have to think it over.

C   Read the script again and circle the phrases that introduce an opinion or a suggestion.

D   🎧 1.69 Listen to the response to the question.

The woman expresses an opinion about possibly applying for the summer internship program. State her opinion and reasons for being concerned about applying.

Read each statement. Circle true or false.

1   The woman feels worried about her history grade.   T   F
2   Even though the man encourages her, she still is not confident about applying.   T   F
3   The woman has a 3.5 grade point average.   T   F
4   The Institute is very competitive.   T   F
5   The woman is going to think about applying for the internship.   T   F

PRACTICE FOR INTEGRATED SPEAKING TASK 3

Do this practice item after you have completed Test 1.

A   Read the following text. (45 seconds)

> **Attention: Residents of Lakeview Dormitory**
>
> As of Oct 1, the use of laptop computers for listening to music or watching videos without the use of headphones in the common areas of the dormitory is strictly prohibited. Also, TV and game boxes and DVD systems are no longer permitted in the common areas and can only be used in students' personal dorm rooms. This is due to the high volume levels and the number of residents who have complained about the noise. In addition, students are required to keep their cell phone conversations to a minimum while in the common areas of the dormitory at all times. We ask that you please respect the quiet study time of your fellow dormitory residents.

 Now listen to a short conversation between a student and a resident advisor.

What is the man's opinion about the new rules and what does he plan to do about it? State his opinion and explain the reasons he gives.

Set your timer for one minute and 30 seconds. Estimate about 30 seconds and make an outline of your response. Then record your answer. When one minute is up play track 76 on CD1. Compare your answer to the answer you hear. Take notes. Play your recorded response again.

Do this practice item after you have completed Test 2.

B   Read the following text. (45 seconds)

> While Robeson Cafeteria is undergoing renovations, students in Monroe and Keller Halls should use Walker Dining Facility until further notice. Please note that due to the large volume of students in Walker Dining Facility, Monroe/Keller students must abide by the following schedule: Please show your ID to the security guard at the door.
>
> Breakfast: **7 a.m. until 8:30 a.m.** Lunch: **11 a.m. until 12:30 p.m.** Dinner: **5:00 p.m. until 6:30 p.m.**
>
> Students residing in Johnson and Jackson Halls may dine at any time from 7 a.m. until 10 a.m.; 11 a.m. until 2 p.m., and 5 p.m. until 10 p.m. daily. Monroe/Keller students who attend evening classes must show their course schedule to the guard to use the facilities during normal dining hours.
>
> Walker Dining Facilities will remain open until 10 p.m. until the renovation of Robeson Cafeteria is completed.

Now listen to a short conversation between a student and the security guard at the dining hall.

The woman has a problem with the dining hall's system. How does the response of the security guard add to the information in the bulletin? State the guard's explanation and use examples and details to support your response.

Set your timer for one minute and 30 seconds. Estimate about 30 seconds and make an outline of your response. Then record your answer. When one minute is up play track 66 on CD2. Compare your answer to the answer you hear. Take notes. Play your recorded response again.

INTEGRATED SPEAKING TASK 4 LISTEN, READ, SPEAK

Speaking task 4 is an integrated task that requires you to read a short academic text and then listen to a lecture that adds information to it, then answer a question about the two sources. You will have 45 seconds to read a 100- to 120-word passage, and will then listen to a one- to two-minute lecture on the same topic. The speaking task is based on what you have just read and heard. You will have 30 seconds to prepare your answer and 60 seconds to respond to the question. If you speak at a normal pace, your response should be 120–125 words long.

SKILL BUILDER 1 READING FOR GIST

Read to increase your speed so that you can understand the main idea of the passage and its most important points. This will be a key skill in preparation for the short lecture and the ability to respond to the question. The reading will give you background information in preparation for the lecture. You will need to take notes on the reading and lecture in order to respond to the speaking prompt.

- Remember to skim and scan.
- You should read the first and last lines of the passage quickly.
- Then read the text and try to find as many of the key words as you can.
- Write down the main points.

SKILL BUILDER 2 SUMMARIZING, SYNTHESIZING AND CONNECTING IDEAS

Synthesis is a way of connecting and combining ideas together. In a university setting, students are expected to synthesize the ideas from their texts and classroom lectures. It is important to think about what has been stated, and evaluate how the information in the lecture expands upon or adds to the information presented in the reading passage. In your response to the task, you are required to give a short summary of what was stated and explain how the two ideas are related. You should also be able to "cite" or quote from the reading or listening passage.

To help you with listening for gist, key words, introductory phrases, and details, read or review the listening skills part of this Further guidance and practice section.

Use these phrases to practice quoting or citing information from the reading and listening passages. Find out the meaning of any words that you do not know.

acknowledges	believes	disputes	observes	thinks
adds	claims	emphasizes	points out	writes
admits	comments	illustrates	reports	
argues	compares	implies	says	
asserts	confirms	notes	suggests	

SKILL BUILDER 3 USING SENTENCE STARTERS AND SIGNAL PHRASES TO ILLUSTRATE YOUR POINTS

A Listen to the sample response for **Test 1, Task 4**. Write down the signal phrases that you hear. Then revise and re-record the response that you recorded earlier when you did the test by using some of the following phrases:

The professor stated that …   It seems that …   The professor made it clear that …

There is a difference between/similarity between …

…………………………… and …………………………… are examples of …

PRACTICE FOR INTEGRATED SPEAKING TASK 4

Do this practice item after you have completed Test 1.

A   Read the following passage. Set your timer for 45 seconds. You may take notes.

> The theory of American philosopher Charles Sanders Peirce (1839–1914) holds that *semiotics*, the study of signs and meaning, was of extreme importance to fields that deal extensively with representation, such as anthropology, cognitive science, epistemology, linguistics, and all the fine arts. According to Peirce, human beings have a desire to place meaning on objects by creating or thinking in signs.
>
> Signs are signifiers for objects. A sign can be an utterance, a spoken or written word, an image, a sound, a smell or flavor, or an action. Peirce stated that nothing is a sign unless it represents an object to something that interprets and translates the meaning, which he called the *interpretant*. The interpretant is the "sense made out of the sign," or the understanding that we have of that sign.

 Now listen to part of a lecture.

Set your timer for one minute and 30 seconds. Estimate 30 seconds to prepare your response to the following question:

Explain how the examples in the lecture represent the theories that Peirce described about placing meanings on objects.

Record your answer. When one minute is up, play track 77 on CD1. Compare your answer to the answer you hear. Take notes. Play your recorded response again.

Do this practice item after you have completed Test 2.

B   Read the following passage. Set your timer for 45 seconds. You may take notes.

> The origins of the American theater are somewhat disputed by historians. Some scholars credit Englishmen Adam Hallam and his sons William and Lewis, with the establishment of the first theatrical company and theater house in the early eighteenth-century American colony. However, prior to the 1919 two-volume *A History of the Theatre in America*, by Arthur Hornblow, the Hallams' troupe is seldom mentioned in historians' sources. In addition, even those scholars who did refer to the Hallams did so rather casually and without offering them their place of significance in the history of the American theater.

 Now listen to part of a lecture.

Set your timer for one minute and 30 seconds. Estimate 30 seconds to prepare your response to the following question:

The professor discusses the history of the early American theater. Explain the professor's description and the reasons why it is difficult to define the concept of American theater.

Record your answer. When one minute is up, play track 67 on CD2. Compare your answer to the answer you hear. Take notes. Play your recorded response again.

INTEGRATED SPEAKING TASK 5 LISTEN, SPEAK

This speaking task requires you to listen to a conversation that might take place on a college campus and respond to a question. The conversation is usually between two students, a student and professor, or a student and a university staff member. In the conversation, you will hear the speakers address a problem and offer **two possible solutions**. The problem may concern one or both of the speakers. The length of the conversation is between **60** and **90 seconds**. When the conversation ends you will have **20 seconds** to prepare and **60 seconds** to respond to the question.

SKILL BUILDER: UNDERSTANDING THE FUNCTION OF LANGUAGE

Formal vs. informal language

When you listen to conversations, there will be different levels of formality and word choice between the speakers. In a consultation between a professor or administrator and a student, the language you hear may be less formal than in a lecture, but it will be more formal than what you hear between two students.

To review academic vocabulary, phrasal verbs, and other expressions, read or review the listening skills part of this Further guidance and practice section.

Listening for phrases used to state a problem or introduce a problem

Recognizing the **set phrases** used to offer suggestions, give directions, ask questions, or give advice will help you to anticipate certain information between the speakers so that you can listen for the key words. There are many phrases that speakers use to "soften" stating their problem because they feel uncertain or unsure about asking for help.

Phrases for introducing a question or asking for help

I was wondering if … ?

Is it possible to … ?

Would it be possible to … ?

Would you be able to help me with … ?

Could I ask you about … ?

Could I talk to you about … ?

There are also phrases that strengthen a suggestion or show that the person feels strongly about the advice.

Phrases for giving directions or making suggestions

I'd like you to …

I have an idea …

This is what I think you should do …

I really think you should …

If I were you I would …

If you don't do {X}, {Y} could happen.

Why don't you try … ?

You could always …

Here's what I think you should do …

Using key phrases in your response

After you have heard the two possible solutions, you can use specific language to begin your response by stating the issues or problem, then explaining which solution you think is better.

Phrases for discussing the problem

{X} seems to have a problem/trouble with …

There is a situation with …

The woman has a problem with …

Phrases for stating your opinion about the solution

I think the [man's] idea about {Y} is better because …

The woman suggests that the man …

This seems to be a better solution, in my opinion, because …

I like the man's suggestion that … because …

I agree with the man's recommendation that the woman …

PRACTICE FOR INTEGRATED SPEAKING TASK 5

Do this practice item after you have completed Test 1.

A 1.57 Listen to the conversation. Then answer the question:

The student and librarian discuss the man's problem searching for books and resources in the computer catalogue. The woman offers two possible ways to limit the search. Describe the problem and then explain which of the two solutions you think is better, and why.

Set your timer for 80 seconds. After 20 seconds, begin your response. Record your response. Then play track 78 on CD1. Compare your answer to the answer you hear. Take notes. Play your recorded response again.

Do this practice item after you have completed Test 2.

B 2.50 Listen to the conversation. Then answer the question:

The students are discussing the woman's problem with her roommate. Describe the problem and then explain which of the man's suggestions you think is better, and why.

Set your timer for 80 seconds. After 20 seconds, begin your response. Record your response. Then play track 68 on CD2. Compare your answer to the answer you hear. Take notes. Play your recorded response again.

INTEGRATED SPEAKING TASK 6 LISTEN, SPEAK

For **Integrated speaking task 6**, you will listen to a lecture or discussion from a classroom. You will then **summarize** the main points of the lecture or discussion, **citing** or **paraphrasing** specific examples and points from the lecture. You will have **20** seconds to prepare your response and **60** seconds to speak.

SKILL BUILDER 1 PARAPHRASING AND SUMMARIZING KEY POINTS

Remember that paraphrasing is putting someone else's words into your own words. You will probably be paraphrasing because you will not have time to write down the lecture word for word. When you summarize the lecture you will be providing a brief discussion of the main points that the professor or speakers made.

FURTHER PRACTICE AND GUIDANCE — SPEAKING

SKILL BUILDER 2 LISTENING FOR STRESS AND WORD REPETITION

Listening for stress on key words can help you focus on the most important information in the lecture. Because you have 20 seconds to prepare, you will want to make sure you jot down the key words and phrases in your notes.

A **Listen for stress on key words**. As you listen, read the script and underline the words that are stressed.

> There are three roles a computer can play in computer crime. It can be the target of the crime, the instrument used to commit the crime, or it can be a source of evidence concerning the crime. And of course it can have multiple roles. If someone uses a computer to steal information or hack into a system, and then they store that information on the same computer, computer forensic experts must tailor their investigation to the multiple roles of the computer in the crime. There are so many factors to take into consideration. You could illegally recover the data or destroy important evidence. Also, you could waste valuable time if you dive into the work without carefully considering the possible multiple roles of the computer in the crime.

SKILL BUILDER 3 USING EXAMPLES AND POINTS IN YOUR RESPONSE

To use phrases that introduce an example, add information, or make a specific point, read or review the listening skills part of this Further guidance and practice section.

Other points to remember:

- Make an outline as you read and listen.
- Use columns to take notes on the reading and listening so you can easily compare the information.
- Remember that you will be provided with all the facts you need.

In your response:

- Give details about the short passage and the lecture so that the listener can understand the overall ideas.
- Use introductory phrases and signals phrases that you have learned.

PRACTICE FOR INTEGRATED SPEAKING TASK 6

Do this practice item after you have completed Test 1.

A 1.60 Listen to part of a lecture. Then answer the question:

Using specific examples and points from the lecture, explain the concept of synergists.

Set your timer for 80 seconds. After 20 seconds, begin your response. Record your response. Then play track 79 on CD1. Compare your answer to the answer you hear. Take notes. Play your recorded response again.

Do this practice item after you have completed Test 2.

B 2.53 Listen to part of a lecture. Then answer the question:

Explain why the Erie Canal was considered an engineering marvel. Use specific examples and points from the lecture to support your idea.

Set your timer for 80 seconds. After 20 seconds, begin your response. Record your response. Then play track 69 on CD2. Compare your answer to the answer you hear. Take notes. Play your recorded response again.

WRITING

There are two types of writing tasks on the TOEFL iBT™: The **Integrated writing task** and the **Independent writing task**.

For the **Integrated task**, you will read a short passage and then listen to a talk connected to the passage. Your essay is a response to the lecture that summarizes the main points and discusses the information in the lecture that differs from what is stated in the reading. You have **20 minutes** to write this essay. The response should be between 175 and 225 words.

For the **Independent task**, you will have **30 minutes** to write a short essay in response to an opinion or preference question. Your essay should be about 250 words.

THE INTEGRATED WRITING TASK

Read the passage and take notes. Write down the major points and be ready to listen for contrasting or additional information in the listening passage.

SKILL BUILDER: OUTLINING

Introduction: this should be a few lines that synthesize the information you read and what the professor states at the beginning of the lecture.

Body paragraph(s): in this paragraph you should make sure to mention the facts that the professor brings up, and use the transition words to show addition and or contrast, such as, *Also*, *in addition*, *in contrast*, *it seems that ... contradicts*, *the ... differs in that ...*

Conclusion: make sure your summary begins with a concluding statement such as, *Lastly*, *In conclusion*, *Finally*.

PRACTICE FOR WRITING TASK 1 INTEGRATED READING, LISTENING, WRITING

Do this practice item after you have completed Test 1.

A Read the passage. Then play the track. Answer the question. Then check your answer with the response in the answer key.

> According to the U.S. government's Environmental Protection Agency (EPA), the main substances that destroy the ozone are chlorofluorocarbons (CFCs) and hydro-chlorofluorocarbons, (HCFCs), which are chemicals found in products like fire extinguishers and pesticides. These ozone-depleting substances are released into the upper ozone layer and destroy it very slowly over time. The EPA has prohibited nonessential use of all products containing CFCs and HCFCs. In order to prevent further depletion of the ozone, the EPA and other agencies around the world have taken precautions. With wider restrictions on products that contain ozone-depleting chemicals, the governments believe that the ozone layer should return to a more normal state by 2050.
>
> Ozone depletion is more commonly known as the *ozone hole*. The ozone hole has notably levelled off in the first decade of the twenty-first century. However, the threat of warming during the spring and summer in the Antarctic may indicate growth of the ozone hole. This is due to the reaction of chlorine with oxygen and the ultraviolet rays that occur from longer periods of sunlight. The springtime ozone has been projected to increase by 5 to 10 percent in the next decade. It is also possible, however, that human activity will have a direct effect on the ozone in the middle to higher stratosphere. This is due to the emissions of gases that occur in the lower layers of atmosphere that are closer to the Earth (troposphere).

Summarize the main points made in the lecture, discussing how they cast doubt on points made in the reading. You can refer to the reading passage as you write.

Do this practice item after you have completed Test 2.

B Read the passage. Then play the track. Answer the question. Then check your answer with the response in the Answer Key.

> Hybrids were the focus of study by biologists such as Charles Darwin and Alfred Wallace. The hybrid, which is a cross between two subspecies within a species of animals, is found to differ greatly from both of its parents in aspects of its *phenotype*—that is, what the animal looks like. The mule is one example. Its mother is a horse and its father is a donkey. The mule is more like the donkey with its ears, its coloring and its temperament. On the other hand, if a female donkey breeds with a male horse, the result is called a hinny—which is not as large as the mule.
>
> There may be as many as 10 percent of the animal species, which, like the mule, are the result of animal species breeding with other species. Most of the offspring of these cross-species hybrids are sterile—meaning that they cannot reproduce. However, there have been many cases in which a fertile female offspring has produced yet another type of offspring. Biologists tend to see these hybrids as "evolutionary dead-ends." This is not always the fate of these animals, as can be noted in "coy dogs," which are the result of crossbreeding between a wild male coyote and the domestic female dog. The offspring of this match are fertile and capable of producing young. It is said that the coy dog crossbreeds will have a reproductive cycle similar to dogs rather than coyotes.

Summarize the points about hybrids in the lecture, explaining how they illustrate the points made in the reading passage.

THE INDEPENDENT WRITING TASK

Follow these steps to aid you in the structure of the independent essay. Remember that as you become a better reader, you may also become a better writer. Writers understand the structure of a good text—how to "hook" or interest the reader, how to support arguments or tell a story, how to prove a thesis, and how to bring the issues or ideas to a conclusion.

SKILL BUILDER: BRAINSTORMING

Whether you have an opinion or preference question, it will be helpful to brainstorm your ideas first. Take a stand and decide while you prepare your answer. You can use a T-chart or brainstorming tree to expand on your main idea and major points.

SKILL BUILDER: OUTLINING

Follow the same type of outline you used for the **Integrated task**. Try to form a thesis statement, which tells the reader your preference or opinion and why you hold that opinion.

The thesis statement usually appears in the last line of the first paragraph. If you know how to "hook" your reader, you can add that to the beginning of your introductory paragraph.

Your first body paragraph should contain **reasons and examples** to support your opinion or preference.

SKILL BUILDER: COHERENCE

Make sure that your paragraphs have strong transition phrases that connect topic sentences to supporting sentences, and the end of the paragraph to the first line of the next paragraph. Refer back to the transitional phrases in the reading and listening parts of this section for examples.

SKILL BUILDER: EDITING AND REVISING

Check your essay for: content—cohesion—grammar—spelling—punctuation.

If time permits, you should try to correct any spelling errors.

Remember to review your punctuation so that you avoid run-on sentences.

Look at your grammar to make sure your subjects and verbs agree, your structure is parallel in listing nouns or adjectives in a series, your tenses are accurate, and that you have used gerunds and infinitives correctly.

PRACTICE FOR WRITING TASK 2 INDEPENDENT WRITING

Do this practice item after you have completed Test 1.

A Many people believe that medical advances are the most important changes in the twenty-first century. Other people believe that advances in space and technology are our most important advances. What is your opinion on this topic? Use reasons and examples to support your opinion.

Do this practice item after you have completed Test 2.

B Compare the contributions of artists or performers and scientists in today's society. Which contributions do you think are more valued today? Give reasons to support your answer.

KEY AND EXPLANATION

TEST ONE

Reading p.6

Passage 1 p.6

1 **B** This is a detail question. To answer this question you need to understand that the word *settlers* is a synonym for *colonists*. A, C, and D are distracters related to the colony as a place instead of a group of people.

2 **D** This is an inference question. To answer this question you need to understand that the captain was "supposed to" take them to Chesapeake Bay, but they failed to reach that destination. A, B, and C contain incorrect facts and distracters.

3 **A** This is a vocabulary question. "Cut into" is a synonym for *etched*. B and C have close meanings to *etched*, but do not make sense in the context. D is a distracter.

4 **A** This is a vocabulary question. *Disappearance* is a synonym for the phrase "vanishing act." B is a synonym for *act*, but does not make sense in the context of the passage. C and D are distracters.

5 **C** This is a purpose question. The author mentions this to help the reader anticipate the information in the paragraph and to support the idea that their disappearance was mysterious. A only connects to the message etched in the tree but does not give enough information. B and D do not provide enough information to support the author's purpose.

6 **C** This is a reference question. The pronoun "it" refers directly back to the singular noun, *mystery*. A, B, and D are also singular nouns, but do not make sense with the passive verb *was solved*.

7 **D** This is a vocabulary question. *Supposedly* is a synonym for *allegedly*. A and C are similar but do not make sense in this context. B is a distracter.

8 **C** This is a fact question. The author mentions that the dates on the rocks could not be scientifically proven. A, B, and D contain distracters and are not mentioned in the paragraph.

9 **B** This is a detail question. To answer this question you need to understand that the professor's reputation was harmed and that *dropped out of sight* means that he left his job. A, C, and D contain incorrect information and distracters.

10 **B** This is a sentence summary question. A leaves out information. C contains incorrect information because the story did not *need* to be told again. D both leaves out information and contains incorrect information.

11 **D** This is a purpose question. The reason that the author mentions this examination of evidence is to highlight the fact that Sparkes was ambitious and seeking monetary gain. A and B do not support this reason. C is not a direct result of White's examination of the evidence about the colonists.

12 **B** This is a vocabulary question. *Notorious* is a synonym for *infamous*. A is an antonym. C is a synonym that does not fit the context. D is a distracter.

13 **D** This is a negative fact question. The author mentions all of the other possible theories about their fate except for moving south.

14 This is a schematic table question. To answer this question you need to distinguish fact from theory. F is neither a controversy, theory, or a fact. B cannot be proven. I is not mentioned in the passage and is neither a fact nor a theory.

| The historical events | A, D, E |
| Theories and controversy | C, G, H |

Passage 2 p.10

15 **C** This is a vocabulary question. The correct synonym for *prevalent* is *widespread*. A and C are antonyms. D is a distracter.

16 **D** This is an inference question. The author mentions the manufacture of vehicles that operate with alternate energy sources, so you can infer that some companies build this type of automobile. The other answers are incorrect because they contain distracting information or information not mentioned in the passage.

17 **C** This is a fact question. To answer this question you must read the second to last line of paragraph 1 and understand that *over-utilization* means the same as *overuse of natural resources*. A, B, and D contain incorrect information or information that is not mentioned in the paragraph.

18 **B** This is a vocabulary question. A and D are antonyms. C is a distracter.

19 **D** This is a fact question. To answer this question, find the information on environmentally conscious design that is mentioned in lines 2, 3 and 4. A is a distracter. B and C do not contain information from the paragraph that is specific enough to answer the question.

20 **A** This is a purpose question. To find the answer to this question, read the first, second and third lines of the paragraph. These lines support the idea that choosing recyclable materials is a challenge, and allow the reader to understand that this challenge is not specific to one type of crew. B, C, and D give incorrect or not enough information to support the purpose.

21 **D** This is a reference question. To answer this question you should understand that the word *they* refers to a plural noun phrase. A, B, and C mention groups who must evaluate the materials, not meet the standard.

22 C This is a negative fact question. To find the answer to this question, look for mention of hazardous materials in the paragraph, such as A, B, and D. Cellulose is mentioned as a *recyclable* material.

23 C This is a purpose question. To find the answer to this question, read the second and third lines of the paragraph. The author wants to show how people now have options to construct green homes and use recyclable materials. A and D are not correct because the author does not mention these factors to give examples of choices for architects. B is incorrect because the author is not trying to criticize past construction practices.

24 A This is a detail question. In order to answer this question you have to understand that two percent of homes is very small. B contains information not stated in the paragraph. C is opposite in meaning to the statement. D mentions architects, not homeowners.

25 C This is a sentence insertion question. The sentence fits best at point C. The connector word *so* means *therefore*, which follows the statements regarding the types of energy sources available to homeowners. This sentence has to follow this fact. A and B do not give the reader enough information. D offers a summary of the paragraph.

26 C This is a vocabulary question. The word *refilled* is a synonym for *renewable*. A is not correct because the sources are not *easy*. B and D contain incorrect information that distracts from the meaning of the phrase.

27 This is a schematic table question. To answer this question you need to sort the types of salvageable material from the non-recyclable materials that are mentioned in the passage. B, C, F, and I are mentioned in paragraph 2 and 3. A, D, and H are mentioned in paragraph 3 as *hazardous* materials, meaning that they are non-recyclable. The author does not mention what would be done with E, plastic cups or take-out containers or G, water pipes from the sewer system.

Salvageable building materials	B, C, F, I
Non-recyclable building materials	A, D, H

Passage 3 p.13

28 C This is a purpose question. The author mentions the novel as an example of how squid were once portrayed as mythical creatures. A contains a distracting use of *illustration* to mean image; B and D are not correct because the author is not discussing or comparing literary styles or types of literature.

29 D This is a fact question. A is incorrect and not stated in the paragraph. B is a distracter because although they were once thought to be mythical, their parts were actually discovered in the twentieth century. C is an incorrect statement.

30 C This is an inference question. In lines four and five, the author suggests that scientists now believe the squid sits and waits for its prey, which is contrary to a previous belief, as mentioned in the previous line. It is not clear that scientists agree. A is not stated in the paragraph. B is the opposite of what is clearly stated in the paragraph. D is incorrect because scientists know how the squid catch prey, but scientists are not sure in what way the squid catch their prey.

31 C This is a vocabulary question. A and D are incorrect synonyms because they do not fit the context. B is a distracter.

32 B This is a sentence summary question. A, C, and D leave out essential information stated in the paragraph.

33 B This is a negative fact question. To answer this question you have to eliminate the fact that all other parts are mentioned as common to both types of squid but only the colossal squid has hooks.

34 A This is a fact or detail question. This is mentioned in the second line of the paragraph. All cephalopods lack a backbone.

35 D This is a vocabulary question. A and C are synonyms that do not fit the context. B is an antonym.

36 C This is an inference question. The author mentions the fact that *dimorphism* has a direct bearing on the size of the squid. The large size of the male indicates that a female could possibly be much larger, however, this is impossible to predict. A is incorrect. B is not factual or stated in the paragraph. D contradicts the fact.

37 A This is a vocabulary question. The phrase refers back to the information mentioned in paragraph 4. The theory means the idea about female squid being larger than male squid. B is incorrect because it only mentions water temperature. C contradicts the fact. D contains incorrect information.

38 D This is a vocabulary question. A is a distracter. B is not a synonym for *lethal* and C is an antonym.

39 D This is a sentence insertion question. To answer this question correctly, you need to understand that the last sentence of the paragraph follows immediately after this sentence because the word *also* is used to show additional information. It cannot be inserted at A, B, or C because it would not link to the ideas in the sentences that precede or follow it.

40 C This is a fact question. The author clearly states in the paragraph that *gigantism* is connected to metabolism, which is also related to the longevity of the squid. A and B are not correct because there is no proof that the icy water makes the squid more aggressive or influences its behavior. D is incorrect

KEY AND EXPLANATION

because the author did not mention that small squid are never found in cold water.

41 **C, D,** and **F** This is a prose summary question. C, D, and F give accurate summaries of the paragraphs based on the most important facts and major points mentioned about when the colossal squid were discovered, details on its size and appearance, and how gigantism plays a part in its development. A, B, and E contain incorrect information or contain minor points mentioned in the passage.

Passage 4 p.17

42 **D** This is a fact question. The answer is in lines 3 and 4. A and B are distracters. C is the opposite of what is stated in line 2.

43 **C** This is a negative fact question. To find the answer to this question, look for the information that is stated in the paragraph. C is incorrect because the "family tree" is a diagram, not ethnography.

44 **C** This is a sentence simplification question. C is the best paraphrase of the sentence. A, B, and D are incomplete and leave out necessary information.

45 **D** This is a purpose question. The author mentions examples of aristocrats, such as Charles and Diana, to illustrate and give an example of the relationship between background and marriage. A is not true. B contradicts the facts. C is too vague.

46 **B** This is a vocabulary question. The word *heritage* is a synonym for *lineage*. A and D are distracters. C is a synonym that does not work in this context.

47 **D** This is a negative fact question. To find this answer you need to identify the facts that have made genealogy a cultural phenomenon. In paragraph 3, television, Internet, and celebrities are mentioned as contributing factors. DNA testing is a possible component of genealogical research but it is not a cause of the cultural phenomenon.

48 **A** This is a vocabulary question. B is a synonym that does not work in this context. C and D are antonyms and distracters.

49 **C** This is a sentence insertion question. This sentence fits best following the sentence concerning ubiquitous television programs. It works best before the topic of one show is mentioned. A would not logically follow this sentence. D refers to "these features," which would include the information mentioned in the previous sentences. B is a distracter.

50 **C** This is a vocabulary question. *Trend* is a synonym for *fad*. A and B are synonyms that do not work in this context. D is a distracter.

51 **D** This is a negative fact question. In order to answer this question, you must find the other facts mentioned in paragraphs 4 and 5. In paragraph 4, the author states that there is no special credential or degree-bearing requirement needed.

52 **B** This is a reference question. The pronoun *It* refers back to the subject of the previous line: a family tree. A and C are distracters. D means a diagram of the family tree, but not all the other factors that the tree represents.

53 **C** This is a vocabulary question. *Complete* is a synonym for *holistic*. A is an antonym. B and D are distracters.

54 **A, D** and **F** This is a prose summary question. In order to answer this question, you must find the major points mentioned in the passage. A is from paragraph 1. D contains a major fact about what genealogists do. F is the important concluding information from the passage. B, C, and E focus on minor points or contain information that is not important to the summary of the passage.

Listening p.21

Conversation 1 p.21

1 **B** This is a gist question. To answer this question you need to listen for key words and phrases, such as "I'm not sure what I should study," "focus your efforts," "going to test us on," "review class" "study group," "good study plan." A is not the main topic of the conversation. C is a detail of the conversation and D is a distracter.

2 **B** This is a detail question. The main reason the student is meeting the assistant is because she missed the class. The fact that the professor is not in his office today is secondary to her absence from class. A is a distracter. C is not true.

3 **A** and **D** This is a detail question. The assistant states that chapter one is basically an introduction, and clearly states that chapter two is on descriptive statistics. B and C contain information that is not mentioned.

4 **A** This is a function question with a replay of part of the conversation. To answer this question you need to understand that the woman is amused by the assistant's statement when she replies, "… don't make me laugh," and realizes that the quiz will not be short. B, C, and D are distracters.

5 **B** This is a detail question. The assistant thinks that the student should attend the study group and gives her information on what to prepare. C would have been true if the student were not going to attend the study group. A is a distracter. D contains information not stated by the assistant.

Conversation 2 p.22

6 **D** This is a gist question. The main reason that the student is visiting the registrar is to get permission to enter a class. His purpose for being there is also the main "gist" of this conversation. A and B are distracters. C is not true because he has already discussed his transfer credits with his advisor.

7 **C** This is an attitude question. Listen to the speaker's tone of voice, as well as the comments she makes, such as "That's quite an undertaking," and "Oh, you did?" A is a distracter. B and D are not correct even though you heard the woman say, "I'm sorry," and "… that's the problem."

8 **D** This is a function with replay question. The woman apologizes because she realizes she might have overlooked something in his file. A is not true. B contradicts what the woman says. C is a distracter.

9 **A** This is a purpose question. The student says he wants to take the class so that he can "fulfill his course requirements." B, C, and D are distracters that contain incorrect information.

10 **A** and **C** This is a detail question. B is a distracter because the student did not need to pick up his transcripts. D is mentioned at the end of the conversation as something the student can do after 3 p.m. when he returns to see the registration officer.

Lecture 1 p.24

11 **A** This is a gist question. To answer this question you have to understand that the main idea of this lecture is how metal movable type was invented, but not C, how it changed, or B, disagreements about it. D is a distracter.

12 **C** This is an inference question. To answer this question, you need to understand that because wood is soft, and the "wooden characters didn't last long," that this meant wood was not an efficient means of printing. A and D are distracters. B is incorrect because the professor said it took a long time to carve characters, but not a block of text.

13 **A** This is a detail question. You need to listen for the key words like "breakthrough," and at the end of the lecture, "advancement." B and C are distracters. D is incorrect because the Jikji document came from Korea.

14 **C** This is a detail question. To answer this question you need to hear the professor say "the only time they were successful was when they used the beeswax method." A is not mentioned. B is a distracter. D is incorrect because we know there were three methods in use.

15 **A** and **C** This is a detail question. The professor mentions these things: copper (metal) and lead, and two types of paper: mulberry bark and sheepskin parchment. B and D are distracters.

16 **D** This is a function question. When the professor says she doesn't want to get into the specifics, she means that she does not want to elaborate on information that is not relevant to the lecture. A, B, and C contain distracters.

Lecture 2 p.25

17 **A** This is a gist question. To answer this question you need to understand that the professor is giving an overview by discussing the many areas that comprise computer forensics. He is not discussing B, reasons for the rise; or C or D which are distracters.

18 **C** This is a function question. The professor assumes that the students understand that the growth of computer crime has been rapid and this is a rhetorical question. A is not stated and cannot be assumed. B contradicts the facts. D is a distracter.

19 **D** This is a purpose question. The professor talks about the abstract nature of data as an example of how difficult it is for the legal system to establish fair laws about computer crime. A is not stated in the lecture. B and C are distracters.

20 **D** This is an inference question. To understand this question, you need to hear the professor mention that in an investigation the forensics experts have to place accuracy above speed. Even though simple data recovery should be done quickly, they must be careful not to destroy evidence. A and B are distracters. C is not mentioned in the lecture.

21 **C** This is a purpose question. The professor uses police tape as an example of quarantine to give the listeners an image of what truly needs to be done to the computer files. A and B are distracters. D is true, but it is not the reason for mentioning the police tape.

22 This is a schematic table question. To answer this question, you need to hear the facts about volatile data: that it is lost when the computer is turned off. The other statements are false.

	True	False
It is a threat to the security of the investigation		✓
It cannot be easily documented without damaging it		✓
It is lost when the computer is turned off	✓	
It results from an attempt to destroy data		✓

Lecture 3 p.27

23 **D** This is a gist question. To answer this question you need to hear ideas expressed in the lecture, such as, the key words "rapidly dominate," and "took over extremely rapidly". The focus on the lecture is flowering plants. A and B are distracters. C is not mentioned in the lecture.

24 **D** This is a detail question. The professor says that "there is nothing in the fossil record to support

KEY AND EXPLANATION

that." And later, that "none of these theories itself constitutes a complete answer." A is not stated directly in the lecture. B contradicts what the professor says. C is not stated in the lecture.

25 **A** This is a detail question. The answer to this question lies in the fact that gymnosperms are "built to last," and that angiosperms needed more nutrition, so when their leaves fell, they created their own nutrients. B and C are distracters. D is not mentioned in the lecture.

26 **B** This is a rhetorical function question. The answer to this question is implied because the professor has already stated that the angiosperms will grow more rapidly. So she thinks the answer is obvious. A is a distracter. C contradicts the question. D is not true.

27 **A** This is a detail question. The answer is stated clearly in the lecture when she talks about how the angiosperms grew and took over—and she says "It's called positive feedback. It leads to explosive growth." B and C are distracters. D is not stated in the lecture.

28 This is an organization question. To answer this question you needed to listen to the key words about gymnosperms and angiosperms.

| Angiosperms | C, D |
| Gymnosperms | A, B, E |

Lecture 4 p.29

29 **B** This is a gist question. To answer this question you need to hear the main ideas in the discussion which posed questions about when American literature actually started and who was considered to be an American author. A is a distracter. C is not true because the professor does not compare the two literary styles. D is incorrect.

30 **B** This is a function question. This phrase means *to put off* or *postpone* something. The professor implies that they may come back to this idea at a later time. A is incorrect. C and D are distracters.

31 **C** This is a detail question. To answer this question you need to hear the key words mentioned by the students and the professor regarding "American style." The student thinks that language is important and that a writer must write in American English to be an American author. A and B are distracters. D is incorrect.

32 **A** This is a purpose question. B is not true. C and D are distracters.

33 **A** This is an inference question. Though the student believes that Smith should be considered an American writer, he also believes that Smith's writing style represented an example of British English, not American.

34 **B** and **D** This is a detail question. To answer this question, you need to hear that though Irving wrote in many different literary genres, he, and Cooper were primarily fiction (novel) writers. They also "paved the way," which means to provide a foundation, for other writers.

Speaking p.31

Speaking task 1 p.31

 Sample response

I think um, to gain experience in life, well … you get just as much from living your life and having things happen to you. I don't think you can only get things like facts from books and really have knowledge. I mean, I know my grandpa didn't um, finish high school … uh, maybe he didn't get to the last grade even. But his experience with people, his job … he travelled around the world too. I think that is just as important as reading books.

Speaking task 2 p.31

 Sample response 1

If I have a choice in how I communicate … um, I prefer face-to-face. I mean, basically, e-mail is OK, and phone is good if you need to talk to someone who is far away, but face-to-face is best. I like to see how people react and I like to uh, see their expressions, you know? People get lost on the Internet these days and maybe they don't, you know, get together in person much anymore. Maybe that's uh, not a good thing. I also think you can make mistakes in reading an e-mail and things like tone get lost. Also, on the phone you can't see someone's expression, so maybe you don't really know how they feel.

 Sample response 2

I prefer to communicate with my friends in person… um, here's why I think so: I don't like to spend too much time on the Internet or computer… you know, playing games or just chatting with instant message. However, I think, uh, I use my cell phone a lot every day and I'm texting way too often. But also, it could be that this is because our society is now more technological. You know, it's easy to do. But I think it's more important to see family or friends face-to-face because when you're in person you can see someone's reaction and body language. So I really prefer to speak in person.

Speaking task 3 p.32

 Sample response

Well, the woman seems kinda worried about her grades and the fact that she needs to um … well she has to have good grades or academic standing to get this internship. And she's worried that if she applies and her grade in history class is not good enough that she will probably be rejected by the committee or whoever, um, is making the decision. I don't know, they didn't mention it, but I'm guessing that she might be OK. Her friend seems to think so too. … Uh, if her résumé and letter are good then she could get the internship. She seems like a typical student, um, cause she is just thinking about grades.

Speaking task 4 p.33

 Sample response

Um, there are some issues about the ozone … it's very controversial. It seems like scientists don't agree about it. The passage says there are some substances … I think, CFCs … and they're damaging. So, one scientist, Dr. Solomon, did some studies on how to repair the ozone hole. The government has this uh, organization … EPA … it makes some restr … restrictions on, um, what kinds of chemicals get released. Well, there is a hole over the Antarctic that shows some of the CFCs were reacting with temperatures and just taking precautions is not enough. Also she said it's happening closer to Earth than we thought. I don't think everybody agrees with her theories, like if the ozone can be repaired … probably if we stop releasing the harmful chemicals it will slow down the depletion, like she said. But it's still controversial.

Speaking task 5 p.34

 Sample response 1

Well, the man has a problem because he can't find the books he needs to write his paper on the animals in film topic. And, um, probably if I had this problem I'd just go to the other library and get the books myself. I think um, this is the fastest way to solve the problem because the student needs the books quickly so he can start reading them. And he said, like something about having to finish this paper in a few weeks, so if he waits to get the book or books that he wants he is not going to have much time to write the paper. And he has to look at the book really, to see if it's useful. So for, me, um, this is the best solution—traveling. And even if it takes a day to go there and back, he's still saving time.

 Sample response 2

The man's problem is uh, that he does not have any books available to him in his university library. And it didn't seem like he knew how to find what he was looking for in the first place, so that librarian, she um, helped him out. But then it seems like he really doesn't know what to do because he wants to get the book quickly but he's not sure he wants to travel. I think I would wait for the books to come because maybe I would think about changing my topic if there is not enough information in my library and what if I go to the other library and then that book is not really the right book? So that would be a waste of time.

Speaking task 6 p.34

 Sample response

Uh, the professor talks about these two types of muscles … um, Ok, one is called brake-e-oradialis … or no, it's synergists. And the other type of muscle is called antagonists. OK, so the thing that is important is that the synergists are the muscles like the biceps that you use to extend and flex your muscles. And the other one is antagonist which … it seems like they are opposite to each other so they are in pairs at the joint. So … the triceps and biceps are examples of antagonists because they, uh, work against each other like when you extend one muscle the other one contracts, and so that's the brake-e-o-radialis again. It's the synergist to the triceps and the antagonist of the bicep. Yeah, that's it.

Writing p.35

Writing task 1 p.35

Sample essay

The author refers to the work of Charles Sanders Peirce, and the professor mentions that the idea of signs was one of his theories. Peirce tried to put meaning on the interpretation of signs in a field known as semiotics, which also is related to linguistics and anthropology.

The lecturer refers to an interesting concept about signs that was illustrated by a Belgian artist, in a painting of a pipe. And it said "this is not a pipe." This concept was presented to illustrate the idea of Peirce and to help the students understand that the image was meant as a sign, as Peirce defined it, because it was not really the pipe.

The idea of what is a sign as opposed to how the person interprets it could be further represented with the example of an icon. The idea of something as a basic unit of meaning. An icon could represent an object like the ancient Egyptians used. If you see a picture on a restroom door of a man or woman you know what that icon means. So this is what Peirce was really trying to say with his theories. People have some kind of need to understand things and use names for signs and this helps us make meaning of our world.

Writing task 2 p.36

Sample essay

People tend to listen to celebrities and actors because those people have a lot of fame and they also tend to speak out more because they can be interviewed in the newspaper, on TV, or in magazines. I don't think that they can always make a difference. For example, I wouldn't listen to someone like Lindsey Lohan or Amy Winehouse unless they made a specific change in their lives to help other kids to stay away from drugs and alcohol.

KEY AND EXPLANATION

It's true that some people, like Oprah Winfrey and Bono, have a lot of money so they try to do humanitarian things that will help people in countries around the world. Oprah gives money to build schools in Africa. And I think Bono does that too, in order to help people with diseases or if they don't have water. This really makes a difference, but I'm not sure if it is realistic for most people because they are not in the same economic class as Oprah or Bono.

But I'm not sure we should look to the famous people to really be our role models. Maybe we should all try to make a difference by ourselves instead.

TEST TWO

Reading p.37

Passage 1 p.37

1 B This is a vocabulary question. B is a synonym for *archetype*. A and C are distracters. D is an antonym.

2 C This is a purpose question. The author states that da Vinci's talents were not typical of men in the fifteenth century. A and B contradict the information in the paragraph. D contains incorrect information.

3 A This is a negative fact question. To answer this question you have to find the other answer choices in the paragraph. C and D are mentioned in paragraph 2 as listed among da Vinci's skills. A can be implied because we know from paragraph 1 that da Vinci is a painter. The Duke of Milan was da Vinci's patron, or, supporter.

4 D This is a fact question. In the last line of the paragraph, the author mentions that his skill was "comparable to any musician … " A and C contradict the information. B cannot be true because the historians reported that he played with great skill.

5 B This is a detail question. The instruments were described as combinations of one or more instruments that had never been constructed. A and C contain distracters; it is not stated that the instruments were too complicated to build or that the directions were not clear. D contains information that is inaccurate.

6 B This is an inference question. The answer to this question lies in the fact that the instrument was carried by the player and powered by the player's leg. A contains information that is not relevant. C contains a synonym for the name of the instrument. D contradicts information in the paragraph.

7 C This is a sentence insertion question. This sentence should follow the line about the "modern-day piano" to explain why this instrument is not named after a type of piano. It does not fit into the paragraph at points A or B because the keyboard has not yet been mentioned. It cannot be inserted at point D because it does not connect to the information in the last sentence.

8 A This is an inference question. The author states in the first line of the paragraph that the notebook at the library in Madrid is "lesser known," which implies that few scholars had read it. B contains incorrect information regarding playing an instrument with wind as opposed to blowing air into it. C is a distracter (*fewer* for *lesser*). D cannot be determined from the information in the paragraph.

9 D This is a vocabulary question. The word *name* is a synonym for *appellation*. A and B are distracters. C is a synonym that is incorrect in this context.

10 B This is a vocabulary question. The phrase is a synonym for *drumsticks*. A, C, and D all contain distracters referring to other parts of the drum that were mentioned in the paragraph.

11 A This is a negative fact question. To answer this question you need to find the other three facts in the paragraph. C is correct because the player could program the speed of the drum by moving pegs. D is correct because the player could pull the cart at a continuous speed. B is implied because the player could come to a stop to adjust the rhythm.

12 B This is a reference question. To answer this question you need to replace the pronoun *it* with the singular noun *the instrument*. A is a distracter. C is the sound the instrument made, but not the instrument itself. D is an incorrect noun to replace the pronoun.

13 B, **D**, and **E** This is a prose summary question. To answer this question, you have to read the sentences and compare them to the paragraphs in the passage that contain the major points of information. A contains incorrect information from paragraphs 1 and 2. C contains information from paragraphs 3 and 4 that is not true. F contains minor details from paragraph 6.

Passage 2 p.40

14 B This is a fact question. The information in paragraph 1 clearly states that planets larger than Jupiter were unlikely to be habitable. A and C contradict information in the paragraph. D is not stated in the paragraph.

15 D This is a purpose question. The author makes a cultural reference to the Goldilocks character to mean that the conditions for habitability must be "just right." A is too general; B and C contradict the information in the paragraph.

16 C This is a negative fact question. In order to answer this question you need to find the three facts stated in the paragraph. A, that the Gliese 581 planet is 50 percent bigger (half the size larger) than Earth is true. B is implied because it is called "Earth-like." D is also true because Gliese 581 orbits a star.

17 B This is a sentence simplification question. A leaves out information. C is not an accurate explanation of the wobble technique. D is too general and does not mention the use of spectroscopic instruments.

18 D This is a vocabulary question. *Indistinct* is a synonym for *blurry*. A and C are distracters. B is an antonym.

19 A This is a detail question. B and C are distracters. D contradicts information in the paragraph.

20 B This is a reference question. The pronoun refers back to the Hubble Space Telescope which is the subject of the preceding sentence. A and C are distracters. D is the closest single noun, but is the object of the verb phrase "exist in."

21 D This is a purpose question. To answer this question you need to understand that the discovery of this molecule supports the theory of life forms in space. A is too vague. B and C contain distracters.

22 D This is an inference question. To answer this question you need to find the information in paragraph 4 which describes the purpose of the Kepler Orbiting Telescope and implies that because it "looks at stars" it is also seeking out habitable planets. A is too vague. C is how it orbits the Earth, but not its purpose. B is a distracter.

23 C This is a sentence insertion question. The sentence best fits the paragraph at point C. This sentence further explains how the Kepler orbits the Earth and the reasoning behind its "trailing behind" the Earth. The other insertion points do not follow logically after or before the phrase "in this way."

24 B This is a vocabulary question. *Emanating* is a synonym for *radiating*. A is incorrect. C is a synonym that does not fit the context. D is a distracter.

25 D This is an inference question. To infer this question, you need to understand that although the Kepler Orbiting Telescope discovered "Earth-like" planets, some are as large as Jupiter, which makes them unlikely to sustain life. A contradicts the sentence in the first line of the paragraph. B is too general. C is not stated in the paragraph.

26 The ground based telescope is C, the La Silla. D, HARPS, is the correct instrument and E, Doppler and G, spectrometry are the correct techniques used with this type of telescope. The correct space-based telescope is I, the Hubble scope which uses A, an infrared camera, and F, photometry ,as its instruments. B, Kepler and H, corrective lens, are distracters. The Kepler Orbiting Telescope is space-based, but only one technique is mentioned that is correct and no other instrument is mentioned. H, the corrective lens, was an adjustment to part of an instrument on the Hubble but is not the instrument itself.

	Type of telescope	
	Ground-based	Space-based
	C	I
Instrument or process	D, E, G	A, F

Passage 3 p.44

27 D This is a fact question. To answer this question you need to find the fact "had a resounding effect …" in line 2 of the paragraph. A and B are distracters. C is a distracter based on the concept of "macro."

28 D This is a vocabulary question. The word *tendencies* is a synonym of *trend* in this context. A and B are synonyms that do not work in the context. C is a distracter.

29 C This is a sentence insertion question. This sentence follows the idea that Keynes first worked in the India Office before he "re-entered" the world of academia. The phrase "post-baccalaureate pursuits" implies that he continued academic work after his BA.

30 A This is a vocabulary question. The word *talent* is a synonym for *adeptness* in this context. B and D are distracters. C is an antonym.

31 A This is an inference question. The author implies that Keynes might not have chosen economics if his mentor had not persuaded him to do so. B is not stated in the paragraph. C is not true. D is a distracter.

32 A This is a negative fact question. To find this answer you need to locate the other facts in the paragraph and eliminate the fact that is an exception. Though he taught a course about the Stock Exchange, he did not work there.

33 D This is a vocabulary question. *Pertained* means *was relevant to*. A, B, and C are distracters and do not fit in the context.

34 A This is an inference question. To find the answer to this question you need to refer to the phrase "controversial book," and look back at the subject in the previous sentence. B cannot be proven from the context. C is not stated. D is not true.

35 D This is a reference question. The possessive pronoun refers to the subject *the government*. A, B, and C are distracters.

36 C This is a negative fact question. To find the answer you need to find the other facts in the paragraph and eliminate this answer choice.

37 B This is a purpose question. The author mentions this as an example of how a recession could be solved, which is "manage or end a recession." A, C, and D are not illustrations of this fact.

38 A This is a fact question. In paragraph 7, the author states that President Roosevelt wanted to improve the country's economy and eventually ended the recession. In the first line, it is clear that his ideas were not popular. B and C are not directly stated in the passage. D is a distracter.

39 A, B, and **D** This is a prose summary question. A, B, and D contain information that includes the major ideas stated in the passage. C contains minor details about his career. E contains minor details about how his theories were put to use.

Passage 4 p.47

40 C This is a fact question. In order to answer this question correctly, you need to find the facts in paragraph 1, line 2. A is not specific enough because it does not mention the exact temperature. B is incorrect. D is not stated in the passage.

41 B This is a vocabulary question. *Layers* is a synonym for *strata*. A is a synonym that does not work in this context. C and D are distracters.

42 D This is a negative fact question. To answer this question you need to verify the three true in the paragraph. The author mentions wind, geographical location and the depth of a lake but does not say that chemicals and minerals are only at the bottom.

43 A This is an inference question. To answer this question you need to understand the statement made by the author that the system is new and it "now includes shallow-lake water," which means that previous classification systems did not include this type of lake. B and C are not correct. D is not stated in the passage.

44 D This is a fact/detail question. Animictic lake water is ice-covered or below freezing, all year. To answer this question you can eliminate A, B, and C, which are not correct facts.

45 B This is a vocabulary question. In this sentence, *transitional* means the middle layer. A and D are distracters. C is an incorrect synonym because it does not fit the context.

46 C This is a vocabulary question. The word *unoxygenated* means without or lacking oxygen. A and B are distracters. D is an antonym.

47 D This is a fact question. In order to answer this question you need to understand the terms "historical stratification system," which is created because the bottom waters of the lake remain undisturbed. A is a distracter. B and C contain information not stated in the paragraph.

48 A This is a fact question. The author says the organisms have survived from ancient times. B is a distracter. C is not true. D is not stated in the passage.

49 B This is a sentence insertion question. This sentence best fits the passage at point B because it logically connects the sentences before and after it. The surface water combined with the bluish calcium creates the aquamarine color. The pink bacteria does not affect the mirror-like surface.

50 A This is an inference question. The professor mentions that this type of lake is found on most of the continents. However, he claims it is rare, meaning not typical. B and C are distracters. D is not correct based on the information in the paragraph.

51 B This is a purpose question. In order to answer this question you need to understand that the professor is making a point about the usefulness of analyzing this type of lake. This science helps geologists determine important information about the history of the Earth. A and C are distracters. D is too ambiguous.

52 This is a schematic table question. The Lake types are A, holomictic, which must have G, lake temperatures above 39 degrees F. This type of lake mixes at least once per year, D. This information is found in paragraphs 1, 2, and 3.

The second type of lake is B, meromictic, for which E is true: only the surface waters mix; I, its surface waters may rise above 39 degrees C and H, its deep layers are cold and contain little oxygen are also true. These are found in paragraphs 4 and 5. C, animictic and F, never mixes, do not contain enough information to complete the table and should be eliminated.

Lake type	Conditions	Mixing
A	G	D
B	H, I	E

Listening p.51

Conversation 1 p.51

1 A This is a gist question. In order to understand this question you need to hear the professor tell the student she could "see that he didn't do well on his last test," and he says it was his "last exam at the end of the semester." B is a distracter for "incomplete." C and D are also distracters.

2 D This is a detail question. To answer this question you need to hear the student say he wanted to take an incomplete in the class. A and B were not stated in the lecture. C is a distracter.

3 B This is a function question. The phrase "here's the deal," means this is the situation or solution. A and C are distracters. D is incorrect.

4 A and **D** This is a detail question. C is a distracter because he said he had already read all the plays. B is a distracter for writing a five-page paper.

5 A This is an attitude question. The student is relieved that the professor is giving him another chance. B was true at first, but the student felt differently at the end of the conversation. C and D are incorrect.

Conversation 2 p.52

6 C This is a gist question. The main reason the student goes to the tutoring center is because she has to do a presentation and says she "has not got a clue about how to do a visual slide show." A is not stated. B is a distracter. D is true but it is not the reason she goes to the tutoring center.

7 A This is a function question. When the advisor asks if she wants "bells and whistles" this is a phrase meaning graphics and animation. He clarifies this when she asks if he meant "like images and graphics …" B and D are distracters. C is incorrect.

8 A This is an inference question. The man tells her that it is intuitive and that she can "figure it out as she goes along." In that way he implies that it is easy to use. B contradicts what he says. C and D are not stated in the conversation.

9 B and C This is a detail question. The woman has two concerns: the first is practicing with the program after she completes the tutorial. The second is speaking in front of other people. She states this directly. A is not mentioned. D is a distracter because she knows how to use a computer.

10 B This is a detail question. To answer this question you need to hear the man tell her to bring her outline. O is incorrect because she only asks if she can bring her laptop at the end of the conversation. A is not mentioned. C is a distracter.

Lecture 1 p.54

11 D This is a gist question. A and B are minor points. C is also a minor detail and is a distracter.

12 A This is a detail question. To answer this question you need to hear the professor mention the effectiveness of the study. B and C are distracters. D is not mentioned in the lecture.

13 B This is an inference question. To answer this question you need to hear the professor say that the audience does not like to see it in critically acclaimed films.

14 C This is a detail question. To answer this question you need to hear the professor say that the audience is engaged in the plot. They are too "absorbed" in the plot to notice the product. Answers A, B, and D are distracters.

15 This is an organization question. To answer this question you need to take notes on the four factors mentioned in the lecture and decide which effects were positive, negative or both.

	+ve effect	-ve effect	Both +ve and -ve
Viewer enjoyment		✓	
Prior notice of placement	✓		
Placement in general			✓
Positive reviews		✓	

16 A This is a function question. To answer this question you need to understand the implications made by the speaker. She implies that the context of the market refers to how the market was performing overall, and the idea of abnormal returns. Answers B, C, and D are distracters because she is not commenting on the research or the effectiveness of the product placement, or suggesting that stock prices are predictable.

Lecture 2 p.55

17 B This is a gist question. The main idea of this lecture is her Changing New York project. A, C, and D are distracters.

18 A This is a purpose question. To answer this question you need to hear the professor say that it was perfect timing for Abbott, and that her "stated purpose was to document and interpret America …"

19 A and D This is a detail question. To answer this question you need to hear the professor mention Abbott's rejection of soft focus in favor of sharpness and clarity, and the rejection of sentimentality of pastoral scenes. B and C contradict what was stated in the lecture.

20 B This is a detail question. To answer this question you need to hear the professor mention that Abbott waited until someone passed by and made sure they were in the frame. A, C, and D are distracters.

21 1 C   2 B   3 A   4 D This is an organization question. To answer this question you need to listen for each of these factors and put them in sequence. The professor described the FAP before Abbott's philosophy, then her project, and last, Doug Levere's work.

22 D This is an attitude question. The professor is complimentary toward Levere's rephotography of Abbott's work. A and C are distracters. B is an antonym.

Lecture 3 p.57

23 B This is a gist question. To answer this question correctly you need to hear the professor say the line "wondering about whether there's a physiological basis for synesthesia." A is not mentioned in the lecture. C is a minor detail. D is a distracter.

KEY AND EXPLANATION

24 A This is a purpose question. To answer this question you need to hear the professor mention the composer Olivier Messiaen as an example to introduce the topic or "hook" the audience. B, C, and D are distracters.

25 D This is a detail question. To understand this question you need to listen for the word "axon" and understand that the professor stated the key word "connectivity" in reference to the axons. A and B are distracters. C is incorrect.

26 C This is a purpose question. To answer this question you need to hear the professor compare highways to the DTI scanning. A is a distracter. B and D are not mentioned in the lecture.

27 A This is a detail question. To answer this question you need to hear the professor state the key word "grapheme-color synesthesia" and mention evidence of a physical basis for the phenomenon, then, "implications of this result." B, C, and D are distracters.

28 D This is a function question. To understand this question you need to know that "back up," means return to a previous point. A, B, and C are distracters.

Lecture 4 p.58

29 D This is a gist question. To answer this question you need to hear the main idea that the professor was discussing various concepts about "Galileo's experiment with falling bodies" with his class. A and B are distracters. C is a distracter that contradicts a minor detail.

30 A This is a detail question. To answer this question you need to hear the professor say, "we owe this story to his biographer," and the key words, "the story has really stayed around as a myth." B, C, and D are distracters.

31 C This is a function question. To understand this question you need to understand the phrase "it makes a nice image," refers to the story and what it represents. A is not stated in the lecture. B and D are distracters.

32 A This is a purpose question. To answer this question correctly you need to hear the professor say that "as far back as the sixth century, other scholars had challenged Aristotle's ideas." B, C, and D are distracters.

33 A This is a detail question. To answer this question you need to hear the professor say "think about air," and then describe what happens in a vacuum. B, C, and D are distracters.

34 C This is an inference question. To answer this question you need to understand that the professor's viewpoint of the moon experiment was a way of showing respect for Galileo's legend, even though it was not an "accurate experiment." A is a distracter. B and D contradict information in the lecture.

Speaking p.60

Speaking task 1 p.60

 Sample response

I think a good teacher should be passionate about teaching and care about her students. I, uh, I've had many different teachers for different subjects and I think if my teacher wasn't interested in the subject then I wasn't learning as much. When the teacher seemed to enjoy, I mean was really into the subject, then I was a lot more interested in the topic too. And I think I learned more. Like in English, I mean. When you work with people every day, especially young kids, then it's really important because you influence those kids. So a good teacher has to have knowledge but has to also be enthusiastic about her job.

Speaking task 2 p.60

 Sample response

Um, I'm not like, opposed to sports or anything, but if I have a choice … I mean, doing something for two hours? Well, then I'm gonna choose to go to a movie. It's much nicer to sit in a quiet theater than go to a noisy event. I know because I've been to basketball games and people are shouting, and it's exciting, and all. Uh … but I really prefer the dark quiet theater, to be honest, and a good movie. And you know, people can eat food … like popcorn, or drink something at a baseball game, but I don't think it's as fun as sitting in front of a good drama. So that's, um, that's what I'd prefer.

Speaking task 3 p.60

 Sample response

The woman is really skeptical about this new book system. I mean, she really doesn't think it's going to work. She … first of all, she doesn't understand how that's going to work because you could get a book that has writing in it. It seems uh, I think that's her main issue because she doesn't want to get a used book that has writing and notes in it from someone else. She thinks they should give out class sets or something, for free. She doesn't think it makes sense to rent used books. Even though it costs less, she's not going to do that because she said, if she can't write in it herself, she doesn't want it.

Speaking task 4 p.61

 Sample response

The professor talks about various hybrids that differ from the ones in the passage. In the reading, uh, there are several animals that are hybrids. These are, like the cross between donkey and horse, which is a mule, and another … hinny. Uh, then the professor adds to that by talking about some of the big cats, like lions and tigers. These are interesting examples of animal diversity because they are unusual looking animals. Once, people thought they were mutations, but they're not. So, she said, um, if you cross a lion father with a tiger mother you get … um, a liger. And then if the other thing happens, it's a tigon. OK, and so these look like the fathers more than the mothers. And then … sometimes some of the animals breed with other cats, like leopards and panthers. And then subspecies can occur. So it becomes more diverse.

Speaking task 5 p.62

 Sample response

First of all, the woman has a problem with her roommate … It seems like they're not compatible. So she needs to move. And she tried talking to the roommate, but that didn't work. So he suggested one option is staying in the dorm but changing roommates. And she might have to talk to the resident advisor … to get a new roommate, or apply in the housing office, but the woman thinks that is too much paperwork. So the man suggests moving to a house off campus. Uh, trying to get a new roommate in the dorm is not such a good idea. So if I were the woman, I'd move off campus. It might cost a little more money to have your own room, but it's worth it because you need to sleep and study, and it's not good to deal with someone who is on the opposite schedule as you.

Speaking task 6 p.62

 Sample response

The Erie Canal was the waterway that connected … actually, so … it was a kind of gateway, as the professor said. Uh, this was Governor Clinton's idea: to make a waterway to connect Atlantic to Great Lakes. His idea was not really accepted in the Senate. I think the lecturer said they laughed him off the floor, or something like that. Anyway, his idea actually benefited the entire country because they built this 363-mile canal, and it was hard work but it created jobs, it actually inspired technology and engineering … an engineering marvel. They took people and they took cargo and those things would not have been able to move that fast otherwise, uh, probably not at that time. That's the 1800s, so there was no other means of transportation except horses pulling wagons. So this was an innovation and opened up the trade routes. That was the main benefit.

Writing p.63

Writing task 1 p.63

Sample essay

The professor speaks about the difficulty in really determining the origins of American theater. It seems that the origins are disputed by historians and that some Englishmen named Adam Hallam and his sons were actually the first to establish a theater company in America in the 1700s. But although the Hallams had a theater space, their repertoire of plays was actually British. They performed plays by British and European playwrights. For the professor the issue is more about what is produced than the actual space it is produced in … so he raises the question: What is American theater? Is it the concept of theater, or, is it the actual, physical space?

So this is where the controversy begins, because although they get credit in some sources for being the "first" theater, for the professor, the idea of American theater meant producing a play that was written by an American and was probably about American culture. Therefore, a Shakespeare play, being an English play, was not really American in the cultural sense. And the first play produced by Tyler was in 1787, in New York City. Maybe that was actually the first truly American play. The professor introduces this idea, which, in contrast to the basic history, sheds a little more light on the true origin of American theater.

Writing task 2 p.64

Sample essay

I think that people usually cause harm to the Earth every day and probably do not realize it. Each time we drop a wrapper to the ground or dump some chemical down the sink, we are putting toxic things into the environment. But most people don't think about this. Human activity might make the Earth better in some ways, but I think that in most ways our activities cause harm to the Earth. The degradation of the environment has occurred in major cities all over the world, where air, water, and soil quality have been compromised due to the pollution caused by pharmaceutical companies, automobiles, and factories. These factors are of course, based on human activity. We're ultimately responsible for the creation and utilization of the resources on Earth, which, in turn, can cause harm to the environment.

For example, in order to survive we need food, clothing, housing, and a means of transportation. We also need water and air. However, in order to create our food, clothes, buildings, and to get those things from place to place, we actually may damage the water and air. When our factories create products, sometimes chemicals harm the water and then the fish. Sometimes we spray too many pesticides on the plants and that harms the food or harms the animals that eat the food. It is a vicious cycle.

Until we really begin to put green living and sustainable lifestyle into practice we will probably continue to harm the environment. Even with cars that use alternative sources of energy, I am not sure that we have a final solution. However we might have one way of improving our air quality if we are not using gasoline or oil. Perhaps over time more people will try to use natural products and more organic or recyclable products to help the environment.

KEY AND EXPLANATION

FURTHER PRACTICE AND GUIDANCE

Reading p.65

Practice for skimming and scanning texts

A Answers will vary
B Answers will vary
C Answers will vary
D Answers will vary

Question type 1 Vocabulary in context p.69

Skill builder 1

A

1 B   2 D   3 C

B

4 The concept of being **environmentally conscious**, or "green," has become more prevalent in twenty-first-century U.S. culture.

5a A problem that has often arisen has been with how a **site crew**—whether it is demolition or construction crew—determines and sorts what is "waste" and what is recyclable.

5b In new "green" construction, insulation that was once asbestos-based can be replaced with recycled denim or constructed with **cellulose**—a fibrous material found in paper products.

6 In terms of energy and natural resources, sustainable architecture may incorporate many **alternative energy sources**—energy that is not harmful to the environment and does not rely on mineral-based fuels like coal or oil.

Skill builder 3

A

1 g   2 e   3 i   4 l   5 c   6 k   7 d
8 a   9 h   10 j   11 f   12 b

B

1 Historians and **archaeologists** alike have still not reached an agreement about this potential physical evidence of the Lost Colony.

2 The genealogical method, or, way of using symbols and diagrams to create a record of kinship connections, is an important technique of **ethnography**.

3 Brain scientists have been wondering about whether there's a **physiological** basis for synesthesia for over a hundred years.

4 It's over the continent of Antarctica and even though there is a great deal of depletion to the ozone, **meteorological** studies have found that there is still a significant amount of ozone there—even during times of extreme depletion.

5 One of the greatest mysteries in **biological** science is why species of flowering plants began to rapidly dominate the earth around 100 million years ago.

6 John Smith's writing style was more like British English. … I saw one of his original texts in the library and it was, you know, a more **archaic** style of writing.

7 **Technological** advances in the nineteenth century helped improve the workers' ability to do things like clear tree stumps and move large amounts of dirt and rocks.

8 I'm looking for information on the way that animals behave like humans, or have human-like characteristics in movies and in cartoons. And I want to focus on live action films.

Oh, you mean **anthropomorphism**?

9 Analysis of meromictic lakes is important to the field of limnology—the study of inland waters—since the deep strata provide significant information about the formation of the lakes and its **geological** record.

10 While many astrophysicists and **astro-biologists** have argued the unlikelihood of life forms on other planets, the data from the Kepler Orbiting Telescope suggests the contrary.

Practice for vocabulary questions

A
1 C   2 D   3 B   4 B
B
5 D   6 D   7 A   8 C
C
9 C   10 C   11 B   12 C   13 D
D
14 C   15 D   16 C

Question type 2 Fact and detail p.78

Skill builder 2

A

Settled by English colonists in **the late sixteenth century**, Roanoke Island lies off **the coast** of what is now **the state of North Carolina**. It is best known as **the home** of "**the Lost Colony**." In 1587, **the explorer** Sir Walter Raleigh dispatched a ship bound for **the new world**, carrying a group of approximately 117 people—including their new governor, John White. **The captain** was supposed to take them farther north, to Chesapeake Bay near Massachusetts, but instead dropped **the passengers** at Roanoke Island—the site of **the first, unsuccessful English colony**. Governor White realized that supplies were low and sailed back to England to acquire more food, promising to return in three months. However, **the war** between England and Spain prevented White from voyaging back to **the island** for three years. When White finally returned to Roanoke in 1590, he found that **the settlers** had disappeared. **The entire site** had been abandoned without a trace of **the colonists** having been there. **The only clue** that White found was **the word** "CROATOAN" carved into a fence post, and **the letters** CRO etched into a tree trunk. There was nothing else to indicate where **the colonists** had gone or **the manner** in which they had left.

B Answers will vary

C Answers will vary but should be similar to the paragraph.

D

A problem that has often arisen has been with how a site crew—whether it is demolition or construction crew—determines and sorts what is "waste" and what is recyclable. Architects and environmental scientists have to decide whether or not a material is appropriate for use in new construction and how it will impact **the environment**. They must evaluate **the materials** from **the demolition** and determine what those materials contain, and if they meet **the standards** set by **the U.S. government's Environmental Protection Agency (the EPA)**. If **the debris** from **the demolition** contains hazardous materials that are harmful to **the environment** or to **the consumer**, such as asbestos, then **the material** is not salvageable. Use of asbestos for insulation and as a form of fire retardation in buildings and fabrics was common in **the nineteenth century**. Asbestos was once used in shingles from **the sides** of an old building, as well as in **the insulation** from **the interior walls** of a home or other construction. In new "green" construction, insulation that was once asbestos-based can be replaced with recycled denim or constructed with cellulose—a fibrous material found in paper products. **The same assessment** applies to wood or wallboard painted with toxic lead-based paints. In addition, gas-flow regulators and meters on both water and gas heating systems constructed prior to 1961 must be carefully evaluated to determine that they do not contain dangerous substances such as mercury. Mercury can be harmful to humans and **the environment** if it is spilled during **the removal** of these devices.

E Answers will vary

F Answers will vary but should be similar to the paragraph.

Skill builder 3

A 1 C   2 A
B 3 D

Practice for fact and detail questions

A 1 C   2 A
B 3 D   4 B   5 D   6 B
C 7 C   8 A
D 9 D   10 C

Question type 3 Negative facts p.84

Practice for negative fact questions

A 1 C   2 D
B 3 D   4 A
C 5 A   6 D
D 7 B   8 B

Question type 4 Identifying pronoun references p.87

Skill builder 1

A

1 Anticipatory

2 R Architects and environmental scientists have to decide whether or not a material is appropriate for use in new construction and how it will impact the environment.

3 R Mercury can be harmful to humans and the environment if it is spilled during the removal of these devices.

4 Anticipatory

5 R The fishermen who caught it also got the squid on video.

6 R The colossal squid differs from the giant squid in that it has hooks on the tentacles.

7 Anticipatory

B

Reference pronouns: Its, it

Demonstrative pronouns: this

8 B
9 C

Practice for reference questions

A 1 D   2 D
B 3 C   4 A
C 5 D   6 D
D 7 D   8 C
E 9 C

KEY AND EXPLANATION

Question type 5 Rhetorical purpose p.91

Skill builder 1

A Answers will vary

B

4 The author discusses the idea of *dimorphism* **to support** the claim that the female squid could be larger its male counterpart.

5 The author mentions that fishermen filmed the squid on video **to offer an example of** one way that scientists were able to examine a live squid.

6 The author states that the scientists preserved the squid in ice **to describe** how they transported the squid to New Zealand for further study.

Practice for rhetorical purpose questions

A 1 C
B 2 D
C 3 D   4 C
D 5 C   6 C
E 7 B   8 D

Question type 6 Making inferences p.95

Skill builder 1

A Inferences: 1, 4, 7

Practice for inference questions

A 1 D   2 B
B 3 C   4 A
C 5 C   6 A   7 C
D 8 A   9 C

Question type 7 Sentence insertion p.98

Skill builder 1

A

The popularity of genealogy as a "cultural phenomenon" has grown to a point where people worldwide are subscribing to various ancestry websites, becoming members of genealogical societies, and even having their DNA tested, all <u>in order to</u> trace their family trees. <u>In addition to</u> a recent rise in the number of Internet-based genealogical research companies, genealogy has <u>also</u> generated commercial appeal <u>by way of</u> television broadcasting. Today, programs on television about "finding your roots" are ubiquitous in several countries. The premise of one show, <u>for example</u>, is investigating the family trees of American celebrities. These features, <u>combined with</u> a celebrity factor, have boosted the interest in genealogy in the U.S. and Canada by nearly half a million people.

This cultural phenomenon may seem like a fad, but <u>at the same time</u>, its historical and more scholarly implications are not lost to cultural anthropologists and researchers in other disciplines. For archivists—the library science specialists who deal with documenting, preserving, and organizing old records—the field of genealogy and the needs of genealogical researchers are very important.

B

	Phrase	Addition or continuation	Contrast	Example or illustration	Cause–effect or purpose
1	in order to				✓
2	in addition to	✓			
3	also	✓			
4	by way of			✓	
5	for example			✓	
6	combined with	✓			
7	at the same time		✓		

Skill builder 2

A

2 These principles are the social building blocks of many nonindustrial-based societies: societies that are "kin based."

3 For example, genealogical records were perhaps most important to the aristocracy of Europe.

5 For example, Charles, Prince of Wales and Lady Diana Spencer marrying because of her impeccable lineage.

4 Throughout history and even today, in upper class families, one's pedigree determined whether a couple could wed.

1 Genealogical research reveals significant facts that can be analyzed in order to see how descent, marriage, and kinship ties play a role in the development of a given society over time.

6 Similarly, in the U.S., one's lineage often played a role in uniting families of a particular socio-economic level—such as the marriage between President John F. Kennedy and Jacqueline Bouvier.

KEY AND EXPLANATION

Practice for sentence insertion questions
A 1 C
B 2 D
C 3 C
D 4 C

Question type 8 Sentence simplification p.101

Skill builder 1

A

1 He systematically **showed** with **verified proof** from experts, that the words written on the rocks in an Elizabethan-era Roman script had been **falsely created** and the dates on the rocks could not be scientifically proven.
2 Sustainable architecture **is constructed by using** environmentally conscious design **methods**.
3 However, despite its **intimidating** size, recent research has speculated that it may not be such an aggressive predator as was **believed**.

4 The genealogist must learn how to **recreate** family trees based on the information provided by an individual, as well as have a deep knowledge and understanding of the sources, in order to create another person's **ancestral line**.

B Answers will vary

Practice for sentence simplification questions
A 1 D
B 2 D
C 3 C
D 4 D

Question type 9 Prose summary p.104

Skill builder 1
A Answers will vary

Practice for prose summary questions
A 1 B, C, F
B 2 A, C, F
C 3 A, B, E
D 4 A, C, E

Question type 10 Schematic table p.107

Skill builder 1

A 1 C   2 E   3 B   4 A   5 D

B

Passage	Title	Field of Study	Pattern
1	Lost Colony	History	Cause/effect
2	Sustainable architecture	Architecture	Problem/solution
3	Colossal squid	Marine biology	Description
4	Genealogy	Cultural anthropology	Description

Skill builder 2

A Answers will vary

Practice for schematic table questions

A 1

Physical	A, B, E
Behavioral	C, G, H

B 2

Media resources	A, E
Printed resources	B, C, F, H

C 3

Viola-organista	C, E
Motorized drum	A, D, F

D 4

Economics courses	B, F, H
Written work	A, D, G

KEY AND EXPLANATION

Listening p.113

Question type 1 Listening for gist p.114

Skill builder 1

A

1 E   2 A   3 B   4 F   5 D   6 C

B

So, last week **we were talking about** bookmaking and the different types of paper. I want **to focus now on** printing—and **by that I mean** the production of multiple copies of an image on paper or some other medium. Now, China … China has a long tradition of woodblock printing that goes back to at least the 800s and well, a lot of these images included written words, or Chinese language characters. So, **you could say that** the Chinese are credited with being the first to actually print words on paper. But **the way they did that** was to carve words into a block of wood, spread ink over it and transfer that to paper. Now, you **have to realize that** carving words into wood is a slow process. And eventually, someone came up with the idea of carving individual characters into separate blocks of wood, so that of course they could move these around into any combination. **This was the beginning of** what is called movable type.

Practice for listening for gist questions

A 1 D   2 C
B 3 D   4 A
C 5 A   6 C
D 7 D   8 B

Question type 2 Listening for a speaker's purpose p.117

Skill builder 1

A

1 D   2 G   3 H   4 C   5 A   6 E   7 B   8 F

B

Purpose	Sentence
to compare/contrast	1 First, I want to call your attention to the differences between American and British literature.
to clarify instructions	2 OK, I want to remind you that the next reading is posted on the class website.
to elaborate	3 Next, I'll get into the specifics on this topic, which is pretty complicated …
to offer an explanation	4 There's not enough time to cover everything I want you to know in today's session.
to confirm understanding	5 I don't need to go into details about the point that the author was trying to make, do I?
to justify a reason	6 I expect you to read the second chapter of the book by our next class.
to give instructions	7 So now I'm going to give you a bit of background on this subject.
to define	8 OK, so, I'll go over this again to make sure you've got this down correctly …

C

1. I want **to focus** now on printing—and by that, I mean the production of multiple copies of an image on paper or some other medium.
2. Remember, I'm going **to put** the notes from today's lecture and your writing assignment on the class website so you can refer to those documents.
3. By saying this, I'm trying **to illustrate** a few of the points that the author tried to make in his book.
4. I would agree with that statement, but then, we'd have **to discuss** the whole idea about letters and script.
5. So, just **to clarify** what we were talking about … you need to file a change of grade form, right?

Practice for listening for purpose questions

A 1 C 2 A
B 3 A 4 B
C 5 D 6 C
D 7 B 8 A

Question type 3 Listening for details p.120

Skill builder 1

A Answers will vary

B

Gymnosperms, **you might say**, are built to last. They live longer, grow slower and their leaves are thicker and store nutrients within them. Angiosperms require more nutrition from the soil than gymnosperms. They also grow much faster. Now **here's the key**: they tend to shed their leaves onto the ground in much higher quantities. And what is it that puts more nutrients into the soil? Leaves. Decomposing leaves deposit nutrients like nitrogen into the soil. So **in a sense** angiosperms create their own food by shedding leaves.

On the other hand, angiosperms and ferns shed their leaves at a much slower rate. And their leaves don't decompose the same way—they really keep the soil low in nutrients. And so it's very difficult for angiosperms to compete in the same area as gymnosperms. There aren't enough nutrients in the soil to give them a foothold.

Practice for listening for detail questions

A
1 C and D
2 A
B
3 C
4 C and D

C
5 B and D
6 A and D
D
7 C
8 A and C

Question type 4 Listening to understand rhetorical function p.122

Skill builder 1

A

Gymnosperms, **you might say**, are built to last. They live longer, grow slower and their leaves are thicker and store nutrients within them. Angiosperms require more nutrition from the soil than gymnosperms. They also grow much faster. **Now here's the key**: they tend to shed their leaves onto the ground in much higher quantities. **And what is it that** puts more nutrients into the soil? Leaves. Decomposing leaves deposit nutrients like nitrogen into the soil. **So in a sense** angiosperms create their own food by shedding leaves.

On the other hand, angiosperms and ferns shed their leaves at a much slower rate. And their leaves don't decompose the same way—they really keep the soil low in nutrients. **And so** it's very difficult for angiosperms to compete in the same area as gymnosperms. There aren't enough nutrients in the soil to give them a foothold.

B

Adding ideas	Compare/contrast
Now here's the key And what is it that	On the other hand
Cause/effect	**Concession**
So in a sense And so	you might say

C

Gymnosperms, you might say, are built to last. They live **longer**, grow **slower** and their leaves are **thicker** and store nutrients within them. Angiosperms require **more nutrition** from the soil **than** gymnosperms. They also grow **much faster**. Now here's the key: they tend to shed their leaves onto the ground **in much higher quantities**. And what is it that puts **more nutrients** into the soil? Leaves. Decomposing leaves deposit nutrients like nitrogen into the soil. So in a sense angiosperms create their own food by shedding leaves.

On the other hand, angiosperms and ferns shed their leaves at a **much slower rate**. And their leaves don't decompose the same way—they really keep the soil low in nutrients. And so it's very difficult

KEY AND EXPLANATION

for angiosperms to compete in the same area as gymnosperms. There aren't enough nutrients in the soil to give them a foothold.

Skill builder 2

A

1 So, **have you already declared** your major?
2 **Really**? That's quite an undertaking.
3 And … which ancient languages **did you study**? I'm just asking because undergraduate students need special permission to take those classes.
4 Oh, **you did**?
5 Wait … I thought you were in your first year … sorry, **am I missing something**?

B

	Rhetorical	Interrogative	Tag	Response?
1		✓		Yes
2	✓			No
3		✓		Yes
4			✓	Yes
5	✓			No

Practice for listening for rhetorical function questions

A 1 B   2 C
B 3 A   4 C
C 5 C   6 C
D 7 D   8 A

Question type 5 Listening to understand the speaker's attitude p.126

Skill builder 3

A

M Hi. Can I help you?
W Hi … um, **maybe, yeah**. Professor McGee isn't in his office today and I missed the last class … so now I'm **not sure** what I should study for the test on Friday.
M **Maybe** I can help … Uh, have you looked at the course syllabus?
W Oh, no. … Um, **good** idea. I **always** forget to refer to that.

B

Recently, two researchers took an **entirely different** approach. Reasoning that none of these theories in itself constitutes a complete answer, they took another look at the available information, looking for common factors. One **intriguing** factor was that early angiosperms **always grew** in areas where there was no competition by gymnosperms and ferns. **Why would that be?** Now **it gets interesting**.

1 F   2 T   3 T   4 F

Skill builder 4

A

1 sarcastic   2 disappointed   3 surprised
4 impressed   5 authoritative

Practice for listening for speaker's attitude questions

A 1 B   2 A
B 3 B   4 B
C 5 C   6 A
D 7 A   8 D

Question type 6 Listening to understand organization p.130

Skill builder 1

A

Well, OK, let's just stop here for a second, because … well, this is really interesting. Remember I said that the Jikji document **was printed in 1377**? Well, **75 years later** and halfway across the world, the first movable type document in the western world was printed by a man named Gutenberg, in Germany. I mean, if you think about the span of human history, 75 years is a very short time, and **yet these two separate cultures** basically made **the same breakthrough** in communication within a very short period of time. There are, of course, **some significant differences** between Gutenberg's methods and the methods of the creators of Jikji. **Like, um**, the kind of metal they used. **For example**, the Korean type was made of copper **while** the German type was **made of lead**. And the uh … the kind of paper they used was **really different too**. Korean paper was made from the bark of mulberry trees and the German paper was **much heavier**. It was parchment … made of sheepskin. But you know, **the similarities** are really **much more fundamental**. I mean, I think you could really argue that the greatest advancement in communication **after** the invention of writing was the invention of movable type. And it happened in **two different places** at relatively **the same time**.

B

3 Recover files that are accessed by a password or are hidden.
1 Isolate all computer files.
5 Take steps to find files that were temporarily stored or lost.

4 Locate files that have been sent to the computer's trash.
2 Take precautions to ensure that files do not get damaged.

C

	WI	JFC
Born in 1789		✓
Born in New Jersey		✓
Named for a U.S. president	✓	
Was born and died in New York	✓	
The elder of the two authors	✓	

Practice for listening for organization questions

A
1 C
2

	A	G
are similar to modern pine trees		✓
were originally segregated but then spread into larger areas	✓	
are flowering plants	✓	
may have been spread by animals	✓	
were dominant more than 125 million years ago		✓

B
3 B
4
4 The DTI scan revealed connections between two areas of the brain.
5 Researchers found evidence of the physical basis of synesthesia.
1 Water molecules move through the brain along the coating of the axon.
3 The DTI generates an image of the brain's nerve pathways.
2 The molecules in the brain are tracked by the DTI scan.

Question type 7 Listening for inferences p.133

Skill builder 2

A
1 talking about
2 focus on
3 goes back
4 came up with
5 get into

Practice for listening for inferences questions
A 1 D 2 C
B 3 A 4 B
C 5 A and B 6 C and D
D 7 A 8 B

Question type 8 Listening to connect content p.136

Skill builder 1

A
✓ Read five of Shakespeare's plays.
✓ Write an opinion essay describing Shakespeare's worst play.
✓ Receive a change of grade after your paper has been submitted.

B
2 Spread clay over the shaped wax.
4 Pour hot molten metal into the mold.
6 Separate the metal from the clay and trim it.
1 Form the wax into the proper shape.
5 Let the metal cool.
3 Bake the formed clay.

Practice for listening to connect content questions

A 1 D

B 2

	JFC	WI	Both
wrote non-fiction books		✓	
wrote novels			✓
wrote a biography of a U.S. President		✓	
was popular in Europe			✓
wrote the *Last of the Mohicans*	✓		
had a story made into a film			✓

KEY AND EXPLANATION

C

3

2 Decide on an appropriate type of presentation program.

4 Make an outline of the presentation.

3 Schedule a tutorial to learn how to use the program.

5 Bring a laptop to the next appointment.

1 Identify if graphics, images, and sound effects are necessary.

D

4 B and C

5

a, d and e are true

Speaking p.139

Independent task 1 p.139

Skill builder 2

A Answers may vary. Adjectives could be: brave, realistic, independent, organized, active, interested, unafraid.

B Answers may vary. Verb phrases could be: takes risks, thinks about learning, experiments with the language, listens carefully,

C Answers may vary

1 I believe that a good language learner has to be **brave**.

2 I think that in order to be a good language learner, a person should be **independent**.

3 In my opinion, a good language learner is someone who is **unafraid**.

4 I think a good language learner **takes risks**.

5 It's my opinion that a good language learner **experiments with language**.

D

In my opinion, a good language learner has to be **brave**. I mean, someone who is not **afraid** of making mistakes in speaking or writing. **I think that** a good language learner **takes chances** with vocabulary and tries to make sure the listener understands them. **To me**, my friend Maria is a good language learner **because** she can **hear** the sounds of language and **repeat** them accurately. She is very good at **pronunciation** and **grammar**. She also **feels** comfortable in conversations with native speakers.

Practice for independent task 1

A Answers will vary. **Sample response**

I'd like to meet Leonardo da Vinci. I think he was one of the most brilliant minds to ever live. He was a genius, no doubt, but I think that his curiosity about the world and his ideas were really an inspiration. He was so innovative because he was fearless in his quest to gain knowledge about all subjects. He would probably be able to talk about all kinds of topics. And I wonder what he would think about computers and technology today. It probably would not surprise him. I like the fact that he thought about engineering and science, and he observed nature and biological processes. So if I could meet him, I'd talk to him about art and his work—but I would also ask him about what solutions he might have for problems we are facing today—with everything from energy and flying to art and health.

B Answers will vary. 2.64 **Sample response**

If I could go anywhere, I'd like to visit France, especially Paris. I've never been there but I've heard that it's really beautiful and I would like to see the Eiffel Tower and the Champs-Elysées, and all the architecture. Plus, it would be great to see the Louvre Museum … and all its great works of art. I'd like to see the Pyramid in front of the museum because it was designed by one of my favorite architects, I.M. Pei, and I would like to stand in it and take in the view. But I'd also go to many other places in France, like the countryside and the Mediterranean Sea. I've always dreamed of going there—I love the language, the films, the food, and the culture—so that would be one of my first choices.

Independent task 2 p.141

Skill builder 2

A Answers will vary. **Sample responses**

I would prefer to live in the city because I like the culture. I like the convenience of public transportation. I prefer the diversity of people.

I would prefer to live in the suburbs. I don't like the noise of a big city. I prefer the quiet and privacy of the suburbs. I like having a car and driving around.

Skill builder 3

A

I prefer to communicate with my friends in person … um, **here's why I think so**: I don't like to spend too much time on the Internet or computer … you know, playing games or just chatting with instant message. **However**, I think, uh, I use my cell phone a lot every day and I'm texting **way** too often. **But also, it** could be that **this is because** our society is now more technological. **You know**, it's easy to do. But **I think** it's more important to see family or friends face-to-face **because** when you're in person you can see someone's reaction and body language. So I **really** prefer to speak in person.

Practice for independent task 2

A Answers will vary. **1.75** **Sample response**

If I could choose between working part time or taking out a loan, I guess I would rather work part time. This is because the idea of having to pay loans back after graduating from college seems really like a lot of pressure. I don't know, um, maybe for some people, it's not a bad thing to have loans and just concentrate on studying. But for me, I would not want to worry about loans. In addition, it's probably good for a person's discipline even if it takes a little longer to graduate. I think it's better to have a job and take classes. You get more variety of life and responsibility that way. That's what I'd prefer.

B Answers will vary. **2.65** **Sample response**

When I'm stressed out, I really prefer to go running or ride my bike. The reason for this is that I'm usually sitting at a computer or something all day and I need to get exercise in order to feel better. It's really important to be active to just give your life balance. In addition, I think it's just good for your overall health, and maybe if a person exercises regularly— not strenuous, but just moderate exercise—then it keeps your stress level down. And for me, that's better to do. I would much rather do some exercise—maybe even play a match of tennis or go dancing—because it really does help release tension.

Integrated task 3 p.142

Skill builder 1

A

The Office of Academic and Research Programs of the World Cultural Institute is **pleased** to announce the Summer Internship Program. Students who **are interested** in the program may apply for full-time summer internships within one of the many divisions of the World Cultural Institute. Internships <u>are offered</u> to both undergraduate and graduate students and all positions <u>are paid</u>.

Please note that only current students of All-State University are eligible.

Applicants <u>are expected</u> to be in good academic standing with a grade point average of 3.5 or above. Applicants should submit a résumé that details their relevant work and educational experiences, along with a cover letter stating their interests and qualifications. If responding by e-mail, please specify the name of the internship in the subject line of the e-mail.

B and **C**

M Hey, **did you** <u>see</u> that the Institute <u>is offering</u> internships this summer?

W Yeah. I really <u>want to apply</u> but, **I'm not sure if** I'm qualified ...

M Why not? What do you <u>mean?</u>

W Well, uh, **I'm not sure** <u>how I did</u> in one of my history classes.

M Oh ... yeah, it <u>says they expect</u> you to be in good academic standing. I guess that means you <u>gotta get</u> good grades in all your classes ... but **how's your** grade point average?

W Well ... **I think** I have a 3.4 ... and this semester I sort of think I did OK, except for that one class. So I'm not sure I will get a 3.5 ... **Anyway**, these internships are pretty competitive.

M OK, but if <u>you have</u> a strong résumé and cover letter, **I don't think** they're <u>going to hold</u> one grade against you. **Maybe you should** send an e-mail and <u>ask</u> for more specific information about academic standing ... like what your average has to be or something like that.

W As **much as I'd like to** ... I'm not sure I should. I'll **have to think** it over.

D 1 T   2 T   3 F   4 T   5 T

Practice for integrated task 3

A Answers will vary. **1.76** **Sample response**

Well, the man is not very happy about the new rules. He thinks it's unfair that you can't watch television or use your cell phone in the common room. And so, he's going to go speak to his dorm mates about it first. Then, he's going to get a petition going to take to the resident director because some small group of students were complaining, and um, that wasn't his group. So he is going to try to get the resident director to pay attention to their idea. Even if this guy is strict about following rules, the student wants to get the petition signed. Maybe if he can show that enough people are against it, then the rule will be changed back.

B Answers will vary. **2.66** **Sample response**

Uh, the woman has a job on the other side of campus. So, she can't get to the dining hall during her scheduled time. The notice is pretty specific about who can eat at the dining hall because of all the construction work or renovations. And there could be too many people if the students don't follow the rules. And the guard said that they might not have enough food or enough space if they don't stick to the schedule. Then there is a problem because if he makes an exception for her, he might have to make an exception for the next student and that could cause a problem. The notice doesn't really give consideration to that ... and so the student isn't thinking about the cafeteria being overcrowded or running out of food.

KEY AND EXPLANATION

Integrated task 4 p.145

Skill builder 3

A Read the script for the sample response for Test 1, Speaking Task 4 on p.158.

Practice for integrated task 4

A Answers will vary. 1.77 **Sample response**
The professor said that there are signs that represent objects that we know. And it seems that humans need to put meaning on objects in order to really understand them. For example, we can see the icon of a woman or man on the door of a restroom and we know what it means. We could also see the difference between the artist's painting of a pipe and the real pipe as the sign representing the real object. I think that the professor made it clear that we interpret those things as signs but that they are just an image. And it was also interesting to think about how the ancient Egyptians used hieroglyphs to be representations of meaning. Like a bird or an eye, or something … I don't know what those things meant exactly, but they represented an object.

B Answers will vary. 2.67 **Sample response**
The professor thinks it's difficult to define American theater because for one thing, the historians don't really give credit to anyone for forming the theater. So even though this family, the Hallams, were the first ones to establish or build a theater in 1753 or something, no one really gave them credit. The professor thinks that you can't really call it American because the Hallams were English and were producing English plays—like Shakespeare plays … and other European plays. So this is what makes it difficult—because is the idea behind American theater the actual theater as a place, or is it the work that gets performed on the stage? This is interesting because in the final comments, uh, the comments that the professor makes, he says that the first American play was written by a man named Tyler and performed in New York City in 1787. So maybe that should be considered as the first American theater experience.

Integrated task 5 p.147

Practice for integrated task 5

A Answers will vary. 1.78 **Sample response**
OK, so the librarian suggests that the man does a Boolean search … and that means he has to enter keywords into the computer. Two words. And he isn't really sure what the main keyword is but he will have a better chance at finding a book if he uses this specific type of search. His other choice, she says, is to go up to the shelves and just look casually through all the book titles to see if anything has information on his topic. I think he should just do the Boolean search and find a few specific books. That way he saves time. If he goes and just browses in the stacks he might find something but it's not clear or for sure that he will. And he could just waste time there.

B Answers will vary. 2.68 **Sample response**
The woman's problem with her roommate is that they are on different schedules and it seems that the woman's roommate doesn't respect her schedule. So she's really tired from her job and taking classes. The man suggests that she talk to the resident advisor, because it seems like the woman talked to her roommate about the problem but that didn't really work. And the second thing the man suggests is that she go to the housing department and just fill out some forms and get a new roommate. I think that's the better idea because they could be really uncomfortable if the advisor talks to the roommate. And that could make the situation worse. The roommate might get upset that the woman spoke to the advisor. So it's probably better just to move out and get a new roommate.

Integrated task 6 p.148

Skill builder 2

A
There are <u>three roles</u> a <u>computer</u> can play in <u>computer crime</u>. It can be the <u>target</u> of the crime, the <u>instrument used</u> to <u>commit</u> the crime, or it can be a <u>source</u> of <u>evidence concerning</u> the crime. And of course it can have <u>multiple</u> roles. If someone uses a computer to <u>steal information</u> or <u>hack into</u> a system, and then they <u>store that information</u> on the same computer, computer <u>forensic experts</u> must <u>tailor their investigation</u> to the multiple <u>roles</u> of the <u>computer</u> in the crime. There are so many factors to <u>take into consideration</u>. You could <u>illegally recover</u> the data or <u>destroy</u> important <u>evidence.</u> Also, you could <u>waste</u> valuable <u>time</u> if you <u>dive</u> into the work without <u>carefully considering</u> the possible <u>multiple</u> roles of the computer in the crime.

Practice for integrated task 6

A Answers will vary. 1.79 **Sample response**
The synergist muscles are muscles like the bicep in the arm and the brachioradialis muscle. As the professor used as an example, those are the um, muscles that you use when you extend your arm out. Like when you drop a pencil and then you stretch your arm out to pick it up. Then you bend your arm. The muscle where the elbow connects to the biceps … they work together. The synergists work together to extend and flex … so I guess when you stretch out your leg then those muscles are also examples of synergist muscles, working together.

B Answers will vary. 2.69 **Sample response**
The Erie Canal was called an engineering marvel for a lot of reasons. First of all, the fact that they built it about 363 miles long across the state of New York in the early 1800s. That's a big challenge. And really,

they didn't have a lot of technology at that time—no tractors or anything. So they had to be innovative to get through all the rock and stones and clear out tree stumps. Like the professor said, they didn't have deep water—it was about 4 feet. So I think it was also an engineering marvel because it was a method of transportation for people and products and it opened up trade to the western part of the U.S. It was like a gateway for travel and commerce … so that made it a real marvel too. And it was Governor Clinton's idea that made the economy of the country really grow.

Writing p.150

Writing task 1 p.150

A Answers will vary. **Sample answer**

The lecture definitely casts some doubts on the text. First of all, the professor discusses the fact that the ozone hole is not exactly where we think it is or should be. The interesting thing too is that the hole is shaped like a column, not a hole—and the fact that scientists are working on patching or repairing it is not mentioned in the reading passage.

According to the professor, Dr. Susan Solomon, who is a Nobel-Prize-winning atmospheric chemist, has done a lot of work examining the ozone layers. And while it is true that there has been a great deal of ozone depletion in the upper layers, the lower layers (the troposphere), has probably suffered more from the depletion. Some of Dr. Solomon's theories have also shown that the CFCs which seem to have had the most effect on the ozone, might not be as vital to the problem as the gas emissions in the atmosphere closer to Earth. The professor also says that Dr. Solomon's studies have shown that there is much more ozone in the Antarctic than we expected to find. The reading mentions that human activity will probably have a more direct effect on depletion in the stratosphere—the higher level of the atmosphere, but the lecturer does not necessarily support this idea.

B Answers will vary. **Sample answer**

Hybrids are a very fascinating occurrence of nature. As the professor says, the examples of hybrid animals are not ones that we would expect to happen very often. However, there are many cases where the offspring of the hybrid has become a very well-known and important part of our society's transportation system—as in the situation of the mule, which is a hybrid of the donkey father and horse mother. The mule was very significant as a work animal. The opposite of that, though, which is the horse father and donkey mother, is much rarer and smaller—and this is known as the hinny. Similarly we can compare the "coy dog" which is the cross between the male coyote and female dog, to the mule in some ways—because these animals seem to be able to breed.

Another interesting fact that the lecturer mentions, is the unusual animal that results from the breeding of a lion and a tiger. If the lion is the father and the tiger is the mother, the offspring that results is called a liger. This animal looks more like its father—it is larger and has the mane of the lion around its head. And when the mother is the lion and the father is the tiger, this is the tigon, which has more stripes like the father. These offspring are not the mutations or "dead-ends" that science once determined them to be. Cross-breeding of these animals may occur— as it might happen in other big cats like jaguars, leopards, and panthers as well. We could end up with many variations and new breeds of animals.

Writing task 2 p.152

A Answers will vary. **Sample answer**

Medical advances are probably one of the most important changes in this century. Although the twentieth century definitely had great advances, I think that this century will probably make important discoveries and find cures to very serious illnesses. It's also true that space travel and the use of probes and satellites that go into space has increased, but I believe that scientists will make the decision to invest their funds in medicine more than space or technology. First of all, there are a lot of inventors who can work independently on technological discoveries. Many of these tech experts, like Bill Gates, have funded their studies and advances in technologies because the companies are independently or privately owned, and not owned by the government. The choice to make advances in medicine is not one that an individual can easily make: a research scientist in the field of health or medicine has to be approved by the government or one of its major organizations, like the Food and Drug Administration, etc.

The twenty-first century will definitely see advances in space travel, discoveries and technology, but the most important ones will come in medicine. I think that with the research done on diseases like cancer, and all the genetic studies that researchers are capable of doing now, with all their knowledge, they will probably find cures or create medications or drugs to slow down certain diseases. This could happen for things like Alzheimer's disease or perhaps multiple sclerosis. There is hope that medical researchers will find cures for these diseases and various types of cancer in the twenty-first century.

B Answers will vary. **Sample answer**

Although a lot of people might think that artists, actors, and musicians—or other performers—have made large contributions to society, I don't think they are as important as scientists. Unfortunately, though, it seems like performers get a lot more attention than scientists. Unless you win the Nobel Prize, most people might not know if you are a famous scientist—or if you cured a disease or something. But we should value the scientists more because they are making a contribution to saving lives and changing our society in a more important way.

In the case of sports or movies, it seems like we place a lot of value on these jobs because the athletes and actors make a lot of money. Most likely, scientists do not make quite as much (like a multi-million dollar sports contract). But this is not to say that performers and athletes are not really valuable—they are. Certainly it is a great contribution to society to entertain and make a film about a topic that gets people thinking, or changes their way of thinking, or inspires them. Even some of the commercial action films could make a contribution to society if they inspire the idea of "good" or "triumph over evil," or something like that. But in the grand scheme, science is still going to be more valuable to humanity because it keeps us healthy and alive—it supports our technological needs and the construction of our homes, or the content of our food. And even though film, music, sports, or other performances can keep our minds active, those other essentials are much more important. And only scientists can make those determinate contributions to our world and societies.

LISTENING SCRIPTS

TEST ONE

Listening

Conversation 1

M Hi. Can I help you?

W Hi … um, maybe, yeah. Professor McGee isn't in his office today and I missed the last class … so now I'm not sure what I should study for the test on Friday.

M Sure, I can help … Uh, have you looked at the course syllabus?

W Oh, no … Um, good idea. I always forget to refer to that.

M I have a copy of it right here. OK. The first statistics quiz is on chapters one *and* two.

W Both? Wow, that's a lot of information.

M Well, if you think about what you've covered, it actually makes sense, since the ideas in the chapters of the book are connected. First, chapter one is basically just an introduction to Business Statistics and chapter two is on Descriptive Statistics. That's got a lot more weight to it.

W So … are you saying we're going to be tested on the material in chapter two, but we should review chapter one as well?

M No, no … that's not what I mean. As far as I know, Professor McGee is going to test the class on *both* chapters, but not equally … in importance, I mean.

W OK, got it. So, um, maybe I should see how the information in chapter one is somehow connected, or … um, what I really need to know before I get into chapter two.

M Agreed … you're right on target. Then, you should focus your efforts on the most important points in chapter two.

W Like … ?

M Well, we know it's on descriptive statistics. And remember, the professor assigned the sections from the text about distributions and variations and …

W Oh yeah, I remember. And those strange things called *quartiles*.

M Right. You studied them when he went over percentiles.

W And he's probably going to test us on percentiles and distributions, and maybe weighted means.

M Definitely. Understanding the concept of weighted means is important. So I'd say you've got about 100 pages to cover for this test.

W Yeah, well, the syllabus calls it a quiz. Doesn't that mean it's gonna be short?

M Come on, you're taking statistics … what's the probability that this test is gonna be short?

W OK. OK. Don't make me laugh … . Uh, so is there a review class or a study group?

M Oh, actually, there is one this afternoon! I've met with a few other students who want to study for the test and we're having a study session today at 3.30. So, I think you should review the things you feel confident about and be prepared to present them to the group.

W Sounds like a good study plan. And I know exactly what I'm good at … percentiles.

M Great. I think you're all set. Make sure to read the case studies too. Then you can describe those as well and be prepared to explain how the case studies represent the statistical problem you're reviewing.

Conversation 2

M Ms. Lee? Hi, I'm James. Um, I have an appointment about getting into the paleontology class.

W Right. Hello James. Have a seat. I was just looking over your transcript.

M OK. Thanks.

W So, have you uh, already declared your major?

M Oh yeah, I did that last semester … I've got a double major in anthropology and archaeology with a minor in ancient languages.

W Really …? That's quite an undertaking. And … which ancient languages did you study? I'm just asking because undergraduate students need special permission to take those classes. Those are generally graduate courses.

M Yeah … uh, well, I spent a semester in Cairo, Egypt … I took an intensive class in Ancient Egyptian and another in archaeology when I was there.

W Oh, you did? Wait … I thought you were in your first year … sorry, am I missing something?

M Well, I'm a transfer student. This is my third year now.

W Oh … I'm sorry … I must not have seen that page of your transcript. OK, OK, so let me get this straight … You studied ancient languages, and then you took archaeology in Cairo for a semester?

M Yeah, that's right. All my credits transferred in … as far as I know … .

W Ah … Well, that's the problem. Mm … I don't see those credits on your transcript from the other university, yet. You know, there's an evaluation system here at the registrar's office. And it takes time to get the paperwork done if you're a new student.

M Oh OK. So … what do I do now? I really want to take this paleontology class in order to fulfill all my course requirements. Do you think I can get into that class?

W Well, you need special permission from the instructor since that's a class for seniors. But, you do realize that there are several prerequisites, right? Have you made an appointment with your advisor yet?

M Yeah, I already spoke to my undergraduate advisor about all of the prerequisites … I took the Archaeological Methods and Analyses course. I also got good grades in Geology and most of the other science prerequisites.

W Well, that's really something. I'll tell you what … I'll check to see how your credit evaluation is coming along … I mean, where it is in the process. OK? Then, come see me after 3 p.m. today and you can fill out the permission form to register for the class.

M Great … thanks. See you later.

LISTENING SCRIPTS

Lecture 1

So last week we were talking about bookmaking and the different types of paper. I want to focus now on printing—and by that I mean the production of multiple copies of an image on paper or some other medium. Now, China … China has a long tradition of woodblock printing that goes back to at least the 800s and well, a lot of these images included written words, or Chinese language characters. So, you could say that the Chinese are credited with being the first to actually print words on paper. But the way they did that was to carve words into a block of wood, spread ink over it and transfer that to paper. Now, you have to realize that carving words into wood is a slow process. And eventually, someone came up with the idea of carving individual characters into separate blocks of wood, so that of course they could move these around into any combination. This was the beginning of what is called movable type.

Movable type allowed the Chinese to reproduce larger amounts of text at a time. But there was a problem. Wood is rather soft. So these wooden characters didn't last very long. So … how did they solve that problem?

Well, the solution to the problem actually came from Korea. And that solution was the invention of *metal* movable type. We know this because of a document that was printed in 1377. It has a very long name, but it's also known as Jikji.

For a time, there was a question about what method was used to create this metal type. I'm talking about how the actual metal is molded into a shape. There were three different methods that were employed at the time. Um … I don't want to get into the specifics of that right now. But, after some experimentation and debate, scholars finally agreed that the shape of the mold was first created in beeswax—you know, the wax that comes from beehives. That's because when they tried to reproduce the style of the original Jikji document, they were only able to successfully recreate the style using the beeswax method.

Here's how they did it: they would form the wax into the proper shape, spread clay over that, and bake it. The wax melted and what was left behind was a baked clay mold. They then poured hot molten metal into the mold. After it cooled, they separated the metal from the clay and trimmed it.

Well, OK, let's just stop here for a second, because … well, this is really interesting. Remember I said that the Jikji document was printed in 1377? Well, 75 years later and halfway across the world, the first movable type document in the western world was printed by a man named Gutenberg, in Germany. I mean, if you think about the span of human history, 75 years is a very short time, and yet these two separate cultures basically made the same breakthrough in communication within a very short period of time. There are, of course, some significant differences between Gutenberg's methods and the methods of the creators of Jikji. Like, um, the kind of metal they used. For example, the Korean type was made of copper while the German type was made of lead. And the uh … the kind of paper they used was really different too. Korean paper was made from the bark of mulberry trees and the German paper was much heavier. It was parchment … made of sheepskin.

But you know, the similarities are really much more fundamental. I mean, I think you could really argue that the greatest advancement in communication after the invention of writing was the invention of movable type. And it happened in two different places at relatively the same time.

Lecture 2

M1 The rise of computer technology over the past decades has created a continually shifting landscape when it comes to the law. And computer crimes are on the rise. Back in 2003 the average bank robbery yielded $6900, but theft by computer averaged $900,000. I don't think we need to see the updated statistics, do we? So, law enforcement organizations like the Federal Bureau of Investigation need guidelines on how to investigate computer crimes, and the challenge for the legal system is to write new laws that retain the fundamental concepts for non-computer crimes. Yes?

W So how does that happen exactly? Can the government both collect data legally from people while at the same time protecting a person's privacy?

M1 Absolutely … and this is where the actual law comes into play. Take for example, the fourth amendment of the United States Constitution. This is the amendment that guards against illegal search and seizure. That means no one can just come into a home and seize someone's data. Most evidence on a computer consists of data. Well, this data is not in a concrete physical form like paper, it's … an abstraction. That's just one example of the type of problems the legal system faces when confronting computer crime.

The establishment of guidelines for *legal* search and seizure of computer evidence has led to the growth of the field of computer forensics. So, what is computer forensics? Well you might think it means getting back your data if your computer crashes—but, computer forensics is not *just* data recovery. It's more … it goes a step further than that. It's about recovering, collecting, and analyzing data for purposes of presenting it in court. And an awareness of computer forensics is not just important for law enforcement specialists. Any business with an awareness of legal methods for recovering data will be better able to protect itself if it is subject to a crime like data theft, because they will be able to present evidence that is admissible in court.

There are three roles a computer can play in computer crime. It can be the target of the crime, the instrument used to commit the crime, or it can be a source of evidence concerning the crime. And of course it can have multiple roles. If someone uses a computer to steal information or hack into a system, and then they store that information on the same computer, computer forensic experts must tailor their investigation to the multiple roles of the computer in the crime. There are so many factors to take into consideration. You could illegally recover the data or destroy important evidence. Also, you could waste valuable time if you dive into the work without carefully considering the possible multiple roles of the computer in the crime.

M2 So, how fast can forensic experts really recover data?

M1 Well, you see, this is where forensics differs from simple data recovery. In computer forensics *accuracy* always takes precedence over speed. Let me be clear: this field is primarily concerned with rules of evidence and legal processes. These are the factors that guide forensic procedures, not the need for speed.

OK … so now, let's turn to an outline of some of the basic steps that a forensics expert takes in identifying and retrieving evidence. First of all, you've got to *quarantine* that computer system. Do you know what I mean by quarantine?

W Isn't that what happens when doctors think someone has a contagious illness?

M1 Yes, good analogy, but in forensics it means letting nothing *into* the area, as opposed to something getting out. Here's an example: You know how police will tape off the area around a crime scene? OK, so that's what you're basically doing. You don't want any new factors to be introduced, like computer viruses or anything else that might change things.

The next step is to recover all the files—normal files, hidden files, password-protected files, etc. After that, recover deleted files. Any attempt to destroy files on a computer leaves behind vital clues.

Investigators are dealing with two basic kinds of data: persistent data and volatile data. Volatile data is data that is lost when the computer is turned off. The investigator must be familiar with all kinds of procedures and software that assist in recovering deleted or damaged files that were stored in the computer's temporary storage and lost when the computer was shut down.

The investigator must provide documentation of the entire computer system. This includes a listing and classification of all files, normal and recovered, and analysis of the system layout. Finally, the investigator must be prepared to testify in a court of law if called upon.

So, next time I really want to start focusing in detail on that first step: how to protect a computer that's being investigated.

Lecture 3

One of the greatest mysteries in biological science is why species of flowering plants began to rapidly dominate the earth around 100 million years ago. Charles Darwin himself, the originator of the theory of evolution, called the spread of flowering plants the "abominable mystery." One of Darwin's central ideas was that species emerge gradually. But relative to other species, they took over extremely rapidly, and globally, over the course of just 30 million years or so.

Flowering plants are known as angiosperms. Angiosperms first appear in the fossil record about 125 million years ago. At that time, the dominant plants were ferns and gymnosperms.

Gymnosperms are non-flowering plants and trees like modern pine trees. Angiosperms were segregated into small areas. Then, around 100,000 years ago, angiosperms began to take over larger areas, starting in the middle latitudes and spreading toward the poles over time.

Well, there have been quite a few theories about why this happened. A lot of the theories have to do with evolutionary improvements in angiosperms, like the ability to pollinate and create seeds that could be dispersed in many ways by animals. Another theory has to do with the population shift from large to small dinosaurs that ate young gymnosperm trees and seeds. It's a nice idea, but there's really nothing in the fossil record that supports that.

Another approach to the puzzle has been to look at the probable environments that the first successful species of angiosperms thrived in. There are a lot of hypotheses about this, like the idea that the first angiosperms grew in wet marsh environments, or conversely in extremely dry environments.

Recently, two researchers took an entirely different approach. Reasoning that none of these theories in itself constitutes a complete answer, they took another look at the available information, looking for common factors. One intriguing factor was that early angiosperms always grew in areas where there was no competition by gymnosperms and ferns. Why would that be? Now it gets interesting.

Gymnosperms, you might say, are built to last. They live longer, grow slower and their leaves are thicker and store nutrients within them. Angiosperms require more nutrition from the soil than gymnosperms. They also grow much faster. Now here's the key: they tend to shed their leaves onto the ground in much higher quantities. And what is it that puts more nutrients into the soil? Leaves. Decomposing leaves deposit nutrients like nitrogen into the soil. So in a sense, angiosperms create their own food by shedding leaves.

On the other hand, gymnosperms and ferns shed their leaves at a much slower rate. And their leaves don't decompose the same way—they really keep the soil low in nutrients. And so it's very difficult for angiosperms to compete in the same area as gymnosperms. There aren't enough nutrients in the soil to give them a foothold.

So, it wasn't just that the early angiosperms grew where there were no gymnosperms. They also grew where the soil was disturbed. Suppose there's a hurricane or tornado … It destroys the existing plant population, leaving behind bare ground. OK, we've got fast-growing angiosperms or slow-growing gymnosperms. What kind of plant is going to take over first after a catastrophe? Do I need to answer?

Once those angiosperms take over fresh ground, they start growing and shedding their leaves. Now the leaves start to decompose, creating nutrients in the soil, causing the plants to grow more in the rich soil. Which causes them to shed more leaves … Do you see what's happening? It's called positive feedback. It leads to explosive growth. Now in areas where gymnosperms dominate, a minor catastrophe can start the process. Say there's some kind of, I don't know, stampede by dinosaurs. And the ferns growing under the cover of tall pine trees are wiped out. Fast-growing angiosperms take over and start altering the soil, filling up every available niche. Slow-growing gymnosperm seeds can't keep up. At some point, the angiosperms take over completely.

Ok, so we've explained potential for rapid expansion of angiosperms. We still don't know what it was that first triggered the expansion. In order for positive feedback to really kick in, there had to be a threshold of abundance of angiosperms. There are many factors that could have contributed.

But the foundation of the expansion, according to the researchers, is the changes in the soil nutrition brought about by flower-bearing plants themselves. Once that process was set in motion, it just accelerated, and other factors started to work in favor of the rise of angiosperms.

Lecture 4

M1 OK, recently we've been discussing how to distinguish works of American literature from British literature. In this unit, we'll read the works of James Fenimore Cooper—who wrote *The Last of the Mohicans*—and Washington Irving, who was probably the first one to be regarded as a man of letters by Europeans. Question?

W Yeah, I've been wondering when American literature actually began? I mean, if you were born in the U.S. or Canada, that makes you a North American. So, Cooper and Irving were born here, and that makes them American authors, right? But what about if you weren't born in the United States but you became a citizen after the U.S. declared its independence from England—so then, wouldn't you be considered an *American* writer?

M1 That's an excellent point. OK, let's hold on a minute and talk about that … specifically, about writers in the United States … . Any thoughts?

LISTENING SCRIPTS

M2 Well, I think that if a writer identified with America—whether he or she had been born in the U.S. or not, but became a citizen—and the style of writing and language the writer used was different from British writing then the writer would be considered an American author.

M1 It would appear that way, wouldn't it? Wouldn't we call the writers of the U.S. Constitution like Ben Franklin or Thomas Jefferson, American writers? Clearly, we can take the argument that they identified with being "American" as opposed to "British" … Can you think of any writers earlier than that?

M2 Uh, but wait a minute. So, when would we say American English really developed—I mean, the way of spelling and some of the vocabulary differences used in the U.S.? For example, I think that Captain John Smith who wrote a book about settling the colony of Virginia in 1608—that's almost two hundred years before the guys we're talking about—well, wouldn't he be considered the first American writer? But his writing style was more like British English … I saw one of his original texts in the library and it was, you know, a more archaic style of writing.

M1 I would agree with that statement, but then, we'd have to discuss the whole idea about letters and script—the orthography that is—as well as the origins of words in American English. So, let's say that we're not just talking about novelists or poets here—we can include essayists, scholars, and other types of writers when we talk about American literature. Everyone follow? OK, good, then let's get back to today's main topic.

So, let's look at our featured authors—again, we're going to read James Fenimore Cooper and Washington Irving and compare their works and how they are similar and different from British writers.

We can call these two writers "contemporaries," since they were born around the same time—right after the American Revolution—and both were children during the presidency of George Washington. Cooper was born in New Jersey in 1789—the year that George Washington became president—and died in Cooperstown, New York in 1851. Irving—who, as I am sure you've guessed was named after George Washington—was born in New York City in 1783, and died in Sunnyside, New York, in 1859.

Washington Irving wrote many works of fiction—short stories like, *The Legend of Sleepy Hollow*, *Rip Van Winkle*—as well as non-fiction, scholarly works. He wrote a biography of George Washington for example, as well as a history of Spain.

James Fenimore Cooper was better known as a novelist. However, both writers gained acclaim in Europe and were admired by British counterparts—like Charles Dickens, for example. Irving and Cooper paved the way for other American writers.

You may all be more familiar with movie versions of Irving's *Sleepy Hollow*, or Cooper's *Last of the Mohicans* than the literary works themselves. So you'll have the opportunity this week to begin reading Irving's short stories. We'll start off with the *Legend of Sleepy Hollow*. Remember, I'm going to put the notes from today's lecture and your writing assignment on the class website so you can refer to those documents. We'll also look closely at the language used by Washington Irving, and then by Cooper, and get back to the idea of how they represent American writers.

Speaking

Task 3

M Hey, did you see that the Institute is offering internships this summer?

W Yeah. I really want to apply but, I'm not sure if I'm qualified …

M Why not? What do you mean?

W Well, uh, I'm not sure how I did in one of my history classes.

M Oh … yeah, it says they expect you to be in good academic standing. I guess that means you gotta get good grades in all your classes … so, how's your grade point average?

W Well … I think I have a 3.4 … and this semester I sort of think I did OK, except for that one class. So I'm not sure I will get a 3.5 … Anyway, these internships are pretty competitive.

M OK, but if you have a strong résumé and cover letter, I don't think they're going to hold one grade against you. Maybe you should send an e-mail and ask for more specific information about academic standing … like what your grade has to be or something like that.

W As much as I'd like to, I'm not sure I should. I'll have to think it over.

Task 4

Now, there's a lot of controversy about the hole in the ozone. Some of the most prominent scientists in the world don't actually agree about what caused it or how to fix the hole in the ozone … But, we do agree that the ozone hole isn't exactly a *hole*. What I mean is, it's kind of shaped like a column. It's over the continent of Antarctica and even though there is a great deal of depletion to the ozone, meteorological studies have found that there is still a significant amount of ozone there—even during times of extreme depletion. One scientist—named Susan Solomon—uh, she's the Nobel Prize-winning atmospheric chemist by the way, has already conducted studies on ozone depletion. In her study she is re-evaluating what causes ozone depletion and how perhaps, the hole can be repaired.

Dr. Solomon examined the ozone depletion in the atmosphere and discovered that it was occurring in the lower layers—closer to the Earth—rather than in the upper ozone layer where it was previously thought to occur. She also realized that the CFC molecules in the ozone layer were reacting with the temperatures of the clouds at the Antarctic pole. Some of her colleagues have had a difficult time accepting her theories—but she actually confirmed her studies during a scientific expedition to Antarctica.

Task 5

M Hi. I have a paper due in a few weeks and I can't seem to find the books and resources that I need.

W Sure. I can help. Have you been using the library's computer catalogue research system?

M Yes, I'm looking for information on animals in films, but for some reason nothing turns up on the subject that I want. I mean, I keep getting documentary films about animals—real animals—and that's not what I want.

W What are you typing in?

M Well, I want to find something on the way that animals behave like humans, or have human-like characteristics in movies and in cartoons. And, uh, focus on live action films.

W Oh, you mean 'anthropomorphism'?

M Ah, yeah, that's it! I knew there was a word for it, but I couldn't come up with it.

W OK. First then, you have to type in the word … next, you will get a list of subjects but then some sub-headings. See?

M Oh wow, but now I have so many results. How do I limit my search?

W You can do two things to limit your search. First, you can do a Boolean search which means you can enter the topic AND another keyword, in this case, anthropomorphism AND film. This will give you specific titles to look for. Or, you can also go to the stacks where the books are located and casually browse for related titles. That way you can skim through the books and see what might be related to your topic. They will all be located in the same area.

M That's great. So how many books on the topic are actually in this library?

W Well, you can see now we get a list of books that were published in the last ten years on that topic. It seems only one of the books related to your topic is in our library.

M Oh, but there is one in a different library that sounds like it's really on my topic. My paper is due in three weeks … as I said. So how can I get that book?

W Well, you can do one of two things: You can go to the other library. It's a consortium library, which means we have a borrowing partnership with them. It takes time to get there, but you can take out the book and have it right away. Or, you can request an interlibrary loan, which will take up to two weeks to process and arrive.

Task 6

Now, we already know that skeletal muscles are connected to bone by tendons—these are special cords that are made of rather tough tissues that attach to bone and help you move the bone and muscle at the same time. Muscles can act in two ways: When the contraction of two muscles acts to support each other, these two muscles are called "synergists." When two muscles work in opposition to each other, they are called "antagonists."

Say you drop your pencil on the floor. What happens when you put your arm down to pick it up? You extend your arm and reach, then, you bend your arm at the elbow to put the pencil back on the desk. There are two muscles that help you flex and extend your muscle at your elbow—the biceps and the brachioradialis muscles. They contract in the same direction at the elbow when it bends. So, that is an example of two muscles that are synergists.

What about an example of muscles that might be considered antagonists? Antagonist muscles also work in pairs at a joint. These are muscles, which—remember—work in opposition to each other. The biceps and triceps muscles are examples of an antagonist pair. When you extend your arm out in front of you, the triceps—the muscle—that's the one right below your shoulder—contracts, and the biceps muscle, which is on your inner arm between your shoulder and your elbow, relaxes. The triceps relax when the biceps contract.

OK. So, let's go back for a minute … Remember, we just said that the synergist muscles act in support of each other. Now, in greater detail, let's make a muscle with our arm again. The brachioradialis muscle at the elbow joint is a synergist to the triceps muscle and an antagonist of the biceps muscle. That's how they work.

Writing

Task 1

So, we've talked a bit about Charles Sanders Peirce's ideas of semiotics—the study of signs. And now we must take that into account when we take a look at this example—the surrealist Belgian painter Rene Magritte's rendering of a tobacco pipe … and beneath this pipe, the phrase: "This is not a pipe." Is this an illustration of what Peirce was talking about when he tried to explain signs and their interpretants? Who would say that this is a pipe … ? No, of course it's not really a pipe, because it is an image of a pipe, not the physical pipe itself. I can take this a step further because I'm actually showing you a photograph of Magritte's painting—which is hanging in a museum. So, you can see how complex this theory becomes, right? This is the paradox—one thing represents another thing, and so on. Magritte, the painter—unlike Peirce, the philosopher—was not actually trying to write a new book on semiotics. Magritte was, as he said, exploring how words and images differ in the ways that they signify things.

So what then, again, is a sign? Some philosophers believe the sign is the basic unit of meaning. We might say that signs can be iconic if we talk about ancient Egyptian hieroglyphic writing—an icon represented an object. When we put up restroom signs we use the figure of man or woman on the door—is this a sign or an icon? The icon represents something we easily recognize. An index, on the other hand, could be the sign you see on the highway that represents a slippery road.

In any case—this is what we do as humans—we use signs to understand and help us make meaning of the world around us.

TEST TWO

Listening

Conversation 1

M So I really appreciate your talking with me about this.

W Well, I was concerned. Generally I think students should get a grade based on your overall work—but I could see that you didn't do as well on the last test … and you had done very well on the first two exams.

M I know. I was right in the middle of moving out of my dorm at the end of the semester and that was my last exam. Normally, I wouldn't ask to take an incomplete, but I just didn't feel that a lower grade really represented my work.

W I agree. But, again, I don't usually like to do change-of-grade forms.

M OK. I understand

W So … well, I was thinking. Perhaps if you want to do an extra credit project … Let's say, something that will help you pull your grade back up to an A minus?

LISTENING SCRIPTS

M I can do that. Look … it's so important that I maintain very good grades. My financial aid package requires that I do …

W I can understand that.

M So what should I do?

W OK, here's the deal: You write a five-page paper on Shakespeare's worst play — and I mean, you have to have read all of them to decide what his worst play was. And tell me why you think so.

M Uh, wow … that's …

W You want to get that change of grade, right?

M Right, yeah. Of course.

W Fine, so you'll have two weeks to write this paper — shouldn't take you too long if you have done your reading.

M Oh, I have. I've read all the plays. And I think I know which one I'm going to choose.

W Fine. Don't tell me … surprise me.

M I will. So, what happens if I do a good job on the paper?

W Then I will fill out the forms for a change of grade. It takes a few weeks after that, but the new grade should go on your transcript afterwards.

M OK … I guess I will have to go to the library over semester break … thanks for your understanding.

Conversation 2

W Hi. I really need your help. I've got to prepare for a presentation and I haven't got a clue about how to do a visual slide show …

M Well, that's why we're here. We have tutors who know all the word-processing and presentation programs. Uh, do you know what presentation viewer program you want to use?

W I have no idea. Which is best?

M That depends on what you want to do. Is your presentation just text or do you want to use visuals with all the bells and whistles?

W Um, you mean like images and graphics, and things that move around on the screen?

M Exactly. You can include sounds or video too …

W Yes, absolutely … the better it looks, the better I hope my grade will be.

M Oh I think it is important that a presentation looks good — but you have to have the substance too.

W I guess so … uh …

M You know what I mean … if you have a good foundation for your presentation, you'll be fine.

W Oh, right.

M Anyway, I would advise you to use this presentation viewer program because it's pretty intuitive — you can figure it out as you go along.

W I've never really tried it.

M After your tutorial, I think you'll find it is pretty simple. Speaking of which, uh, when do you want to schedule your tutoring session?

W As soon as possible! My presentation is next week and I'm nervous about speaking in front of other people anyway. It would be bad if I had no time to practice using the program.

M That's true. So … then, how about tomorrow at 2 p.m.? Bring your outline.

W Great. I'll do that. Can I bring my laptop with me?

M Sure … see you then.

Lecture 1

W1 Last week we were talking about consumers' changing attitudes toward traditional modes of advertising. To remain effective, advertisers have to employ a variety of methods. One of those methods is *product placement*. Can anyone think of an example of product placement?

M Uh, like when a morning TV talk show host is drinking a cup of coffee from a famous coffee shop and you see that on camera?

W1 That's right. Product placement is the practice of including branded products in mass-media broadcasts, whether by mentioning the product by name or showing the product or brand logo visually. So, if a character in a movie or in a TV show drinks from a can that shows the brand name, that's product placement. It's been a key strategy over the last ten years, especially in film and television. But until recently, no one has really answered the key questions: Is product placement effective? And if so, how much?

One way of defining effectiveness in this context is to look at how the company's stock price changes. If you can demonstrate that a specific product placement campaign caused the stock price to go up significantly, then you can say it was worth doing. And recently, a pair of marketing researchers devised a study to address the fundamental question of the value of product placement.

The method they chose is pretty commonly used. It's called an event study. Basically, that just means that they analyzed an event from the past for which they have a lot of data, and they have the benefit of hindsight. Because time has gone by, they can isolate the event in time to look at long-term effects. In this case, the event they chose to examine was the placement of products in the most successful films of 2002.

If you just look at the stock price after a movie's release, you can't just say, oh, they placed Crunchy brand potato chips in a scene and the Crunchy brand stock price went up, so it was worth it. You have to look at the context of the market at the time. What was the expected stock price of the product's company when the movie was released to the public? What the researchers are looking for is something called abnormal return.

Abnormal return refers to the deviation of the actual stock price from what can be projected from the general stock market movement at the time. Those projections are based on a lot of factors and they've been shown to be extremely reliable. The researchers are confident that any abnormal returns, up or down, can be attributed to product placement.

So, in 2002 there were 31 movies that made 20 million dollars in the U.S. over their first weekend. Twenty-four of them had product placement and those are the ones they studied.

W2 So what factors in the placement situation affected the stock prices?

W1 Good question. Well, one hypothesis the researchers had was that the mere fact of product placement would have positive effect, and overall, it did. In this case they looked at the change in price between two days before the film and the actual premiere of the film. Investors get prior notice about a placement through a number of sources. And that generates investor interest, which translates into a positive abnormal return.

There are a couple of other factors that didn't surprise the researchers. Let's say a film comes out and the critics just love it. And a top company has placed a product in the film, and the ad execs read the great reviews—how do you think they feel?

M They're probably excited about it.

W1 No—surprisingly, the opposite happens. They're miserable. Because good reviews create a negative abnormal return. It seems people don't like to see product placement in a high art context. They want critically acclaimed films to be protected from advertising tactics …

M OK … But what if audiences love the film? Aren't viewers more apt to buy the products if they see actors using them?

W1 Well, you see, when audiences love the film, they become very engaged in the plot. They're transported into another world. That's great for the filmmakers but *not* for product placement. Truth is, audiences don't notice the product! They're too absorbed in the plot—it's the "audience absorption" factor. Yes?

W2 Uh, how did researchers measure the audience absorption factor?

W1 Well, they looked at records of audience surveys from the opening night for each film. Audience surveys include a rating for how "enjoyable" a film was. And according to past studies, enjoyability is a good indicator of how absorbed the audiences were in the film.

But on average, the researchers found that product placement generates positive returns. There are a lot of other factors that can create a beneficial product placement that I haven't mentioned. But the value of this study is that it sheds some light on the product placement scenarios that generate the best payoff.

Lecture 2

With unemployment rampant in the economic depression of the 1930s, the government established a program to put people to work. It was called the Works Progress Administration, or WPA. The WPA funded the construction and maintenance of schools, parks and highways. A small subdivision of the WPA, uh the Federal Arts Project, or FAP, was dedicated to employing artists.

The reasoning behind the FAP was that the arts, as much as schools and bridges, contributed to the public welfare. And of course artists at the time of the Depression were extremely vulnerable.

Photographers were uniquely suited to the requirements of the FAP, not least because much of their work constituted documenting the achievements of the WPA. But documentation in the larger sense of capturing the reality of an entire country was the mission of many of the FAP photographers. One of the photographers funded by the FAP beginning in 1935 was Berenice Abbott.

It was perfect timing for Berenice Abbott—she'd been photographing New York City since her return from Paris in 1929. Long before the FAP came into being, her stated purpose was to document and interpret America with love, but without sentimentality. And she felt that New York represented the essence of the changing nature of American society.

I want to just go back to that word, sentimentality. Because it relates to how we can define Abbott's approach to her art. As we talked about last week, photography in its initial stages had been used in a very painterly fashion. People like Abbott realized early on that photography's strengths had not been recognized or utilized. Abbott and her contemporaries rebelled against the widespread painterly use of soft focus in favor of the sharpness and clarity naturally inherent in photography. And they also rejected the sentimentality of typical pastoral scenes and landscapes in favor of a realistic depiction of fast-paced, modern urban life. It was this sensibility that she brought with her to New York from Paris, where she had been living for eight years.

Abbott's project was, simply put, to photograph New York City. She called her project "Changing New York." And the way she approached this project was to try to depict, through photography, the, uh, interaction between human beings and solid architectural constructs. Or something like that … I don't have the exact quote. See, she was trying to find a balance between buildings and activity. So she decided to use more than just a hand-held camera … which was perfect for, you know, capturing the hustle and bustle of the city, but would not have done justice to the giant buildings that also define the city. At the same time, she didn't want to just overshadow everything with those buildings.

So she began to use a large format camera. One of those rather bulky cameras you have to put on a tripod and then you have to view the image under a black hood … difficult to carry around, but it widened her vision. It allowed her to capture the size of massive modern buildings and also to juxtapose them in a shot with older, humbler ones. And to keep the life in her shots she would often wait until someone passed by and make sure they were in the frame. Or she would ask people to walk through or stand in the frame. So, she ended up using the large view camera for most of the work.

Well, this "Changing New York" collection of 305 photographs is really a remarkable achievement. Its images are so powerful that Abbott is considered by many to be one of the twentieth century's greatest photographers. In fact, one more contemporary photographer—Douglas Levere—was so inspired by her work that in the 1990s he decided to *re*-photograph Abbott's New York photos. Imagine this: Levere went to the same locations, on the same day and same time with the identical camera that Abbott had used. He reframed Abbott's shots as exactly as possible. Why would someone do that? I have to admit; when I first heard about this I was skeptical of one artist copying another so completely. But then I saw the photographs. And the amazing thing about them is that if you put them side by side with Abbott's, you see that they are a logical extension of her work. They take you even deeper into the contrast between the old and the new that Abbott so expertly revealed in the 1930s.

Lecture 3

The twentieth-century composer Olivier Messiaen wrote his musical compositions with accompanying color descriptions. Sounds interesting, right? Well, for Messiaen, musical sounds were associated with different colors. Now, Messiaen didn't just decide to assign colors to sounds. I'm talking about perception. He actually saw colors when he heard or imagined music. This involuntary association of one sense with another is a phenomenon called *synesthesia*.

LISTENING SCRIPTS

In Olivier Messiaen's case, synesthesia involved a combination of the senses of hearing and sight. But synesthesia can take many forms and involve any of the five senses. For some people, their synesthesia takes the form of an association between words or letters and colors. That's called grapheme-color synesthesia.

For someone with grapheme-color synesthesia, the letter 'A' might always appear tinged with red, or the number 5 might be light blue. Grapheme-color synesthesia is the most common form of synesthesia and it's also the form that has been studied the most. Brain scientists have been wondering about whether there's a physiological basis for synesthesia for over a hundred years.

One theory about the cause of synesthesia has to do with the neural connections between different parts of the brain. As we talked about last week, different parts of the brain are active when the brain is performing different tasks. Could it be that certain areas of the brain are more connected in people with synesthesia? In the case of grapheme-color synesthesia, this would mean that the area of the brain concerned with color perception would be more highly connected to the area concerned with graphic shapes. And it just so happens that these areas are right next to each other. And it's those two areas that some researchers focused on in a recent study of grapheme-color synesthesia.

What they did was ... well, let's back up. I want to be clear on what is meant by connectivity. The actual physical connections between nerves are tiny filaments. They're like ultra-thin wires. They're called axons. Well each of these axons is surrounded by a covering, a sheath of fatty tissue, much like an electrical wire is coated with plastic. And, the more axons, the more connectivity.

So let's get back to the recent study. The researchers studied 36 subjects. Half of them were synesthetes—that's what they call people who have synesthesia—and the other half were not. And they used a couple of different brain imaging techniques to see what kind of differences they could find between the two groups. We have various means for detecting activity in different regions of the brain. We can detect blood flow and electrical activity and convert this information into images. But these techniques can't actually detect these axons in the brain. In order to really detect connectivity, these researchers used a special technique called diffusion tensor imaging.

Let's call it DTI. DTI is able to track the movement of water molecules in the brain. It has to do with that sheath of fatty tissue I mentioned, the one that surrounds the axon, and how it interacts with water. As water molecules move through the brain, they tend to move along the coating of the axon, instead of penetrating toward the center of it. And so by tracking the movements of water molecules, DTI scanning can generate an image of the nerve pathways kind of like ... if you took a picture of a landscape from above at night, the lights from the cars would tell you where the highways are. Well, the images generated by DTI scanning revealed significantly more connections between the two areas for the synesthestes than for the non-synesthetes. So that's the first solid evidence we have for a physical basis for the phenomenon of synesthesia. The implications of this result may go beyond grapheme-color synesthesia. And I think they may go beyond synesthesia itself. Think about it. We're talking about perception and experience and the differences in the brain between people who have identifiably different experiences of the world. And that means that connectivity might explain a lot more about our individual differences than just synesthesia.

But let's not get ahead of ourselves. There's certainly a lot more to learn about synesthesia in relation to neural connectivity before we can comfortably generalize that far.

Lecture 4

M1 Has anyone ever seen this? There's some famous film footage shot on the moon from 1971. There's an American astronaut, Commander David R Scott, standing on the moon holding a feather in one hand and a hammer in the other. And then, he releases the hammer and the feather, and watches how they fall to the ground. Now, why did he do that?

W He wanted to see which one would hit the ground first.

M1 Well you could say that, and you wouldn't be wrong, but I think he already knew that they would both reach the ground at the same time. And you know what he said? He said, "How about that? Galileo was correct in his findings."

M2 Oh! Isn't that like what Galileo did, at the Leaning Tower of Pisa in Italy? He went up to the top of the tower and dropped two different-sized cannonballs to see if they would land at the same time ... to, um ... test the nature of gravity and bodies in motion.

M1 Well, yeah, that's the popular story about Galileo. It's funny, though. This story is probably not true. We owe this story to his biographer. He talks about how Galileo climbed the Leaning Tower of Pisa and "in the presence of other teachers and philosophers and all the students," showed through repeated experiments that the velocity, the speed, of moving bodies of different weights did not vary. But that story has really stayed around as a myth. I mean you can sort of picture all these scholars standing around with their mouths open in disbelief and there's Galileo up in the tower with a triumphant smile on his face. It makes a nice image because it represents such a powerful and sudden break with the prevailing beliefs of the time.

W You mean like Aristotle's theories about gravity?

M1 Yes, exactly. I mean, here you had an ancient Greek philosopher whose ideas about bodies in motion had been around for over 1700 years ... But let's come back to that in a minute. Because I want to also mention that Galileo was not really the first person to conceive of this experiment. As far back as the sixth century, other scholars had challenged Aristotle's ideas. And what were Aristotle's ideas?

M2 Um ... he believed that an object should fall at a uniform speed to be determined by its weight: so a heavy rock would fall faster than a lighter rock. Something that weighs 50 pounds should fall faster than something that weighs 20 pounds.

M1 And you know Aristotle wasn't entirely wrong, was he?

W Um ...

M1 Think about air.

W Oh, right ... of course. If you take the resistance from the air into account, well, yeah he's right—a heavier object would fall faster.

M And that's another reason why people have always been fascinated with this experiment. Because unless you can do the experiment in a vacuum—and by that I mean take the air out of it—you can't really test the theory completely.

Now this is interesting. Because after Galileo, scientists tried doing the experiment using hand pumps to take air out of a glass chamber and drop things inside of it; there was a famous experiment performed for the King of England where they dropped a coin and a feather in one of those chambers. And, Sir Isaac Newton was able to prove Galileo's theories mathematically, which is now called Newton's Universal Law of Gravitation.

And many physics students see this same demonstration even today. So in 1971, because the moon has no atmosphere, Commander Scott was able to do the experiment in a true vacuum. He saw clearly that Galileo had been right.

M2 But what he did doesn't seem very scientific. I mean, were there any measurements … ? I think that if you just drop something by hand, there is no way to make sure that the two objects release at the exact same time.

M1 Well, that goes back to what I was saying earlier. In a way, you could say that he was paying tribute to Galileo, not really doing a strict experiment. And you're right—there was room for error because he released them at the same time by hand. But think about it: there's no way humans would have gotten to the moon if they'd still believed *Aristotle* was right! So, although Commander Scott didn't really perform the experiment accurately, we can use this as an example of the far-reaching effects of Galileo's laws of falling bodies, and his legend.

Speaking

Task 3

M Did you see that new policy at the bookstore … ? You can actually rent a book. That's gonna save me a lot of money next semester.

W Huh … well, I have to say … it seems a bit strange to me. Half off the price? So … that means it's a used book, right?

M I don't know … probably. Interesting idea. I suppose it could work.

W Well, I don't know about you, but I don't like the idea of using someone else's book—I mean, they might have marked it up already. And if I want to write in my textbook, then well, I might have a different system of making notes.

M Oh, I see your point. But, it doesn't say that the books are used.

W They must be used. Why would the bookstore risk people writing in them? And if they are going to give out that many new texts for rental, then why don't they just get class sets, or something? Well, don't we borrow books from the library for free? So why should we rent them?

M Well, you pay a lot less than buying the textbook at its usual price.

W True, but like I said, if I can't write in it myself, it's not something I'm interested in.

Task 4

So, let's get back to the idea of hybrids. Hybrids can happen with many animal species. The most common one we know is the *mule*—a cross between a donkey father and a horse mother, whereas the reverse is called a *hinny*. So the hinny has a horse father and a donkey mother. Both animals are sterile—meaning they don't reproduce, but there have been many cases where the animals were in fact, able to breed. This kind of diversity was important in a way, because mules were a new kind of work animal for farmers and for transportation purposes.

Another unusual-looking hybrid occurs between lions and tigers. The appearance of these hybrid animals is striking. When the parents are a lion father and a tiger mother, the resulting cat is called a *liger*. Like the example of the mule compared to the hinny—the liger is also much larger than the *tigon*, which is what we call the offspring of a tiger father and a lion mother. Ligers seem to have the features of their fathers—they are lion-like in coloring. The tigon usually has more stripes, similar to its tiger father.

These hybrid animals have long held fascination for biologists. Some perhaps first perceived them as mutations. However, this was not true … These hybrids are not only limited to lion and tiger cross breeding. In fact, it is possible for jaguars and tigers to mix, as well as leopards with panthers. The hybridization of these big cats can also result in subspecies if the offspring are able to breed.

Task 5

M Hey, Amy, you doing OK?

W Not really … I'm exhausted from trying to juggle my work schedule and my studies. Plus, my roommate is really noisy and, she's on a completely different schedule than I am, so I never sleep!

M That's not good … what are you trying to do to fix it?

W I have no idea what to do. I tried talking to her about it but you know, she's not really open to suggestions about her behavior.

M Really? Have you thought of getting someone else to talk to her?

W I'm not sure that would solve anything now … she'd think I was interfering.

M Well I have a couple of ideas … OK. First … you could talk to your resident advisor, because it's part of the advisor's duties to make sure dorm residents maintain respect and you know, get along. Or, you could go to the housing office and make a request for a new roommate.

W Yeah, I thought about that. But that's a lot of paperwork.

M Or, I have an even better idea. I know some girls who live on the third floor of my dorm … and they have the same problem as you do. They're planning on moving off campus and renting a house together. As far as I know, everyone gets their own room and you'll only share a kitchen and common areas … The only thing is that it's more expensive than the dorm and you'd have to cook for yourself too.

W That's a lot to think about. I don't mind cooking … but … I don't know if I can afford a more expensive place.

M If you want me to, I can give you Jenny's cell phone number. She's the one who found the house.

Task 6

We can thank Governor Dewitt Clinton—who proposed the idea for the Erie Canal in 1808 to the members of the New York state legislature—for the fact that we have this waterway connecting the Atlantic Ocean to the Great Lakes. Uh, at first, the senate was not interested in building a canal across New York State. In fact, they often called it "Clinton's Ditch." And they laughed him right off the senate floor. However, this ditch would connect the Hudson River to Lake Ontario and enable both cargo and passengers to move more easily. The canal would become the "gateway to the west," and open up the trade routes from Chicago to the western part of the United States.

Now, Governor Dewitt Clinton was really tenacious—I mean, he held on to his belief and really fought for this idea. And guess what? In 1817, builders finally began construction on the canal. The Erie Canal took eight years to complete, which may seem like a long time to you and me. But, considering the distance—363 miles—and all the obstacles its builders would encounter along the way, it was pretty fast. Technological advances in the nineteenth century helped improve the workers' ability to do things like clear tree stumps and move large amounts of dirt and rocks. When it finally opened in 1825, it stretched from Albany—the state capital—to Buffalo, New York, on Lake Erie. So—to repeat—the Erie Canal was 363 miles long. It was also 40 feet wide but only 4 feet in depth. Uh … though it wasn't very deep, boats with 30 tons of freight could easily float on it. And on the towpath—a narrow dirt path along the side of the canal—mules pulled the boats through the still water at a pace of four to five miles per hour. Not fast by today's standards—but in that time, it was really innovative!

The Erie Canal is an important part of United States history because it opened up travel and trade across the state. Before it closed in the twentieth century, it was an important method of transportation. The Erie Canal was called an "engineering marvel." So … even though people don't use the canal for transportation today, it is an important historical site and many parts of it have small museums and cultural centers for visitors and tourists.

Writing

Task 1

We're really just getting started on the history of American theater. We touched upon the earliest theater—built in 1716 in Williamsburg, Virginia. In the early eighteenth century, when the whole idea of being "American" began, and I say this because many people saw the colonies simply as an extension of England until 1776, the American Revolution … well, the first troupe that was really credited with creating a theater in the U.S. was that of Adam Hallam and his sons. And all of their repertoire, their collection of performed pieces, were works by British and European playwrights. Most historians, other than Hornblow in 1919, hardly mentioned the Hallams in their books. So even though there is this, um, concept of American theater, it's hard to call it American in a cultural sense. Perhaps because the Hallams were English, the theater and its productions were still considered "English."

What was American theater? To the Hallams, it was the space as well as the repertoire of fine plays that they brought with them. Lewis Hallam established New York City's first theater in about 1753, on Nassau street in Manhattan. It must have been thrilling for those people who had never seen Shakespeare plays before.

But, still, I think we can't really call this "American" theater until the first "American" play was produced—which was the playwright Royall Tyler's piece, "The Contrast," performed in 1787 at the John Street theater in New York City.

Further practice and guidance

Integrated speaking task 3

A

M Hey, Mary. Uh, is this notice for real?

W You mean the bulletin about the TVs and laptops?

M Yeah. I can't believe it … I mean, my friends and I hang out in the common room after class and watch movies or play video games … especially on Friday nights. Is this rule in effect even on weekends?

W That's a good question … well, yeah, according to the way this announcement is worded: It says, "not permitted," so, yes.

M And … no cell phone calls allowed in the common room? It's harder to make calls in your room. Is there anyone to talk to about this?

W Uh, you'd have to speak with the resident director— you know Joe Montgomery?

M Right. Yeah. Oh … he's kind of a stickler for the rules, isn't he?

W Mm. Well, we had a meeting and he said this is what many students have been complaining about—too much noise. And that makes it hard to study.

M I bet it was just a small group of students … it wasn't me. Uh, what if I get a petition going and have everybody who is against the new rule sign it?

W You can try.

M OK … I'm going to talk to some of my dorm mates now.

B

W Hi. I don't know what to do … I left my class schedule back at the dorm. If I go all the way back to the dorm, I won't have time to eat before my 7 p.m. class …

M Well, the schedule is set up to keep the traffic in the dining hall at a minimum. Otherwise we have two problems—one, there won't be enough food, and two, there won't be enough space.

W Uh, my problem is that I have a work-study job on this side of campus until 6 p.m. and my dorm is on the other side of campus. If I try to get back to my dorm to get my schedule, I won't have time to eat dinner.

M So … you're trying to get me to let you in at an unscheduled time, right?

W Yeah … and I only have about half an hour before my class …

M The problem is, every student is going to ask me for the same thing, and then we get overcrowding and chaos in the dining hall.

W Well, if you could make an exception for me just this once, I'll make sure my schedule is permanently in my bookbag for next time.

TEST ONE AND TWO CD TRACKS

CD1

Tracks	Task
1–7	Listening 1
8–14	Listening 2
15–21	Listening 3
22–28	Listening 4
29–37	Listening 5
38–47	Listening 6
48	Speaking 1
49	Speaking 2
50–52	Speaking 3
53–55	Speaking 4
56–58	Speaking 5
59–61	Speaking 6
62–63	Writing 1
64	FPG Listening p.128
65	FPG Speaking p.144
66	Speaking 1 sample answer
67	Speaking 2 sample answer 1
68	Speaking 2 sample answer 2
69	Speaking 3 sample answer
70	Speaking 4 sample answer
71	Speaking 5 sample answer 1
72	Speaking 5 sample answer 2
73	Speaking 6 sample answer
74	FPG speaking 1 sample answer
75	FPG speaking 2 sample answer
76	FPG speaking 3 sample answer
77	FPG speaking 4 sample answer
78	FPG speaking 5 sample answer
79	FPG speaking 6 sample answer

CD2

Tracks	Task
1–8	Listening 1
9–14	Listening 2
15–19	Listening 3
20–25	Listening 4
26–34	Listening 5
35–40	Listening 6
41	Speaking 1
42	Speaking 2
43–45	Speaking 3
46–48	Speaking 4
49–51	Speaking 5
52–54	Speaking 6
55–56	Writing 1
57	FPG Speaking p.145
58	Speaking 1 sample answer
59	Speaking 2 sample answer
60	Speaking 3 sample answer
61	Speaking 4 sample answer
62	Speaking 5 sample answer
63	Speaking 6 sample answer
64	FPG speaking 1 sample answer
65	FPG speaking 2 sample answer
66	FPG speaking 3 sample answer
67	FPG speaking 4 sample answer
68	FPG speaking 5 sample answer
69	FPG speaking 6 sample answer

CD TRACK LISTING

FURTHER PRACTICE AND GUIDANCE CD TRACKS
In order to do the Further Practice and Guidance sections it is necessary to listen to certain tracks from the CDs. These tracks are listed below, for reference.

CD1

Tracks	Task
2	Listening p.120 and p.128
3	Listening p.115
4	Listening p.121
6	Listening p.135
9–10	Listening p.118
10–11	Listening p.125
12	Listening p.125
13	Listening p.129 and p.137
16	Listening p.115
19	Listening p.137
20	Listening p.129 and p.131
24	Listening p.119
25	Speaking p.149
27	Listening p.131
30–31	Listening p.132
30	Listening p.135
31	Listening p.116
32	Listening p.128
33	Listening p.121 and 123
41	Listening p.125
42	Listening p.125
43	Listening p.121
45	Listening p.132
46	Listening p.137
54	Writing p.150
57	Speaking p.148
60	Speaking p.149
63	Speaking p.146
70	Speaking p.146

CD2

Tracks	Task
2	Listening p.116
4	Listening p.126
4–5	Listening p.137
7	Listening p.135
10–12	Listening p.122 and p.129
13	Listening p.119
17	Listening p.136
21	Listening p.122
23	Listening p.126
28	Listening p.119
31	Listening p.132
32	Listening p.133
33	Listening p.130
36	Listening p.116
47	Writing p.151
50	Speaking p.148
53	Speaking p.149
56	Speaking p.146
57	Speaking p.145

SCORING SHEET

Test 1 Reading		Test 2 Reading	
1–13	1 point	1–12	1 point
14	3 points for 6 correct answers	13	2 points for 3 correct answers
15–26	1 point	14–25	1 point
27	4 points for 7 correct answers	26	4 points for 7 correct answers
28–40	1 point	27–38	1 point
41	2 points for 3 correct answers	39	2 points for 3 correct answers
42–53	1 point	40–51	1 point
54	2 points for 3 correct answers	52	4 points for 7 correct answers
Test 1 Listening		**Test 2 Listening**	
1–21	1 point	1–14	1 point
22	2 points for 5 correct answers	15	2 points for 4 correct answers
23–27	1 point for 4 correct answers	16–20	1 point for 3 correct answers
28	1 point	21	2 points for 4 correct answers
29–34	1 point	22–34	1 point

Reading conversion scores

Total points (raw score)	Scaled score (estimated)
60–61	30
58–59	29
55–57	28
53–54	27
51–52	26
50	25
48–49	24
46–47	23
45	22
43–44	21
41–42	20
40	19
38–39	18
35–37	17
34	16
32–33	15
30–31	14
28–29	13
25–27	12
22–24	11
20–21	10
17–19	9
13–15	8
10–12	7
9	4
1–8	0–4

Listening conversion scores

Total points (raw score)	Scaled score (estimated)
36	30
34–35	29
32–33	28
30–31	27
28–29	25–26
26–27	23–24
25	22
23–24	20–21
22	19
20–21	18
18–19	17
15–16	16
13–14	15
10–12	13–14
9	10–11
5–8	8–9
0–4	3–7
	0–3

ically

TEST 1 ANSWER SHEET

Reading

For questions 1–13, write the letter corresponding to the correct answer (A, B, C, D).

1 _____
2 _____
3 _____
4 _____
5 _____
6 _____
7 _____
8 _____
9 _____
10 _____
11 _____
12 _____
13 _____

For question 14, write the letters that correspond to the correct answers (A, B, C, D, E, F, G, H, I) in the column.

14

The historical events	
Theories and controversy	

For questions 15–26, write the letter corresponding to the correct answer (A, B, C, D).

15 _____
16 _____
17 _____
18 _____
19 _____
20 _____
21 _____
22 _____
23 _____
24 _____
25 _____
26 _____

For question 27, write the letters that correspond to the correct answers (A, B, C, D, E, F, G, H, I) in the column.

27

Salvageable building materials	
Non–recyclable	

For questions 28–40, write the letters that correspond to the correct answers (A, B, C, D).

28 _____
29 _____
30 _____
31 _____
32 _____
33 _____
34 _____
35 _____
36 _____
37 _____
38 _____
39 _____
40 _____

For question 41 write the letters that correspond to the correct answers (A, B, C, D, E, F).

41 _____

For questions 42–51, write the letters that correspond to the correct answers (A, B, C, D).

42 _____
43 _____
44 _____
45 _____
46 _____
47 _____
48 _____
49 _____
50 _____
51 _____
52 _____
53 _____

For question 54, write the letters that correspond to the correct answers (A, B, C, D, E, F).

54 _____

Listening

For questions 1–21, write the letter or letters corresponding to the correct answer (A, B, C, D).

1 _____
2 _____
3 Choose 2 _____
_____
4 _____
5 _____
6 _____
7 _____
8 _____
9 _____
10 Choose 2 _____
_____
11 _____
12 _____
13 _____
14 _____
15 Choose 2 _____
_____
16 _____
17 _____
18 _____
19 _____
20 _____
21 _____
22 For question 22, write T for True; F for False.

1 _____   3 _____
2 _____   4 _____

23 _____
24 _____
25 _____
26 _____
27 _____
28

Angiosperms	
Gymnosperms	

29 _____
30 _____
31 _____
32 _____
33 _____
34 Choose 2 _____
_____

Reading

For questions 1–13, write the letter corresponding to the correct answer (A, B, C, D).

1 _____
2 _____
3 _____
4 _____
5 _____
6 _____
7 _____
8 _____
9 _____
10 _____
11 _____
12 _____

For question 13, write the letters that correspond to the correct answers (A, B, C, D, E, F).

13 _____

For questions 14–25 write the letter corresponding to the correct answer (A, B, C, D).

15 _____
16 _____
17 _____
18 _____
19 _____
20 _____
21 _____
22 _____
23 _____
24 _____
25 _____

For question 26, write the letters that correspond to the correct answers (A, B, C, D, E, F, G, H, I) in the columns.

26

	Type of telescope	
	Ground-based	Space-based
Instrument or process		

For questions 27–38, write the letters that correspond to the correct answers (A, B, C, D).

28 _____
29 _____
30 _____
31 _____
32 _____
33 _____
34 _____
35 _____
36 _____
37 _____
38 _____

For question 39, write the letters that correspond to the correct answers (A, B, C, D, E, F).

39 _____

For questions 40–51, write the letter corresponding to the correct answer (A, B, C, D).

40 _____
41 _____
42 _____
43 _____
44 _____
45 _____
46 _____
47 _____
48 _____
49 _____
50 _____
51 _____

For question 52, write the letters that correspond to the correct answers (A, B, C, D, E, F, G, H, I) in the columns.

52

Lake type	Conditions	Mixing

Listening

For questions 1–14, write the letter or letters corresponding to the correct answer (A, B, C, D).

1 _____
2 _____
3 _____
4 Choose 2 _____
5 _____
6 _____
7 _____
8 _____
9 Choose 2 _____
10 _____
11 _____
12 _____
13 _____
14 _____

15 Place a check next to the effect of each factor on returns

	Strictly positive effect	Strictly negative effect	Both positive and negative
Viewer enjoyment			
Prior notice of placement			
Placement in general			
Highly absorbing plot			

For questions 16–20 write the letter or letters corresponding to the correct answer (A, B, C, D).

16 _____
17 _____
18 _____
19 Choose 2 _____
20 _____

21 Fill in the chart with events in the order that the professor discusses them.

1	
2	
3	
4	

For questions 22–34, write the letter or letters corresponding to the correct answer (A, B, C, D).

22 _____
23 _____
24 _____
25 _____
26 _____
27 _____
28 _____
29 _____
30 _____
31 _____
32 _____
33 _____
34 _____